"Dr. Z. has been treating OCD for many years, and passi
OCD keeps her approach to treating it fresh, merging th
new. In her new book, she demonstrates how ERP and
tackle OCD and how readers can make a shift from reactive moves to wise moves,
with many exercises to help the reader understand and apply these skills. Thank you,
Dr. Z., for your dedication and service to the OCD community!"

– **Stuart Ralph,** *The OCD Stories*

"This is a very helpful book for anyone who has been struggling with obsessive-compulsive tendencies – and who is sick and tired of allowing them to hold them back from the life they really want to live. This workbook will help you identify what truly matters to you and start you moving in those directions with determination and kindness toward yourself. Dr. Z uses her extensive clinical experiences, knowledge and skills to offer you many practical examples and exercises that can truly make a difference in your life. Through different chapters, readers will gain an understanding of how obsessions became a problem, learn to watch their mind, recognize ruling-thoughts, clarify values, and take actions towards values-based exercises. Dr. Z wrote this book with a compassionate heart and open mind in a non-technical, clear, concise, and personable style that makes it easy to work with it. I recommend this book wholeheartedly and without any reservations."

– **Georg H. Eifert, PhD,** Chapman University Professor Emeritus of Psychology,
coauthor of *Anxiety Happens* and *The Mindfulness
and Acceptance Workbook for Anxiety*

"This is much more than a workbook: it's an engaging and informative travel guide for the journey to OCD recovery. A passionate expert in OCD, Dr. Z is your wise and caring companion, offering step-by-step guidance for how to make choices that put you, not OCD, in the driver's seat. Her tips, tools, and insights provide not only a roadmap to recovery but also a process for enjoying the journey – and your life – along the way."

– **Shala Nicely, LPC,** author, *Is Fred in the Refrigerator?
Taming OCD and Reclaiming My Life*

"Even the best OCD clinicians struggle to provide effective treatment with clients who have strong belief in their obsessions, avoidance of emotions, and wavering motivation. Adults with OCD often present this way and many clinicians refer them out as they feel inadequate to help. This workbook offers a way forward using Acceptance and Commitment Therapy (ACT) as a model for how to provide exposure therapy and get back into your life. Regardless the type or form of OCD a person is dealing with, the intersection of Acceptance and Commitment Therapy and Exposure Response Prevention applies to all of them, and those key skills are highlighted in every chapter in a skillful and accessible manner. Dr. Zurita Ona's vast clinical experience shines through in this excellent workbook. I highly recommend it to any clinician treating clients with OCD!"

– **Nate Gruner, LCSW,** Staff Therapist,
McLean Hospital OCD Institute

Living Beyond OCD Using Acceptance and Commitment Therapy

This user-friendly workbook provides adults with obsessive compulsive disorder (OCD) the tools they need to move beyond their disorder using Acceptance and Commitment Therapy (ACT). It also serves as compact text for clinicians/practitioners to use with clients suffering from OCD at any point in treatment.

This workbook offers readers hands-on ACT and Exposure Response Prevention (ERP) skills for taming disturbing obsessions and filling the gap between where one stands and where one wants to go. Dr. Zurita provides evidence-based exercises to guide adults through the process of ACT. This includes learning to step back from one's thoughts and memories, opening up to all types of unwanted thoughts and feelings, paying attention to the physical world, observing one's thoughts and feelings, getting rid of barriers to values-based living, and developing consistent patterns of values-based behavior.

Written from the office of a full-time therapist, in a simple, uncomplicated, and unpretentious manner, this workbook will be useful for all clients suffering from OCD and for the therapists who work with them.

Patricia E. Zurita Ona, PsyD, is a clinical psychologist specialized in working with children, adolescents, and adults struggling with OCD, anxiety, and emotion regulation problems. Dr. Z is the founder of the East Bay Behavior Therapy Center, a boutique therapy practice, where she runs an intensive outpatient program integrating ACT and Exposure Response Prevention (ERP). She is also a fellow of the Association of Contextual Behavioral Science (ACBS), member of the OCD San Francisco Bay Area (affiliate from the International OCD Foundation), and a chair of the committee for the Anxiety and Depression American Association (ADAA).

Living Beyond OCD Using Acceptance and Commitment Therapy

A Workbook for Adults

Patricia E. Zurita Ona

Routledge
Taylor & Francis Group

NEW YORK AND LONDON

First published 2021
by Routledge
52 Vanderbilt Avenue, New York, NY 10017

and by Routledge
2 Park Square, Milton Park, Abingdon, Oxon, OX14 4RN

Routledge is an imprint of the Taylor & Francis Group, an informa business

© 2021 Taylor & Francis

Library of Congress Cataloging-in-Publication Data
No Cataloging-in-Publication Data is included as expendable educational materials such as laboratory manuals, teacher's manuals, programmed instruction test sheets, workbooks, etc., are ineligible for this program.

ISBN: 978-0-367-17844-4 (hbk)
ISBN: 978-0-367-17847-5 (pbk)
ISBN: 978-0-429-05803-5 (ebk)

Typeset in Caecilia
by Apex CoVantage, LLC

To my clients: everything I have done in my career has been always thinking of the people I work with.

To the people who believed in me, my accent, my heels, and my skills.

To the quiet innovators who continue to do what matters because it matters.

Contents

Contents

Contents

Figures

Tables

Exercises

Introduction

I ran out of space when writing this workbook, and I didn't want to bother my publishers negotiating the numbers of words and becoming a headache for them. So I have few words for you:

In this workbook you won't read academic theories, long statistics, or abstract advice to tackle obsessive compulsive disorder (OCD); while this workbook is based on solid scientific-ground, you will find very few nerdy comments. I wanted to write a workbook that shows you how to overcome OCD and live a purposeful, fulfilling, and rich life. So you will get real skills, real how-tos, and real takeaways to handle obsessions and related behaviors to live the life that works for you.

I genuinely did my best to write something that is uncomplicated, unpretentious, and as real as it gets. Hope you make all the skills of this workbook yours, and most importantly, I urge you to put them into action and do what matters to you!

Okay, let's dig in!

Dr. Z.

How to Use This Workbook

To give you a full picture of what lies ahead, let's go over the most frequent questions readers have about this workbook.

Who Is This Workbook for?

If you are newly diagnosed with OCD, are currently in treatment, or suspect you have OCD, this workbook offers you hands-on Acceptance and Commitment Therapy (ACT) skills for taming your disruptive compulsions caused by obsessions. This workbook also helps to close the gap between where you are and where you want to go, freeing you to live the vital, rich life you're seeking.

If you have received treatment for OCD and are in the post-treatment phase, this book refreshes your skills and adds ACT techniques to help you move forward.

How Is This Workbook Organized?

This book is divided into 10 parts. Each part begins with a brief introduction of main topics and finishes with key takeaways. Each part also ends with a life tracker exercise, which invites you to pause and reflect on how you're living your life as you work through this workbook.

Each chapter focuses on one or two topics, teaches skills to use in daily life, offers exercises to practice, poses questions for you to answer, and provides worksheets for you to complete. (There are also extra worksheets on the website: www.actbeyond.ocd.)

Part I gives you the basics: what OCD is, what maintains it, how your brain works, and the different types of obsession.

Part II goes into the details of ACT, describes how it blends with Exposure Response Prevention (ERP), and explains how it will help you to overcome OCD episodes.

Part III is where you identify two things: (1) all the compulsions and avoidant behaviors that are fueling OCD episodes and (2) all the ruling-thoughts – such as obsessions, anxiety, and unhelpful thinking strategies – that are running your life in unproductive ways.

Part IV asks you to assess how compulsions, avoidant behaviors, and holding onto ruling-thoughts are working in your life and in your relationship with yourself. It also asks you to determine what you really have control of when dealing with annoying obsessions.

Part V gives you all the tips you need to create a new relationship with your mind and thinking – one in which you're not bossed around by or blindly following what it says. In this part, you'll learn how not to believe everything your brain says!

Part VI teaches you specific ACT skills to handle obsessions as they show up and as they are, along with the anxiety, panic, or fear that immediately follows. You will learn a bunch of defusion skills, acceptance prompts, and tips to ride the wave of your overwhelming emotions.

Part VII asks you to go in-depth into discovering your values. You'll figure out how you want them to show up in different areas in your life and what steps you can take, wherever you are, to put your values in action. This part ends with a chapter on taking a break from reading this workbook so you can practice all the skills you have learned so far to handle those unwanted obsessions that come your way. Why? Because more than rushing and mechanically practicing skills, this workbook is about building awareness of what skills you practice, how you practice them, and why you do so. Besides, who doesn't need a break from time to time.

Part VIII guides you through the process of values-based exposures: how to use your values as a guide, how to prepare for them, and what to expect when doing them. The chapter "Make W.I.S.E. M.O.V.E.S. When Practicing Values-Guided Exposures" *teaches* you what to do when facing a situation, object, activity, or people that the pattern-making machine of your brain associates with obsessions. The part finishes with a chapter on how to handle compulsions and different ways to do so.

Part IX prepares you to handle potential blocks that may come your way: values-conflict, reason-giving thoughts, lack of values clarity, and doing exposures as a compulsion.

Finally, Part X guides you with how to move forward with your life by facing obsessions as they arise, upsetting situations as they happen, and overwhelming emotions as they roll. You will learn how to practice self-compassion on the go and how to make mini-W.I.S.E. M.O.V.E.S. when life gets messy.

What's Next After Reading This Workbook?

You can find additional notes, ideas, and exercises at my website. Take a peek at it when you have a chance! Here is the url www.actbeyondocd.com.

How Did You Come Up With the Examples for This Workbook?

The examples of clients you will read about in this workbook are fictional; they are a combination of different people I have encountered in my personal life, clinical work, and own narratives I created to illustrate a particular point.

Is There an Acronym?

There is only one core acronym: "W.I.S.E. M.O.V.E.S."

You will read about it in Part VIII, "Making W.I.S.E. M.O.V.E.S." After learning about it, I urge you to make this acronym yours all the way! Take it as a reminder of the skills you can use to handle triggering moments effectively.

Am I Going to Get Triggered?

Many types of obsessions – fear of germs, contamination, symmetry, harm, sexuality, violence, and others that vary from being not-so-weird to ultra-weird – and compulsions are mentioned throughout this book.

Some of the words, examples, or narratives may be distressing, and in those moments my invitation is for you to pause, take a deep breath, and notice what is happening. If necessary, take a mini-break and then continue reading.

Where Do I Start Reading?

I recommend you work on this workbook from cover to cover. Although it is tempting to skip some sections, I encourage you not to skip any chapter, including the introductions to each part, even if there is information, skills, or content you're already familiar with or that doesn't seem to apply directly to you. The different pieces of information and skills are interwoven, and they build on each other, so skipping chapters or parts may get you confused, head you in the wrong direction, or minimize the outcomes of the vital work you're doing in this workbook.

If you're reading this book on your own, without also working with a therapist specialized in ACT or OCD, it is even more essential that you read all chapters and not skip any.

And in case you are familiar with ERP and are tempted to jump into those chapters right away, from a place of caring, I discourage you from doing so. Without reading the chapters that precede them, you will miss out on learning foundational core skills that will help you approach those triggering moments in a way that can be helpful to you and unique to ACT. Please take my word for it!

At What Pace Should I Read?

When we're struggling, it is natural to want a quick fix, a quick repair, or a quick solution as soon as possible. I'm the first person to want all those things when something goes wrong.

But as much as there is a strong need to get the obsession under control as quickly as possible, I urge you to read this workbook at a slower rhythm – one that gets your life back on track and full of vitality, meaning, and presence. It does no good to attempt to help yourself by rushing through skills and becoming exhausted, scatterbrained, and overwhelmed in the process.

I'm not asking you to read at the pace of a turtle or saying that reading at the speed of a rabbit is wrong. I'm saying that to make the best of the skills from this workbook, it's important to focus on what's key: learning, practicing, and keeping track of how this process goes with curiosity, intention, and flexibility.

I encourage you to learn the skills at a pace that helps you to create a new way of relating to your mind and the work you're going to be doing when facing values-guided exposures and taking steps toward discovering what makes you tick.

At the end of the part VI, you will take a two- to three-week break from reading this workbook, but you will continue to practice the skills you've learned. This is because practicing ACT skills again and again is key to making the best of this workbook.

Sometimes amazing things happen not because of how fast or how slow we walk but because we keep walking at a steady, firm pace, full of curiosity about the process and with commitment. Try it!

Make This Workbook Yours

This workbook has been written for *you*! When coming across information, exercises, activities, skills, or tips you like and find helpful, make sure to circle, underline, or highlight them, or to make any mark you want, so you can easily locate them later.

There is no wrong way of doing anything in this workbook. Your courage to face obsessions and your commitment to learn skills and get your life back on track are more important than anything else.

Make a Habit of Using Your Skills!

It would be nice if forming a habit to use your skills was as easy as a magic trick. But habit formation takes time and consistency. Set a regular time to do your reading, complete all exercises, make use of the tracking logs in the Appendix, and stick to your personal commitment.

The format of this book allows you to work on it after dinner, during lunch, on your coffee break, on your commute, or even at 3 a.m., when you cannot fall asleep. The chapters are short and light, so you can flip through them in different settings and at different times.

Talk to Others About It!

When dealing with OCD, anxiety, worry, or any other psychological struggle, the tendency is to shut down, hide, isolate, and stop living your life. But by doing so, you deprive yourself of one of the most powerful tools for getting back on your feet: connecting with others.

Think about it for a moment. How much effort, energy, and stress does it cost to keep this secret? I'm not suggesting you should tell everyone about what you're going through, and I certainly respect your privacy, but I encourage you to speak with those who care about you, because nothing can replace the experience of being seen, loved, and accepted by others as we are, as we come, and as we strive to be.

You might like to jot down notes from this workbook, your learnings, or your experiences, and share them on social networks. Or you might make copies of the takeaway summaries and post those. These tiny steps are not only ways to reinforce the skills you're learning, but they can also keep you accountable to your commitments, destigmatize mental health problems, and help you to foster real, caring, and long-lasting relationships.

I have genuinely done my best to provide you with ACT skills in a simple, uncomplicated, unpretentious, and jargon-free manner. I've shared with you all the skills I teach my own clients, and use in my life day by day.

I don't have a recipe for how you should live your life, but I can tell you that learning to have a better relationship with your mind, watching what it does and taking it lightly, figuring out *how* you want to show up every day, and doing what matters in every possible way can lead to an amazing range of opportunities for finding your way in life and shifting from surviving into thriving!

Let's get you started!

PART I

Getting to Know Your Mind

A Pattern-Making Machine

This first part gives you the basics to start where you are. It's about unpicking the stories we tell ourselves about thinking, how our mind works, and how we relate to fear. You'll learn what OCD is, the many ways in which it's reinforced, and the different themes it comes up with.

Your mind is very good at playing tricks, and learning how it does this is liberating!

1

Obsessions Are the Norm!

I know that we don't know each other and that we haven't met, but if I were next to you and we were going to start talking about OCD, I would share with you a memory I have of one of those warm and humid summer nights in Bolivia, my country of origin.

I was driving back to Santa Cruz, one of Bolivia's main cities, after a long camping trip. I was sweaty because of the high temperature and elevated humidity of the tropical weather. I could feel the hot air slapping my face, moving through my nose every time I breathed in and breathed out. My face was shiny with perspiration. I was listening to music, as I usually do on a long trip. Despite the heat, I was feeling refreshed from my time in the forest, thinking lightly about conversations I had, and ready to go to sleep wrapped in the clean sheets on my bed.

I was driving at a regular speed on the freeway when, suddenly, the white lights of a truck driving toward me on the opposite side of the road made me suck in a deep breath. Instantly, I saw in my mind this awful scene of being hit by the truck, my car pushed to the side of the road, my body covered in blood, and me dying quickly. The image was so clear and vivid that I began to hyperventilate and sweat even more. I gripped the wheel really hard with both of my hands. And then the truck passed. The experience lasted only seconds, but it felt like an eternity to me. I pulled over, still hyperventilating. I couldn't shake the image in my mind – it was very clear and very real.

The image I created in my mind has never left. In fact, it pops up from time to time, even when I'm not driving. And at times my mind tells me that this image "proves that I'm going to die young." I sometimes get anxious when driving next to a big truck, and I hold the wheel really hard with both hands. This image is so real that, no matter where I am, who I'm with, what I'm doing, it can show up any time.

Looking back, it's clear that I had an intrusive thought and a panic attack. And because this image continues to show up and is sticky, I can classify it as an obsession. Obsessions are thoughts or images that are unwanted, repetitive, scary, hard to let go of, and come with a strong sense of urgency; they also include urges or impulses, which is a way of describing an intense bodily sensation (like washing hands) paired with an unwanted thought (like *My hands are covered in germs!*). In this workbook, we'll use the terms "obsessions" and "intrusive thoughts" interchangeably when referring to "thoughts, images, and urges."

Let me clarify right away that obsessions are *not* a personality trait, a symbol of your unconscious mind, or a hidden intention. Intrusive thoughts can be confusing because they vary in degrees of bizarreness and incongruence with your character and your values, so they can range from being *ego-syntonic* or benign to *ego-dystonic* or *ultra-weird*. In other words, some obsessions – the ego-syntonic ones – are more consistent with a person's view of the world, feel natural, and are not distressing. The opposite goes for ego-dystonic ones.

If we think about the "weirdness" of thoughts, or thinking in general, as a naturally occurring phenomenon that everyone's mind has, we may see it as a continuum:

ultra-weird	weird	a bit weird	not weird at all

Let's take a look at how this frame applies to some random intrusive thoughts:

Images of having sex with another person than your partner
Fears of people stealing your knowledge
Images of punching a person
Doubts about your existence being real
Fears of losing control
Random images of blood in a curtain
Fears about your partner cheating on you

How about your own intrusive thoughts? Think about the obsessions you have been having over the last month and mark an X under the category where it fits best.

Intrusive thought	ultra-weird	weird	a bit weird	not weird at all

But, again, it's important to keep in mind that all obsessions are content generated by our mind, and at their core, they're annoying, aggravating, and, as little dictators, demand you do something about them right away.

Is It Only You?

There's been a lot of research studies around obsessions. Don't worry, I won't go into all of them. But here are just a few studies that are important for you to be aware of.

Rachman and de Silva (1978), Salkovskis and Harrison (1984), and Radomsky and his colleagues (2014) assessed how obsessions show up among adults in the United States and college students in 13 countries across six different continents. Guess what they found? Obsessions are part of the brain chatter in *everyone*'s daily life, whether we are diagnosed as having OCD or not.

Here is a take-home message from those studies: everyone has bizarre thoughts.

For instance, Melissa, a 45-year-old saleswoman, has chosen to work part-time to spend quality time with her kids. On a Sunday afternoon, she is lying down on the couch with her 7-year-old son, and her arm, by accident, touches her kid's genital area. At that moment, Melissa has the thought, "Did I like it? Am I a pedophile? Am I going to abuse my kid?" She quickly moves off the couch and sits apart from her son.

I don't know the annoying obsession your mind comes up with, but you're not alone, you're not crazy, and you're not defective. It's absolutely normal to have weird, unwanted, scary, or disturbing thoughts. They're part of being human, part of what our normal mind does – whether we have OCD or not.

Our minds are constantly coming up with theories, hypotheses, problems to solve, thoughts about the past, images, patterns, wishful thoughts, revenge contemplations, romantic memories, worries, stories, doubtful thoughts, and so on, nonstop and without taking any breaks, vacations, or holidays. Don't believe me? Try the next exercise.

Exercise: Watching Your Mind

Get a timer and set it for 3 minutes, and in those 3 minutes watch the stuff that your mind comes up with. Just do your best to notice all the things your mind conjures up. When the alarm sounds, jot down the thoughts and images you had:

What did your mind do? Every time I watch my mind, it never surprises me the amount of blah-blah-blah it comes up with. Sometimes that blah-blah-blah is interesting, fun, and insightful, and other times it's a massive stream of images, random thoughts, and a bunch of nonsensical noise. Our busy minds also come up with intrusive thoughts; that's the norm, and not the exception.

You may be wondering, "If everyone has all types of thoughts, including dark obsessions, how do I have OCD?" We'll answer that in the next chapter.

If Obsessions Are Normal, What About OCD?

What starts obsessive-compulsive disorder? How does a person go from having a disturbing thought to spending hours dealing with OCD?

To start, let's think for a moment about Theo, a 26-year-old art graduate student who loves history classes. Theo is fascinated by modern European history, loves to read all types of books, watch movies, and debate about them.

One afternoon, while Theo was listening to his teacher lecturing about the Cold War, he noticed a weird sensation while swallowing, as if he wasn't swallowing on the right side of his throat and there something was wrong with it. His mind quickly had thoughts about how important swallowing is for eating, drinking, talking, etc., and he started panicking about having a problem with his swallowing. Theo swallowed multiple times, faster, slower, and when doing so, he noticed that at times his swallowing felt a bit normal.

He tried to continue listening to the history lecture, and then, when swallowing again, he noticed that there was a sensation of dryness, so this time he put his hands on his throat while swallowing and checked what was wrong – he even tried to stop swallowing for a minute to see if his swallowing went back to *normal*. Theo went to the bathroom, turned on the water faucet, put his hand under it, and brought it to his mouth, hoping that extra water would help his swallowing and the weird sensation that something was wrong. Theo went back to class and moved his tongue inside his mouth multiple times to help his swallowing. But while he found at times his swallowing was okay, he continued to have thoughts about something being potentially wrong with his swallowing and it being an indication of chronic illness.

Later that night, Theo was careful how much he was talking to his girlfriend, checked the amount of saliva he had, how his swallowing felt when eating and snacking, drank more water than usual and refused to drink a beer with his dad (as they usually did), and when going to sleep he searched "swallowing problems" online. Theo found all types of information, from chronic medical conditions like cancer and autoimmune disorder to transitory ones like a cold. Theo just had a medical check a month ago, and the doctors didn't find anything of medical concern. He didn't have any other symptoms of flu, cold, sore throat, or any other related condition, but despite knowing all that, Theo couldn't let go of the thought "Something is wrong with my swallowing." The next day, Theo decided to skip breakfast just in case coffee would make his swallowing worse and to monitor the dryness of his throat to compare whether he had more saliva the moment before.

Here is a connection that Theo's brain made: a weird sensation with swallowing equals danger, distress, and anxiety. Keeping Theo's experience in mind, let's unpack it to answer two questions. What starts OCD? What maintains it?

How Does an OCD Episode Start?

Theo's OCD struggles started with not-so-weird unwanted thoughts that he couldn't let go of. "Is there something wrong with my saliva? Do I have a serious medical condition that I don't know about?" Theo managed the discomfort that came along with those obsessions by doing all types of checking.

And even though it seems natural that any person would check whether they have a medical condition or not, what's different is that Theo was very bothered by these obsessions. He was in distress, couldn't continue with his day, couldn't dismiss those thoughts. He often checked the amount of saliva he had, changed the pace of his swallowing, researched online, and checked the symptoms of other illnesses. Every time Theo did any of those behaviors, he felt a bit better momentarily about the quality of his swallowing. But it was only a matter of time until the obsession about something being wrong with his swallowing showed up again in Theo's mind. And he tried to manage it, again and again, using the same short-lived strategies.

Theo kept doing those checking behaviors for a single reason: to get rid of the obsession. He was determined to minimize the impact of the thought, making sure there was nothing wrong with his swallowing. All those behaviors are called compulsions. And the tricky part with compulsions is that, while they can calm you down quickly, they only calm you down until get triggered again.

Figure 2.1 is a graphic to explain how Theo went from having an obsession to an OCD episode, and how it starts.

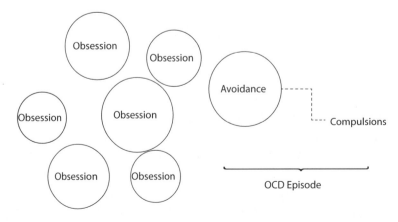

Figure 2.1 From an obsession to an OCD episode.

Theo went from having an obsession to having an OCD episode because his brain quickly learned that one way to let go of the distress, fear, and panic of the obsession is by doing a compulsion. Who wouldn't? Acting based on the fear, distress, panic, and agony that comes with obsessions is like a scratching an itch – there is a sense of relief that comes right away. That's how OCD starts.

Compulsions and avoidant behaviors – things you do right away to avoid the discomfort, distress, and anxiety that comes with intrusive thoughts – work immediately. And any person struggling with these very sticky obsessions will quickly develop patterns of compulsions – doing different types of checking, rituals, and so forth – or different types of avoidance.

So now you know how your mind works when triggered; in the next chapters, you'll learn more about compulsions and avoidant behaviors.

What Keeps OCD Going?

OCD doesn't keep going on its own. OCD keeps getting bigger and bigger, worse and worse, because compulsions and avoidant behaviors work – but only in the short term. They alleviate your distress, take the edge off the fear, but they last only seconds. And that's why you keep doing them, over and over.

Let me go into nerdy behavioral land for a bit, because this information is important to understand: how do you go from one OCD episode into another one? Behaviorally speaking, doing compulsions and avoidant behaviors "negatively reinforces" the cycle of an OCD episode. If you recall, one of the first associations that Theo's brain made was that a weird sensation when swallowing equals danger. Next, Theo's brain learned that, when doing compulsions and avoidant behaviors, he could quickly decrease the awful experience that came with those thoughts and feel safe, better, and less anxious for a bit.

What do you think is the consequence of that learning? Naturally, Theo will do more and more compulsive and avoidant behaviors, because they worked. And that's how compulsions and avoidant behaviors "reinforce" Theo's associations of: (1) uncomfortable sensations when swallowing equals fear, distress, and anxiety and (2) compulsions and avoidance get rid of those obsessions. This is a classic example of negative reinforcement, which is called negative reinforcement because the yucky stuff that comes with the thought of "am I getting sick?" is removed.

As you can see, because of behavioral reinforcement, Theo went from having a benign obsession to having an OCD episode, and from having a single episode to multiple ones a day.

Imagine for a second that an obsession is like a ball in a pool. And because it's scary, you try to push it down. But every time you push it down, the ball not only bounces back up, but a new ball shows up in the pool representing an obsession in a different place in your life. Now imagine one of your worst fears inside a ball in the pool. You give all your attention to it, as you have done so far, and you push it down – as you have done with all those compulsions and avoidant behaviors – but then quickly a new ball shows up. So you try to pay attention to the second one, and as you try to make the second ball go away, a third one pops up, and then a fourth, and a fifth, and so on, to the point that the pool is filled with balls, and you have no space for swimming.

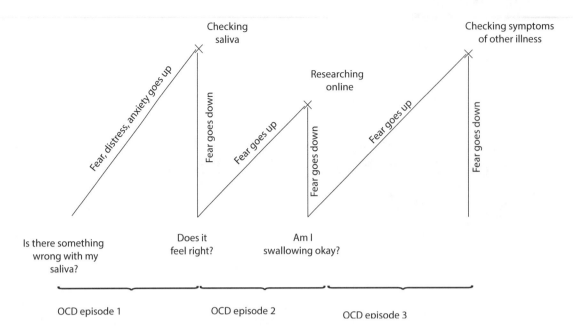

Figure 3.1 What keeps OCD going?

Your mind is a pattern-making machine. How so? Well, when having an obsession, your mind is constantly checking whether that unwanted, bizarre, or distressing thought or situation is similar to another one that made you anxious in the past. If so, then *boom!* it registers a thinking pattern and then generates reasons to be scared and terrified and to take the obsession as the absolute truth.

Your brain quickly learns that the only way to get rid of the fear that comes along with the obsession is by doing a compulsion or avoiding the triggering situation, people, activity, or object. And if you keep doing the same thing over and over, OCD episodes continue happening, one after another.

With time, if your brain continues to reinforce the association between an obsession and fear and these pairings get activated in different situations, your brain starts developing new associations of threat in those new areas or anything related to them. This process is called *fear generalization*. And that's how you went from having an obsession to having an OCD episode (fear acquisition), and from having a single OCD episode to having multiple OCD episodes (fear maintenance), and, lastly, how you went from experiencing regular day-to-day activities to triggering ones (fear generalization).

Because obsessions by nature are repetitive, sticky, and hard to let go of, at some point the same intrusion that initially showed up in your mind appeared again in a different or similar situation, and you did what you learned the first time: you did a compulsion or avoided the situation. And as you went through the obsession-compulsion cycle over and over, each one of the subsequent episodes reinforced the first one.

For example, if you have a fear of causing harm to your loved ones by not paying attention to them and their safety, as a compulsion you might start to check the stove, the outlets, and the fans in the bathroom multiple times when leaving the house and before going to sleep. Over time, you may start to avoid watching movies with scenes about disastrous mishaps. Or you might stop listening to the news because there might be stories about parents who made mistakes at home and caused harm to their kids.

As you can see, behaviorally speaking, negative reinforcement strengthens, increases, and augments OCD episodes, on top of that, and it causes them to happen anywhere, everywhere, no matter who you're with. Negative reinforcement is tricky, right?

Within ACT, as a behavioral approach, there is a saying: "We cannot understand behavior without looking at a context." By "context," I'm referring to a specific situation in which behavior takes place, what happens before it (antecedents), and what happens afterward (consequences). Every time we do something, there is a consequence for that behavior, whether we're aware of it or not, and those consequences can either increase or decrease the likelihood of that behavior in the future. For example, I continue breathing because it keeps me alive; if I don't go to work, I don't pay my bills; if I don't finish writing this book, my editor will be extremely mad with me. All those consequences increase the likelihood of my behaviors happening over and over, multiple times.

Every time we do something in response to our unwanted thoughts and the yucky stuff that shows up under our skin, there is a consequence that makes it decrease or increase. Understanding this behavioral framework allows us to make sense of all of our behaviors and why we keep doing one thing over another. In this case, I hope you can see how compulsions and avoidance keep you stuck when dealing with obsessions!

Exercise: How Did Your OCD Episodes Start?

Let's explore how OCD episodes became a problem for you. Consider an obsession you have and answer the following:

What are the associations that your brain made? Jot them down in each line that corresponds.

Obsession:

_____

Feelings that came along with it:

_____

Triggering event: what started the obsessions?

_____

Compulsions: what did you do right away when having the obsession?

_____

Avoidant behaviors: what did you avoid because of this obsession?

_____

Other related triggering events for the same obsession:

You're not crazy, and nothing is broken within you. It's just that your brain has learned a repetitive, recurring, and cyclical pattern to handle obsessions that don't serve you in the long run.

It's estimated that, worldwide, 112 million people have OCD (Williams & Wetterneck, 2019). OCD can afflict anyone.

If you're reading this workbook, it's probably because you have been struggling to control your obsessions, what you think, or what you feel. You have taken the obsessions literally, so you see your life through the lens of obsessions. Or you may even see yourself as the content of your obsessions: "I'm a horrible person, I'm a mess, I'm a murderer." But, as you move forward with this workbook you will learn that intrusions come and go, and they don't have to dictate what you do, who you want to be, and how you want to live your life.

Now that you learned how a person goes from having an obsession to having OCD, you may be wondering what makes obsessions so powerful that they take you in a downward spiral. That is the topic of the next chapter.

Why Are Obsessions So Hard to Let Go Of?

As you've now learned, obsessions are normal for all of us. For most people, however, obsessions are in the background of our minds. For those with OCD, they come front and center in the mind for four core reasons:

1. how your brain relates one thing with another,
2. how your brain overworks,
3. how you handle the yucky and overwhelming fearful emotions you experience with obsessions, and
4. how you take your thoughts (very seriously and as the absolute truth).

Let's go through them one by one in this chapter.

Your Brain Is Constantly Connecting Everything With Everything

If you look at the history of humanity, cave people had to survive all types of potential challenges – wild animals, poor weather conditions, lack of food, aggressive enemies, unknown illnesses, unknown causes of death – you name it. It wasn't an easy time for our ancestors.

In order to survive, not only they needed to learn to work together but also to keep track of what went wrong, what could possibly go wrong, and any cues of potential danger. Basically, all of the safety-based behaviors that the cave people practiced kept them alive, and as necessary as they were, they also reinforced a particular way of thinking: associative learning. Our ancestors learned to connect one thing with another hundreds of times, over and over for millions of years as a survival response.

Here's how it worked: if you saw a tiger close to the trees, that experience would unfold in your mind as "Tigers can be around all trees, so watch out!" These days, even though our environment has changed, and tigers are rarely lurking behind trees, our brain still responds to that program. As ridiculous as it may sound, when feeling anxious, scared, or worried, our brain – as a young organ in our body – is doing its job in the only way it knows how to do it: enforcing all types of things to protect, watch over, and guard us against getting hurt.

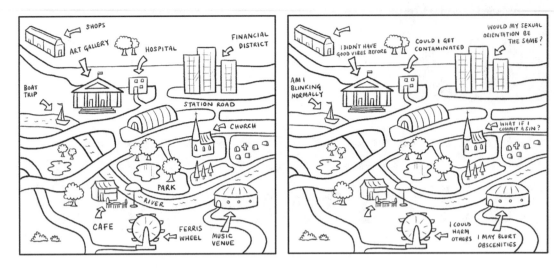

Figure 4.1 Maps.

In Chapter 3, you learned that your brain is pattern-making machine. And now, thanks to evolution, you can see that your brain is also content-generating machine. Reality is that our brain never stops making content and finding patterns!

Your Brain Is Overworking

Our brain has the capacity to anticipate danger and tell us "Watch out: something is wrong." The hypothalamus, like a kitty, checks when there is danger and communicates this information to the *amygdala*; the amygdala, in turn, acts at the speed of a rabbit to release neurochemicals and mobilize your body for a fight, flight, or freeze response. After receiving the message from the amygdala, the *hippocampus* acts like a turtle and, at its own pace, checks with the *prefrontal cortex*, the area of planning and decision making. Our brain will do this whether or not the danger signal is real in that particular moment. Based on the prefrontal cortex's response, your body makes the necessary adjustments for you to respond appropriately to the situation.

That's how the hypothalamus, amygdala, and hippocampus interact together. But what happens when obsessions show up in your mind accompanies by those overwhelming emotions, and this regulatory process gets started? Here is what happens: A hardworking and overactive amygdala keeps screaming and yelling "This is dangerous!" to the hippocampus, but the hippocampus, which is already slow, gets much slower, because the amygdala doesn't shut off. The struggle in the back of our brain doesn't give much of a chance for communication with the prefrontal cortex to check out what's really happening and readjust a response accordingly to the situation.

Anxious people struggle with having a hyperfunctional and hardworking amygdala and an underfunctioning hippocampus, which quickly makes them prone to mobilize the body for a fight, flight, or freeze response. When you're in flight mode, your sympathetic nervous system is activated and your brain releases stress hormones that make your heart beat faster and your breathing accelerate. You have tunnel vision, shaking, muscular tension, and other reactions. In flight mode, you get out of the situation. In freezing mode, the amygdala is so overactive that you can't fight or flee. When that overstimulation happens, the dorsal vagal nerve of your parasympathetic nervous system prepares your body to shut down as a survival response: your breathing and heart rate slow down, your mouth generates more saliva, you get quiet, and you basically freeze (Porges, 2001).

All these bodily reactions, as annoying as they can be, prepare you to handle a threat in the best possible way, by: (1) running away as fast as you can, called flight; (2) fighting back; or (3) freezing or playing dead. Sometimes, my clients are surprised to learn that, when dealing with anxiety, you can also experience a freezing response. Think about a person with flying phobia; in a plane, that person may experience a full freezing response. A person with agoraphobia may also experience freezing responses if walking in the streets. A person who struggles with social anxiety may go blank when giving a presentation. A person with spider phobia may check out completely when seeing a spider in the room.

Wherever you go, wherever you live, and regardless of your age, sexual orientation, or gender identification, you're wired to experience fear, anxiety, worries, and all related emotions. It's unavoidable. It's just that, when dealing with OCD, you have a reactive brain that prefers to overreact, overprepare, and overrespond when facing dangerous situations, so it shouts at your signs of danger at a high volume and at a high speed.

Exercise: Where Do You Feel Fear?

On the blank silhouette below, locate all the places in your body where you experience fear when having an obsession. Label the places with the physical sensation that you have.

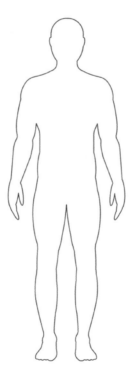

Figure 4.2 Human silhouette.

You Don't Like the Fear, Panic, and Anxiety That Come with Obsessions

We are all wired to experience all types of emotions: the unpleasant, pleasurable, fun, annoying ones, and all the variations in between. And to clarify, I'm referring to feelings and emotions interchangeably.

Emotions have been present throughout the history of humanity, from the cave person to *Homo sapiens*. We're emotional beings. However, despite this reality, the function of emotions in our regular day-to-day life was only acknowledged with the work of Antonio Damasio when neuroaffective science arose in 1995. Prior to that, emotions were seen as purposeless.

Emotions are present in every single thing we do. For example, think about a time when you walk into a grocery store and decide to get some cheese. You walk to the respective section, look at the dozens of cheese options on the shelf, and then you decide. That simple decision, right there, was influenced by your emotions. It may have happened when you chose one type of cheese over the other: when looking at all the options, you may have had a visceral reaction about some of them, a quick reaction in your body, and then you may have put that piece of data together with other variables – like the specific dish you want to cook with the cheese, your budget, type of gathering, and so on – so that, finally, you made a decision.

Generally speaking, emotions serve important purposes for our survival as a species, as a group and as individuals. They help us: (1) communicate with others, (2) figure out what's going on with us, (3) survive dangerous situations, (4) motivate ourselves to take action toward what's important to us, and (5) connect with others. If you do a short inventory of different periods in your life, you will likely find more than one event that shows how your emotions fulfilled each one of these functions.

As much as we don't like all emotions – especially the stressful ones – they are not good or bad. They just are. Emotions rise and fall and don't last forever, even though our mind tells us they do. But despite what we know about emotions at a scientific level, let's face it: uncomfortable emotions have a bad rap in our society, and consequently, fear has a bad rap, too.

Exercise: My Inventory of Emotions Related to OCD

List all the emotions you have had related to your OCD.

It's likely that you listed fear, anxiety, panic, or worry – and maybe all four emotions! But even if you haven't, let's check what you believe to be true about these emotions.

Exercise: What Have I Learned About Fear and Related Emotions?

In this space, write down everything you believe about the emotions you listed in the previous exercise. You may have picked up beliefs about certain emotions from parents, peers, teachers, or in all messages from pop culture. For example, if you wrote "panic" in your list, you might write here "Panic is a feeling only weak people have. It's for delicate people, and I'm ashamed to feel it."

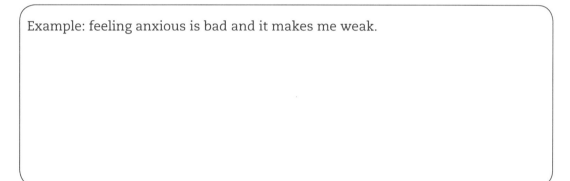

Example: feeling anxious is bad and it makes me weak.

When I ask my clients these questions, I usually hear responses along the lines of "Fear, anxiety, worry are signs of weakness; there is nothing to be afraid of, it's an annoying emotion; they block me from being happy," and so on. What came up for you?

In spite of what you have learned about your uncomfortable feelings over the years, here's the real-deal truth about fear, worry, panic, distress, and anxiety.

You Don't Decide What You're Afraid of, Worry, or Are Anxious About

When emotions happen to us, our brain quickly labels an emotional experience as good, bad, great, awful, awesome, terrible, and so on. Quite likely, your brain has labeled all those moments when you felt scared, panicky, worried, or anxious as terrible things that happen to you and as things to avoid at all costs. Am I close?

Here is a fact: having all those uncomfortable feelings is not a choice. We don't have control over them, we don't decide what to be afraid of. *But* – and this is a big but – as challenging as it sounds, we can learn to choose how to respond to them, feel whatever we feel, think whatever we think, and still do what's important to us.

Let's do a quick experiment. What if, right now, I ask you not to feel uncomfortable with all those bizarre intrusions that are showing up in your mind? What happens? Can you do that? Can you just stop feeling distressed about them? It's impossible to do that because, as much as we want to, we just don't have control over what we feel – it just happens that we feel what we feel.

Fear Can Be Handy at Times

Anxiety, fear, disgust, or anger – they're all different masks that our evolved threat-detection system wears. Our minds have evolved to always have our "threat-detection system on" and to be "better safe than sorry" for the benefit of our species. When I discuss this with my clients, they think that it's a crazy idea to consider that our fears, worries, and anxieties can be helpful at times. But what if you look back and check for yourself whether fear and its related feelings have ever been helpful to you?

For example, Rebecca got scared when her kid had a high fever, so she called the doctor; it turned out that her daughter had an infection. Her feelings were helpful in getting her daughter a diagnosis and medication. Another time, Rebecca received a one-line email from her boss asking her to meet him in his office in the next half-hour. Rebecca instantly got panicky and thought she would be fired, so she spent the next 30 minutes listing all the projects she had finished on time to present to her boss. She could barely think straight during the meeting, which turned out to be about a new program he wanted her input on.

Your turn.

Exercise: Checking How Fear Has Worked in Your Life

List here those situations in which **fear** has been helpful to you	List here those situations in which **fear** has NOT been helpful to you

No matter where we go or what we do, we carry this natural capacity to experience fear and all types of related emotions. In certain scenarios, especially if there are life-or-death situations, taking action based on those fearful feelings is going to be helpful. In others, it won't be.

You May Be Afraid of Feeling Afraid

Turning off fear and its related emotions is impossible. It's doubly hard for you, because having a reactive brain means that your hardworking amygdala is telling you to be scared and throwing danger signs at you every time an obsession shows up. Your reactive brain tries really hard to convince you that your automatic response to fear or your compulsion is good to do, the right thing to do, and that you should act on fear. It's like your brain says, "Hey, do what you need to do to keep yourself safe. Just do it."

And when you act on the automatic feelings that come with intrusive thoughts, then your brain learns that the only way to handle those disruptive moments is by acting on them, which could easily morph into developing *a feeling of being afraid about feeling afraid.* So tricky, right?

Think about it: when feeling frightened because of the content of disturbing thought, the most common response is to dislike those feelings. It's also natural to do whatever you can to make that feeling go away. But it's not so simple because, as you know, your brain will push you to do what you feel, and it will also judge what you feel; it's like your brain says things like "That was an awful emotion. I don't want to feel it ever again, it sucks . . . ." Yet the problem is that when you avoid an unwanted feeling, it festers and comes back stronger, causing you to repeat the obsession-compulsion cycle.

Are you fearful about feeling fearful? Keep in mind that there is really no such thing as "good" or "bad" feelings; there are only "helpful" and "unhelpful" reactions to your emotions.

In this workbook, you will learn to be the one deciding how to live your day-to-day life while having all types of obsessions and all the feelings that come along, *like the private stuff you experience and not like the private stuff that you have to act on.* You can't choose to feel what you feel; you can't choose what thought pops up in your mind, but you can choose how to respond to all those experiences and how to act moment by moment. It's hard work and not impossible!

You Take Your Thoughts Too Seriously

Years ago, Daisy found herself walking the streets of London, when suddenly she saw a kitchen-supply store. She got curious, walked inside, and, while browsing around, saw a couple of Japanese knives that looked perfect for making sushi. Daisy grabbed one of them, held it, passed her fingers over the blade and, out of the blue, she had this pretty disturbing thought: "What if I stab my children? What if I stab my husband?" She quickly dropped the knife, went out of the store, and called her mom. "Mom, did I ever do anything violent?" Her mom said, "None that I remember." For hours, Daisy walked the streets, going over and over her mom's words, "None that I remember." Daisy felt petrified at the idea of hurting her family, and it was worse hearing the words "I don't remember" from her mom. Daisy kept thinking, "Maybe I did something violent when I was a kid. Maybe I never told my mom. What if I did it – could I do it again? Is my family going to be safe?"

You may wonder why in the world Daisy would be thinking about hurting her family. Why would her mind come up with stuff like that? Could anything good come from it?

Every day, when you wake up, your mind wakes up, too, and that's the beginning of its incessant activity. It comes up with all types of content, about everything and anything, connecting all the dots, forward and backward and in all directions, putting together all types of possibilities and relating one thing to another thing.

As you are just learning, and will continue to do so, obsessions are another product of the mind, a bizarre, disturbing, and obnoxious one, and yet just another product of the mind. It's not that you have "wrong" thoughts, it's just that your mind and my mind come up with all types of content, including creepy themes at times. We are all capable of having unwanted obsessions, but regardless of how disturbing those obsessions can be, an obsession is just an obsession.

But why is our mind capable of coming up with bizarre content? Where is this capacity of our mind coming from? That's a million-dollar question, isn't it?

Here is a short response: evolution. The cave people before us had to survive dangerous, unpredictable, and unforgivable conditions, and overcome hundreds of obstacles for the *Homo sapiens* to evolve and for us to be here. Can you imagine how it was to be alive those times, doing what you could 24/7 to keep breathing and surviving from one moment to the next moment? Our ancestors had a really rough time for thousands of years, and their highest priority was to avoid danger. Through all those efforts they made over and over to avoid death, their brains acquired special capacities, such as scanning the environment for danger at all times, problem-solving as quickly as possible, keeping track of what went wrong in the past, what could go awfully wrong in the future, what rules to follow in the present, and many other ones that kept them alive. As a species, we morphed from *Pliopithecus* to *Australopithecus* and from *Homo erectus* to *Homo sapiens*, with many variations in between. We made it!

And, as our species made it, our brain made it too, with an important caveat for our times: *our environment has drastically changed, but our brain hasn't.* Basically, we're no longer surrounded by ferocious saber-toothed cats, volcanoes, wild rivers, and unreliable sources of food. We certainly have other types of dangerous situations, but most of us are not waking up every day with the constant fear of death. But remember, while our surroundings are really different, our brain is predisposed to behave exactly as it did millions of years ago. Our brain carries with it the capacity to scan the environment for danger, problem-solve dangerous situations, keep track of what went wrong in the past, anticipate what could go wrong later, and decide what safety-based rules to follow in any given moment.

Let's go back to Daisy and the question of why the mind would come up with such bizarre obsessions. Daisy's brain, my brain, your brain, and everybody's brain is predisposed to do so – no exceptions. But, you may wonder, why does it feel so real? Because the brain is not error-free.

As you are learning, the brain's ability to do all types of things that kept us alive as a species is not 100 percent perfect. The brain's job is to call your attention to what could put you in danger, and it's not exempt from making mistakes; those mistakes are called "prediction errors." Here is an example. If an ancestor got attacked by a mountain lion when drinking water from a river, it's quite likely that the next time the same ancestor needed to drink water from any river, he might hold onto the belief that there was a mountain lion around and do all types of things to avoid death, such as spending a couple of hours preparing tools to kill the lion, asking other members of his group to do the same, waiting for hours for the mountain lion to show up, and asking his group to measure how much water they're consuming, in case they run out of it, and so on. This particular cave person learned that river = mountain lion and mountain lion = death.

The academic term for this type of learning is *aversive associative learning*, and it has been a key role in explaining how OCD, trauma, and all types of anxiety – social anxiety, specific phobias, chronic worry, and panic attacks – get developed and maintained. Assuming, thinking, and anticipating that there will always be a mountain lion when one drinks water from a river is an evolutionarily adaptive process that helped our species to survive. But in contemporary times, responding quickly to any sign of danger around us in the same way that our ancestors did, without checking what's really happening in a given moment (is it really a mountain lion or a squirrel?) or noticing whether we are simply scared of a thought, image, or an urge, is a recipe for limited, narrow, and restricted living.

Having the brain that we have, as it is, is both a gift and a curse. The structure and functioning of our brain differentiate us from other species. The alarm system for danger that our brain is equipped with – the reticular activating system – helps us to survive. The constant scanning for danger that our brain does keeps us safe. And as part of our biological inheritance, our brain also pushes us to be risk-averse at all times to minimize what could hurt us and get rid of potential harm. Along with all those amazing attributes of the brain, the brain scans for threats not only outside of you, but also within you, and those bizarre thoughts, images, and urges are perceived as an internal threat that could harm you. And as with any tendency, some people have more of it and some people have less of it.

When your brain comes up with disgusting, disturbing, bizarre, or strange obsessions, it is just doing it what it is supposed to be doing: alerting you to potential danger, and that's the purpose of that content. But here is the big but: if you don't check what wild animal your brain is identifying as dangerous and take it literally as it is, then (and only then) do you have an OCD episode.

Are obsessions your enemy? Are obsessions a real enemy? Or are they just creations of your hardworking mind? Write down your response here:

_____

_____

_____

_____

_____

Now it's time to jot down all the obsessions that your mind has come up with. You may be dealing with a single obsession or a couple of them. You may have had one type of obsession in the past and new ones today. See if you can jot them all down on the next form, as if you're completing an inventory of those pesky obsessions.

I know you don't know me and I don't know you, but chances are that if you're like one of the clients I work with, you don't like having obsessions. And yet keep in mind that I'm not inviting you to like them or love them. In this moment, I'm inviting you to jot them down as they are: letters consonants and vowels put together.

Exercise: Inventory of Obsessions That Your Mind Comes Up With

Jot down all the obsessions your mind has come up with:

What reactions do you have when you notice that your mind is saying stuff like that? Did you have those reactions as you were simply writing them down? Is it when you take those thoughts too seriously that you end up getting fooled by those thoughts and believing them?

For now, keep in mind that obsessions, even the wackiest ones (as with any thought), cannot hurt you! You just have an overworking brain that is bossing you around, coming up with overwhelming feelings of fear, and trying to protect you at the same time!

5

Are There Different Types of OCD?

When I was the clinical director of a training site for doctoral students, I worked with a student for two consecutive years in a work-study position. Among the many memories I have from our time together are ones when I used to walk into the office and see colorful sticky-notes beautifully arranged on the whiteboard for different tasks and priority levels. To be honest, it was like a piece of art to see that degree of organization.

Our minds crave organization, categorization, and classification, and some of us, like my student and me, just love it! Sometimes, grouping pieces of data together makes things just more manageable to track, remember, make decisions about, and so on. And psychologists may well be prone to assembling, classifying, and putting things together, as you will see next.

Because intrusive thoughts are more common than not, the academic literature has grouped the different obsessions and compulsions into themes, and that's why most of the literature on this subject – whether academic, self-help, or blog posts – end up referring to the different types of OCD.

You may have heard about OCD subtypes, such as contamination OCD, washers, checkers, existential OCD, harm OCD, and so many others. While thinking of subtypes of OCD is very popular, what starts and then maintains OCD is the same for all of these forms, and the principles of the treatment are also the same for any form of OCD.

Some specialists agree that there are just *four* dimensions of OCD: harm, unacceptable thoughts, contamination, and symmetry Abramowitz, Taylor, and McKay (2009). In Table 5.1, I list alphabetically the most common subtypes of OCD that different types of literature, academic and self-help, have recognized so you can understand and manage better the cycle of OCD.

Table 5.1 Types of OCD

What's the theme?	What is this theme about?	What does this theme look like, and how does it feel?
Aggressive OCD or **Harm OCD**	The theme of these intrusions is about harming yourself or others as either a direct or indirect result of your actions. Aggressive obsessions can involve fears of self-harm or of causing harm to others, either by lethal forms of harm (e.g., stabbing, suffocating, strangling, shooting, poisoning oneself or another) or because of carelessness (e.g. "if I don't pay attention, they may fall down on the stairs" or "If I trip when holding a knife, I may stab them"). People dealing with aggressive or harm obsessions usually hold onto the thoughts of "Because I think so, it makes me so" or "If I don't do anything, if I don't prevent it, it's the same as me causing it." It's as if having these violent images or thoughts makes them a violent person or reveals their true aggressive persona, and if they don't pay attention to them, they believe that they may act on them or accidentally harm others. Avoidant behaviors may include the avoidance of people who could cause harm, of tools that could be used to harm, and of news, books, movies, or any other material related to harm.	Let's take a look at Sebastian and Thomas's experiences with this form of obsession: Sebastian, a college student, went to visit his parents for the summer. He did the usual summertime activities: going camping, cooking meals together, going for runs with his brothers, watching movies, and teasing his sister on and off. Sebastian was very close to his family and always looked forward to spending time with them after a stressful semester at school. After watching a documentary about typography, he went to sleep around 11 p.m., as he usually does. While sleeping, Sebastian had a nightmare about "slicing his parents" and woke up thinking about it the following day. Sebastian was shocked at having had that image, because deep down he loved his parents and wouldn't ever do anything to hurt them or his siblings. Sebastian didn't know what to make of it, but he kept thinking about whether he actually wanted to do this, so he checked his feelings toward his parents and started writing down the good moments he had with them to prove to himself that he didn't want to harm them. He started avoiding being in the kitchen with his parents because he was afraid about holding knives around them and preferred to be with both of them, rather than just one of them, in case he ended up attacking one of them.

Thomas, a stay-at-home dad, was doing the laundry as part of his regular weekly activities while the kids were at school and his wife at work. When pouring the laundry detergent into the laundry machine, he suddenly had an image of blood pouring out instead of detergent. He shook his head and felt a bit confused. As he continued doing errands in the house, picking up clothes and cleaning the mess the kids had left, he again saw images of blood, this time covering the curtains. He shook his head again and took a deep breath.

Thomas, not wanting to alarm his wife, went to the kitchen to have a glass of water and then saw dead bodies and mutilated parts. Thomas became petrified, thinking he'd lost his mind. He had never experienced these types of violent images before and didn't know what to do or who to talk to about them. He felt lonely, horrified at himself for having those images, and confused about his character. On his worst days, he would sit for hours, holding his head between both hands as if he could make it stop.

Let's think about the following contamination obsessions that Patricia has:

When Patricia walked into an office to fill out a job application, she carried her own pen because of her fear of getting contaminated and becoming ill when using pens from a public area.

Aggressive or harm compulsions may include checking that someone is okay; asking others if they did anything weird; checking your own intentions ("Did I really want to hurt my kid?"); anticipating future scenarios in case of causing potential harm to yourself or others; analysis of past scenarios or reviewing past scenarios to make sure that nothing has happened and, therefore, you're innocent.

Contamination OCD

This is, perhaps, one of the best-known forms of OCD, since it has been disseminated through social media quite often.

People with fears of contamination get hooked into the fear of "being contaminated" due to direct contact with different substances, such as toxic chemicals, dirt, germs, garbage, sticky substances, bodily fluids (saliva, semen, feces, etc.), and objects that are infected by any of the contaminants.

(Continued)

Table 5.1 (Continued)

What's the theme?	What is this theme about?	What does this theme look like, and how does it feel?
	Everyday compulsive behaviors may include excessive handwashing, excessively long showers, wearing gloves, sanitizing different areas, changing clothing that has been exposed to the street environment before letting it come into contact with furniture in the house, asking others if it's safe to go to a particular place, or asking if a stain or contaminant that a person stepped in is safe. Avoidant behaviors usually include staying away from contaminated places such as hospitals, public bathrooms, people who have a particular illness, shaking hands with people who could potentially contaminate them, and so on. In the past, the literature has included emotional contamination within the subtype of contamination obsessions. However, in recent years, the literature has mentioned a new theme of OCD, metaphysical OCD, that includes obsessions about emotional contamination. Metaphysical OCD is described further in this table.	On her way to the grocery store, Patricia saw a reddish stain on the ground. She immediately had the thought, "This could be blood. Did I step on it?" She checked the stain from different angles, trying to figure out if it was dry or not, looking at its size and its texture. She called her friends to ask what they would do or whether she should throw away the shoes she was wearing. When hanging out with others, Patricia generally avoided shaking their hands, or she waited for others to open doors in public spaces. Throughout all these episodes, Patricia felt very embarrassed about having to do all these checking behaviors. She worried about people seeing her doing them, and she felt frustrated with herself for not being able to stop them.
Existential OCD	This theme of obsessions involves philosophical thoughts, existential matters, and reflections about life issues. While they seem like natural reflections that every person has at one time or another, at some point these thoughts arise alongside extreme distress that is hard to let go of.	Here is how existential obsessions showed up in Theresa's daily life: After meeting with a financial advisor, Theresa agreed that it was important for her to get life insurance to protect her family.

Most well-known existential obsessions are about death, life after death, feeling love after death, making the best of life, whether emotions are the right ones in a given situation, immortality, life-after-death experiences, and other similar matters.

Compulsive behaviors may include scanning memories about life events in which a person experienced particular feelings, replaying emotional experiences (such as falling in love, being excited about life, etc.), dissecting past encounters when having a particular feeling to make sure it was the right one, discussing existential topics or life issues as a form of "figuring them out" and hoping to find the "right response," searching online about existential matters, and reading books about philosophical matters.

When signing the life insurance form, the advisor lightly asked, "Do you think that you're living your life as you wanted to?" Theresa paused for a moment and thought about the question. It was as if she was wondering about it for the first time, and she became quiet. After signing the documents, she found herself walking toward her car trying to answer that exact question: "Have I been living my life as I wanted to?" Theresa mechanically started driving the car and couldn't stop thinking about the question. She started replaying moments in her life, times when she felt connected with others, times with her family that were difficult, and times when she had dating issues. Theresa kept wondering whether she was living life at her best, whether she was making the right choices about how to spend her time and her money, and on and on.

Theresa also pondered at length about the impact of her behavior on others: "Am I doing right by others? Am I having an impact on other people? Am I balancing things out in my life?"

At times, she was able to answer those questions with a partially satisfying response, but the thoughts kept showing up nevertheless, again and again, forcing her on a deep downward spiral of thinking about matters that didn't have a definite answer.

These thoughts were very stressful for Theresa because she could not let them go even as they exhausted her completely.

(Continued)

Table 5.1 (Continued)

What's the theme?	What is this theme about?	What does this theme look like, and how does it feel?
Hyperawareness OCD	This form of OCD is also known as somatic OCD or somatosensory OCD. This group of fears relates to concerns about the quality of specific involuntary bodily reactions or bodily functions, such as breathing, swallowing, amount of saliva, itching, ringing in the ears, blinking, body smell, and the like. Compulsive behaviors typically include contacting doctors, searching online, and checking the quality and intensity of bodily functions (for example, "Am I breathing the same amount of air as this morning?" or "Is this tingling sensation moving from one finger to another?"). Because the focus of these obsessions is on functions that happen automatically in a person's body, people with this form of OCD fear not being able to stop being aware of them (e.g., "What if I cannot stop paying attention to them and it ruins my life?") or not being able to distract themselves from them because they're present at all times. People struggling with hyperawareness obsessions usually engage in massive dosages of body checking and body scanning. Some carry on with regular day-to-day activities like work and school and so on; on the surface they appear fine, because they're not avoiding any situations or activities. Yet they're internally preoccupied and hyperfocused on their bodily sensations.	Consider Shareen and Rudolph's day-to-day experiences with hyperawareness OCD: Shareen gets triggered when perceiving any movement or light changes in her peripheral vision – she checks around, moving her eyes slowly, looking to see if something is there. She continues checking until she feels comfortable. Shareen is concerned that if she doesn't check around, her peripheral vision will be affected. When Rudolph was getting a routine teeth cleaning, he noticed that the technician spent more time on his bottom right teeth. At the end of the procedure, Rudolph felt a bit of an itch and sharp sensation in that area, so he immediately asked for a mirror; he checked whether there was an irritation and whether the redness was different than the rest of his gums. He asked the technician multiple times about the irritation and was told that the reaction was normal, but as soon as Rudolph left the dental facility, he searched on his phone about those reactions. Rudolph found multiple websites. While reading all types of information, he continued to inspect his gums in front of a mirror, asked his wife to contact another dentist just in case, and got hooked on the thought, "I'm afraid that if I don't do anything about it, my gums can have major problems later on, get weak, and I may even loose bone in that area."

Despite doctors ruling out medical conditions, people with hyperawareness obsessions get hooked on thoughts about something being wrong with their health, feel a strong need to prevent that potential medical condition from occurring, and continue to engage in checking behaviors and mental compulsions.

Rudolph struggled with a fear of having an undiagnosed condition that would get worse, even though doctors had denied that possibility. He got hooked on this obsession and couldn't let it go, to the point that he concentrated all his efforts, energy, and resources trying to "figure out" what could go wrong with his body in the future.

But he did feel temporarily better when reading blogs, asking his wife to book appointments, monitoring the redness and sharp sensation of his gums when eating different types of food, testing if the temperature of food affected that area, trying different toothpastes, and taking pictures on a daily basis. Rudolph was sad that he couldn't pursue his passion for art since often he spent most of his time making sure he wasn't sick.

Just-right OCD

This classification of OCD usually refers to obsessions about a sensation or feeling that is interpreted as weird, uncomfortable, distressing, or off. Because these obsessions are so sticky – meaning they're extremely difficult to let go of – a person engages in compulsions related to symmetry, ordering, arranging their physical environment, or any other form of compulsive behavior until the "weird" situation "feels right." Because of these organizing behaviors, this form of OCD is also known as perfectionistic OCD.

Let's see what Allyson, Theresa, and Todd's struggles with just-right OCD looks like for them:

When Allyson walks into her living room, she notices a weird feeling when detecting the position of the TV in regard to the painting on the wall, so she arranges both objects until they feel right to her. Sometimes she arranges them symmetrically and sometimes not.

Allyson leaves her house every morning to go to work, but when walking through the back door she walks in and out multiple times. Sometimes four times, sometimes eight. But as a rule, she only stops going back and forth until it feels right and satisfying to her.

(Continued)

Table 5.1 (Continued)

What's the theme?	What is this theme about?	What does this theme look like, and how does it feel?
	Just-right OCD also includes mental compulsions characterized by a person repeating sayings, making lists, counting words, praying, or the like until the person or their situation feels right.	Allyson also engages in mental compulsions related to keeping track of her activities, because she is afraid of losing her mind and decompensating. So every day she matches a word or term with a specific activity. For example, "waking up" is matched to her morning routine, "book" is repeated every time she picks up a book. "Breakfast" is matched to the action of preparing her usual cereal, but if a different milk or cereal is used, Allyson adds an additional word to her list, such as "breakfast-vanilla." If she has breakfast at her parents' house, she creates the word "breakfast-mom-vanilla."
	A popular misconception is that people dealing with these types of obsessions or compulsive behaviors are, in general, very organized, neat, and like perfection, but this is an assumption that is usually very far from the truth.	
	Yes, some people dealing with this form of obsession may prefer and like to keep things organized, but not everyone who has an obsession or any form of OCD will automatically inherit those preferences.	The list of "matching words" grows longer and longer as Allyson moves throughout her day. As she tracks every activity, she sometimes repeats the entire word list a different number of times until they feel right to her.
	And just to make it crystal clear, the compulsions (organizing behaviors) are driven by the wish to avoid the discomfort that comes with the uncomfortable feelings that "something is wrong and off" about an environment or situation. These compulsive behaviors are not necessarily meant to prevent something bad from happening – they're meant to neutralize, get rid of, or minimize the distress they feel.	If someone talked to Allyson when she was in the middle of doing a mental compulsion, she would get very upset, because she had to restart the mental compulsion. However, people only witnessed her getting abruptly angry; they didn't have a clue that Allyson was stuck in her head.
		At the end of the day, Allyson continued her mental compulsion and analyzed whether the list of "matching words" was different than the one from the day before and whether there was a particular meaning inherent in that.

Allyson felt exhausted most of the time because she spent a significant amount of time in her head, and while she genuinely cared about connecting with others, she didn't know how to manage. She felt scared about the outcome of not completing her mental compulsion.

Theresa was concerned about not explaining things properly and about not using the right words when delivering a presentation at work. So afterward, she asked her teammates if they understood what she had said and whether her ideas had been conveyed properly. At home, she replayed in her mind how her delivery went.

Todd was dealing with his obsession about making mistakes when completing writing projects in his English class, so he compulsively wrote down all the directions given by the instructor, asked classmates to share the directions as they understood them, and compared notes. Todd couldn't start working on essays or projects unless he was reassured that he was doing them perfectly. When working on the essays, he rewrote and retyped them multiple times, but he would get stuck because he would question if a particular word was the right one to use.

Let's think for a moment of Sidney, who has been struggling with obsessions since adolescence because of fears of contamination and harm. After getting diagnosed with OCD and starting exposure exercises, he

(Continued)

Meta OCD   This is a fairly new topographical description about obsessions and related matters; in other words, the theme of meta OCD is about OCD itself. Meta OCD may involve issues related to (a) making obsessions worse, (b) doubting about the diagnosis, (c) fears about your character or who

Table 5.1 (Continued)

What's the theme?	What is this theme about?	What does this theme look like, and how does it feel?
	you are because of obsessions, or (d) concerns about the appropriateness of treatment or the treatment itself. As you can see, this is another example of how the brain can latch onto anything and everything as an obsession and as compulsion. Some examples of obsessions involve questions like: what if I actually don't get better? Do I have OCD? Am I faking OCD? How do I know I'm in a good place to leave treatment and not go back to where I was before? Am I lying about having OCD? Some examples of compulsions could be asking for reassurance from others or searching for all types of mental health resources (self-help books, forums, OCD tests, etc.).	spent significant time in his therapy sessions asking his clinician about whether he's doing the exposures correctly, whether they could make his OCD worse, and if it's possible he's faking OCD to get attention. After therapy, he usually spent a couple of hours searching for the highest-rated self-help books, mental health resources, podcasts that focus on personal growth, anxiety, and OCD. On a weekly basis, Sidney also completed an online version of the Yale-Brown Obsessive Compulsive Scale to check his scores and see whether his OCD symptoms were worsening.
Metaphysical OCD	This form of OCD has been recently mentioned in the literature, so there is not much written about it, although quite likely, it has affected the lives of many before now. When dealing with this theme of obsessions, people get triggered with particular feelings, vibes, or energies as if those internal experiences are symbols, cues, or omens that could cause harm to themselves or others. Some past literature has referred to this theme of obsession as emotional contamination OCD.	Here is how Fernando experiences metaphysical obsessions: Fernando loves to explore different types of food, learn different languages, and become immersed in different cultures. He always takes the opportunity to travel with his parents, uncles, and cousins, whether locally, within the country, or internationally. Traveling is Fernando's passion. During his senior year in high school, his cohort decided to travel to Bolivia, Peru, Paraguay, and Ecuador. Fernando was looking forward to the trip for months, since he hadn't been to South America before.

He wanted to practice Spanish and see indigenous cultures. During his trip, Fernando had strong vibes when visiting some sites, and when talking to some indigenous people, he started compulsively dissecting the meaning of those vibes and energies.

Fernando's obsession grew quickly. He started hugging people in different ways based on whether he was feeling bad energy or good energy; he was afraid that something bad would happen to him if he was around bad energy. As he continued traveling, he also continued checking his vibes, or intuitions, about colors, shapes, and activities. With every situation, activity, or person he encountered, he immediately scanned his feelings about them.

One day, Fernando met a girl who didn't have good energy, and hours later he got laid off from his job as camp counselor. When he received the email, Fernando's brain made the connection that the girl's negative energy caused him to lose his job, and he couldn't stop thinking about it.

Fernando's list of compulsions and avoidant behaviors grew to include day-to-day activities such as chewing enough times until it felt right, changing clothing when having a bad vibe with the piece of clothing, not reading a book if it had a bad energy, stopping watching a movie when having bad vibes, avoiding specific workout machines at the gym that had a bad energy, and avoiding saying words that had a bad vibe.

(Continued)

Strong beliefs in metaphysical or alternative energies are common in some cultures; and just to clarify, I'm not saying that holding these beliefs is inherently problematic. What is problematic is when an over-reactive brain gets hooked on obsessions and compulsions triggered by energies, feelings, or vibes and this cycle gets socially reinforced because of cultural messages. For instance, in the area where I live, doing "manifestations or creating manifestos" is a very popular practice; when creating a manifesto, you are asked to visualize your future in any area of your life, and you're encouraged to ask the universe for that future to become a reality. Creating a manifesto assumes that by imagining your future, you will make it happen, which reinforces the idea that you have control over your thoughts and that all those feelings and sensations you experience have a particular meaning.

In other words, there is a difference between practicing some activities flexibly (e.g., doing a visualization exercise of your future) versus rigidly attaching meaning to them ("If I say this, it always means this" or "I cannot say this, because it means this" or "I cannot say this, and it may happen"). A reactive brain can easily get hooked onto thoughts such as "because I think so, it makes me so", "I feel it, therefore it's true", "thinking about it makes it happen," or "feeling this, means this . . . ." As with

Table 5.1 (Continued)

What's the theme?	What is this theme about?	What does this theme look like, and how does it feel?
	many forms of OCD, a person with a metaphysical obsession can easily end up attributing power and meaning to every single word, sentence, or feeling, thus establishing a problematic cause-and-effect relationship.	Fernando felt very stressed about catching and neutralizing the vibe of things, but he got hooked with the thought that "indigenous people have lived for years in this way, so energy experiences must be true." Fernando lost his ability to organize his life around what he cared about. He couldn't show up as the friend he wanted to be. Fernando felt down, depressed, and sad about his world getting narrower and narrower. He didn't know how to handle all those horrible feelings he had about many things around him.
Moral OCD See **Scrupulosity OCD**.		
Pedophile OCD	Pedophile OCD encompasses thoughts about molesting children, feeling sexually attracted to children, and committing incest. Unfortunately, this may be one of the most misunderstood forms of OCD. There is a variable that makes pedophile obsessions complicated, but not unworkable,: groinal responses – groinal responses experiences groinal responses – and everyone experiences tingling, itching, scratchy reactions – and everyone experiences arousal reactions that vary in intensity from moment to moment. These responses are dynamic instead of ecstatic experiences. They are triggered when we're with our romantic partners or without them and when hanging out with people of all ages, including children.	Let's consider the situations that Suni went through. After Suni gave a bath to her 2-year-old daughter and touched her vagina while washing her, Suni had an image of her daughter's naked body and with it the thought "Am I a pedophile? Did I like touching her parts? Why did I have that image? If I touched her private parts and have this image, it's because I'm a pedophile." Suni spent hours and hours replaying other times she gave her daughter a bath, changed her daughter's clothes, or held her daughter on her lap. She began to panic. When having these images, Suni started telling herself, "I'm not a pedophile, I'm not a pedophile. I didn't do anything, didn't feel anything." The thought of being a "pedophile" was 100 percent incongruent with who she wants to be, her character, and her personal values.

The challenge is that these uncontrollable reactions are quickly interpreted by a reactive brain, eager to prove that something is wrong with the person that has them: it is as if when they have those groinal reactions, it means the person wants to act on them.

A person dealing with pedophilia obsessions can easily spend significant amounts of time compulsively replaying past scenarios when dealing with triggering situations, checking their bodily reactions for potential signs of sexual attraction, or anticipating and preventing how they would handle future situations if they were to have them.

A person struggling with this type of obsessions does not want to hurt children; their obsession is with their unwanted thoughts about what could happen.

Perfectionistic OCD
See "Just-right OCD."

Postpartum OCD

This class of obsessions includes intrusive thoughts about either intentionally or accidentally harming one's own baby (e.g., contaminating one's baby with toxic products, doing something inappropriate, transferring bad energies, and so on).

It's extremely distressing and panicky for a parent to experience and acknowledge these intrusive thoughts when they are expected to be happy and bubbly about becoming a parent, and because of this social pressure, there is much secrecy around this type of obsession.

On top of all those painful moments rushing through her mind, Suni didn't share any of this with anybody, because she was hooked on the thought that "saying it out loud" would somehow prove the validity and accuracy of the thought.

Suni felt that she was crazy for having these thoughts, that there was something fundamentally wrong with her for having them, and she didn't know how to get unstuck from her own mind.

Let's look at Sheela's experience with postpartum OCD following the delivery of her first baby.

Sheela brought her newborn baby home and, in her first weeks, she began to experience all the peaks and valleys that come with caring for a newborn: loving the baby every day, feeling exhausted for not sleeping, learning the baby's needs, bonding with the baby, watching the baby sleeping, and just living motherhood all the way.

(Continued)

Table 5.1 (Continued)

What's the theme?	What is this theme about?	What does this theme look like, and how does it feel?
	While most of the literature has suggested that only mothers are affected by postpartum obsessions, there is preliminary research that suggests that fathers experience this form of obsessions as well (Abramowitz et al., 2001). This, of course, makes sense, given that the brain could latch into anything as an obsession and as a compulsion; there is no reason why the overreactive brain of a father cannot latch onto fears of harming a baby, doing something inappropriate, and so on. Obsessions, in the end, are not a matter of gender but a matter of a brain perceiving danger when bizarre and non-bizarre thoughts, images, and urges pop up. Compulsions may include: repeatedly checking that the baby's blankets are not close to his face when he is sleeping, so he doesn't suffocate; checking multiple times that there are no other objects in the crib; holding a mirror to check if the baby is breathing; checking with sitters to see if the baby is okay; asking people to be come over so that the parent isn't alone with the baby; and so on. Avoidant behaviors usually include resisting the following: being alone with the baby, changing the baby's diapers, being around sharp objects, giving the baby a bath, holding the baby, walking while holding the baby, feeding the baby, and the like.	One day Sheela's baby had a high fever, so Sheela spent time next to her, checking her temperature, giving liquids to her, and changing one diaper after another. While changing diapers, Sheela had the thought "What if I insert my finger in my kid's vagina?" and she got really terrified and disturbed about this thought, as if having it meant she wanted to do so. Sheela couldn't let go of this thought. She prayed at night hoping it would go away and that it had never happened. She kept it secret and, a week later, told her husband he needed to take time off from work because she couldn't continue taking care of the baby alone. As time passed by, Sheela couldn't stop thinking about the bizarre thought about touching her daughter inappropriately, and she replayed mentally over and over how she had changed her diaper. Sheela couldn't bear this obsession. She felt terribly guilty about having it, and she took it as an indication that she maybe secretly wanted to harm her baby – which only made things worse for her. Sheela was physically exhausted from all the chores that come with taking care of a baby, and on top of that, mentally exhausted for all the efforts she was making in her head to deal with this obsession.

Pure O, Pure OCD, or Mental OCD

"Pure OCD" is a term that has created controversy among clinicians, researchers, and OCD sufferers. Because of the way it's written, it conveys the message that a person dealing with pure OCD only has obsessions, with no compulsions.

Here is my take: there is no need to argue about this label but to understand it within its context. If you look at the literature on OCD, most of it was focused on public compulsions that are visible to the eyes of everyone, and while there were some writings about people that have mental compulsions, not much was written about it. In fact, we don't know how many people got undiagnosed because of the lack of awareness of mental compulsions and not knowing they were suffering with OCD.

With that premise, let's briefly clarify that pure OCD or mental OCD is a myth given that all OCD episodes include both obsessions and compulsions. Even if a compulsion is private, not visible to others, it's still a compulsion.

These obsessions can be prompted by all types of triggers, such as fears of getting contaminated, existential themes, doing things right, and everything in between. The key characteristic is that once triggered, the compulsions are private, no one sees them, and even the sufferer doesn't know that they are engaging in a mental compulsion, because all they're focused on is getting rid of the distress that comes along with these wacky obsessions.

Let's go over Jessica and Jack's struggles to make sense of mental OCD. Keep in mind that you will read many other examples of mental compulsions in Part III, "The Trilogy That Makes Your Life Miserable."

Jessica battles with her obsession about forgetting key information about her personal life. When triggered, she creates mental lists and pictures all of the different tasks she has to complete during the day. She matches the activity to a word that both describes the activity and the memory of it. If, for whatever reason Jessica was interrupted in the middle of her compulsion, or if she became confused about a particular task, she would start the matching activity all over again, from the beginning of her day.

Jack was a lawyer in transition between firms, so he had some extra time on his hands to do fun things. He was watching movies, reading books, going for mini road trips here and there, and generally enjoying his month off. On his way back from eating Thai food, he saw a woman on the train reading the book *Zen and the Art of Motorcycle Maintenance*. He was kind of curious about the title and asked this person a few questions. At the end of their ride, Jack was quite curious, so he ordered the book on his cell phone.

When reading it, Jack found himself pondering about the purpose of life and whether he was living the life he was supposed to live. He found himself sad, confused, and scared about not being able to respond to these questions with any certainty. Jack spent hours trying to remember different life memories from his

(Continued)

Table 5.1 (Continued)

What's the theme?	What is this theme about?	What does this theme look like, and how does it feel?
	To make it crystal clear, obsessions may show up as thoughts like "did I? could I? would I? do I want to do x, what if I do . . .?" And then the response to those thoughts is more thinking, dwelling, repeating sentences, dissecting, figuring out, and so on.

Table 9.1 in Chapter 9 charts the different forms that mental compulsions have, so you will read more about them there. As an example of what you will read in that chart, some mental compulsions look low-key, like saying sentences, repeating words or counting numbers, but they can also be very complex, like replaying past scenarios over and over until they feel right, because your brain is holding on to a memory that feels safe and right and blocks the disturbing obsessions. | childhood right up to the present, thinking about whether those moments were truly meaningful for him, if he was living at his best. Sometimes, the more he did, the more he found moments of relief, but at other times he kept going, because he was worried about missing important indicators that could repeat in the future.

When Jessica and Jack experienced those thoughts – natural reflective thoughts as they may appear – they came with tons of desperation, distress, and fear, because they could not fully figure them out.

Jessica and Jack didn't know that all the overthinking, replaying, and overanalyzing they were doing when trying to solve their obsessions were exactly what was making them feel as if they were losing their minds. |
| Relationship OCD (R-OCD) | R-OCD covers obsessions relating to relationships. While initially this category only included obsessions affecting romantic relationships, these days the academic literature also reports cases between parents and children, and even relationships with spiritual authorities.

While it's natural for all of us to deliberate about the "fit" of a romantic relationship – whether our feelings for our partner are real or not – the high degree of panic, fear, and anguish that comes with these reflections is considered a form of OCD. Reflecting on life matters is one thing, but having obsessions about relationships that are hard to | To understand R-OCD thinking better, let's briefly think of David.

David is the father of three children and has been married for over 18 years. He works full-time and does his best to have a regular rhythm between work and family life.

One day, his teenage daughter, Martha, started arguing with him about wanting to go for a sleepover. The argument ended up with her being upset and running to her bedroom, and David talking to his wife about how difficult it was to raise teens. The next day, David woke up thinking "Do I love Martha? I guess I do, but is it possible that I don't?" He felt awful that day and |

(Continued)

let go of, that are more like sticky thoughts, and that, when unresolved, stop a person from moving forward in their day-to-day activities is quite another, and can be extremely painful.

Current writings recognize relationship OCD as having two variations: relationship-centered and partner-focused (Doron et al., 2014). In plain language, these variations can be seen in three types of common obsessions and many variations or combinations of them:

(1) "Is this the right relationship for me (e.g., "Am I just settling down?" "Would this relationship be a long-lasting one?")?"

(2) "Do I really love this person? (romantic partner, parent, child, religious figure)?"

(3) "Does this person really love me?"

People struggling with this type of obsession can spend years not fully committing to a partner in a relationship, and it may even appear as if they have "commitment phobia," whereas they may well be struggling with intrusive thoughts about relationships.

Frequent compulsions may include a person testing their feelings when spending time with their partner (e.g., "Am I in love?"; "Do I feel love?"); searching for that "Aha!" moment or for warm feelings inside; checking their sense of attraction or their romantic memories; or comparing current feelings with feelings they had with previous partners.

called his wife to ask her if he had ever treated their daughter differently than the other kids. Even though she answered that she'd never noticed anything, David couldn't stop thinking about it.

At the end of day, when driving to pick his children up from school, he started checking how he felt about his daughter when she was talking, laughing, or listening to music. David even asked his daughter to recall the most challenging conversations they had had together, so when she was recalling those events he could try to remember how he felt about her in those moments, to make sure "he loved her."

David couldn't understand what was going on. He was upset with himself for thinking in such a bizarre way, and he was petrified at the idea of "not loving his daughter" – as well as at the thought of "talking to others about it." He would ask himself "What type of monster am I, if I don't love my daughter?"

Table 5.1 (Continued)

What's the theme?	What is this theme about?	What does this theme look like, and how does it feel?
	Common public compulsions may include asking for reassurance about being loved, asking others if they observed cues that their partner loves them, and discussing the quality of the relationships with their partners. Avoidant behaviors may include steering clear of the following: saying "I love you" to a partner; responding to compliments about the relationship; or having intimate relationships with romantic partners. The challenge with these obsessions is that they can go unrecognized for years because they can appear as natural reflections that any thoughtful person has. However, in the day-to-day life of a person suffering with OCD, they're painful, take them into agony, and keep them in an analysis-paralysis state. Usually sufferers cannot make sense of what's happening to them because they're fighting thinking with more thinking.	
Religious OCD See **Scrupulosity OCD**.		
Responsibility OCD	This category of OCD refers to the unsettling fear of being irresponsible and causing harm or potential harm, whether intentionally or by accident. It is very similar to harm OCD. The academic literature has highlighted that these OCD sufferers present with an extreme sense of hyper-responsibility about their behaviors and the impact of them on others.	To understand this form of obsessive thinking better, let's consider Frank: Frank was very thoughtful about protecting the environment, and during college he participated in different grassroots activities to create awareness about the interaction between the environment and human behavior.

Other authors have tagged obsessions about responsibility as a theme, and that's how the name of responsibility OCD emerged.

Obsessions about being responsible for causing harm to others can vary from causing death, emotional harm, or other types of harm (such as environmental harm or moral harm). See **Harm OCD** for a more elaborate explanation of this.

A subtle difference that some authors note is that, at the core, clients with this form of OCD are engaging in compulsions to prevent not only harm but also to prevent feeling guilty, remorseful, or regretful.

After graduating from college, Frank decided to go to law school to pursue environmental law.

During a lunch gathering, he couldn't help noticing how his classmates didn't recycle plates or cups, threw everything to the garbage, and didn't care about how many plastic utensils they used. Frank felt a strong wave of heat going through his body and thought "What if I don't do anything about it? Then global warming is going to accelerate. The islands of plastics will grow – and I cannot live with it. What if I don't do anything about it? Does that make me a bad person? I can't live with it!"

Frank started to pick up his classmates' trash discreetly and to separate the recycling items in a corner of the lunch room. At the end of the gathering, Frank wondered if he was recycling all the items properly – whether he was leaving toxic residues that could harm the earth and cause death to other species. Frank got hooked onto that thought: "Did I do it right, so the planet doesn't get more damaged?" After replaying in his mind what he recycled and how he did it, he felt still uncomfortable, so he couldn't stop asking a classmate next to him: "I did separate recyclable items from non-recyclable ones properly, right?"

Frank's fear about harming the environment was not so weird (remember the discussion in Chapter 1 about the different forms of obsessions), but the degree of guilt, distress, and agony that Frank experienced because of the thoughts made it hard for him to keep going with his learning and school activities. It tortured him.

(Continued)

Table 5.1 (Continued)

What's the theme?	What is this theme about?	What does this theme look like, and how does it feel?
Scrupulosity OCD, Moral OCD, and Religious OCD	Scrupulosity OCD refers to obsessions related to the fear of intentionally or accidentally committing immoral acts, being an immoral person, saying or doing things wrong, or engaging in any form of behavior that goes against a person's morals, standards, or religious beliefs. The specifics of an obsession that is incongruent with a person's religious beliefs varies from person to person, given their religious background. For instance, within the Jewish community some examples of obsessions are fears of violating dietary restrictions or disrespecting the Shabbat (Sabbath). For a person from a Christian background, some obsessions involve offending God, going to hell, or disrespecting religious authorities (Huppert & Siev, 2010). Most common efforts to neutralize those obsessions may include compulsions like: excessive praying, asking for reassurance, figuring out or replaying a religious practice, asking God for forgiveness, confessing sin, repeatedly checking to see if a sin was committed, avoiding spiritual contamination, or avoiding spiritual services or figures that may be triggers. Unfortunately, those who struggle with this form of obsessions find it difficult to distinguish religious behavior from compulsive responses to an obsessive fear of not living according to their	Let's look at the daily struggles that Tammy and Tim encountered. Tammy was talking to her mom about how her marriage was going, but she felt weird about not saying the truth, as if she was intentionally lying. Tammy said things like "I think this is what happened . . ." and "I'm not fully sure, but I think this is what I said . . ." After the conversation, Tammy was struggling with trying to figure out her compulsions: "Did I say the truth? Is that what really happened? What exactly did I tell my mom? If my mom saw me looking downward, she may think that I was lying." When Tim was walking in the street, he heard a teenager saying, "Oh gosh, fuck this." Tim got hooked on the obsession of "what if I'm associated with this person? Then that means I'll be committing a sin" and got fearful about the possibility committing a sin. On another occasion, Tim was at a service and got distracted listening to two children talking and playing. He started thinking, "If I wasn't paying attention, does it mean my faith is not strong enough? Does it mean I don't care about God?" As a compulsion, Tim told himself, "God knows my heart; God sees what I'm made of; God trusts me." For Tammy and Tim, having obsessions about their morality was really sad, because they grew up valuing their morals and religious principles. Having to question their behavior as immoral or sinful made each

religious beliefs. In fact, they may see a compulsion as a commendable behavior, even though it's exhausting, stressful, and hard to handle in their lives.

Sexual Orientation OCD, Homosexual OCD (HOCD), Gay OCD

This is another form of OCD that is usually misconstrued and underdiagnosed. Common obsessions are about sexual orientation, infidelity, sexual deviations, and, at times, sexual thoughts related to religious authority figures or religious figures (Gordon, 2002).

These forms of obsessions have nothing to do with a person's view of homosexuality but with intrusive thoughts, worries, and fears about feeling attracted to or wanting to be with someone of a different sexual orientation than they're usually attracted to. This applies to people of all genders and sexual orientations. For instance, a homosexual person could have intrusive thoughts about being straight, and so on.

And just to make it crystal clear, a core difference between sexual orientation obsessions versus being confused about sexual orientation or having sexual fluidity is that obsessions are extremely upsetting, stressful, pop up out of the blue, and are inconsistent with a person's history of sexual preferences. Sexual obsessions are also different than sexual fantasies or horny thoughts, because these latter ones involve pleasure, fun, and are enjoyable.

one of them overly focused on their thinking, as they spent hours and hours searching for the truth; at the end of each one of those moments of search, they felt discouraged about not finding an absolute answer and felt confused about what type of person they really were or what their true morals were.

Consider Tom's experience with these forms of obsessions to make sense of what he went through.

Tom had felt attracted to boys since he was a child. He had a crush on his best friend in elementary school but didn't say or do much about it because of his religious background. During his adolescent years, he had sexual encounters with both boys and girls and, as time went on, around the age of 16, he came out as gay. He continued with his life, living as a homosexual and having different partners, went to college, graduated, and started his own company, but in his late thirties he had a dream about being straight and having sex with a woman. Tom woke up in the middle of the night, hyperventilating and feeling frightened.

Tom started journaling all the reactions he had when interacting with women – watching movies, shows, or commercials involving women, checking if he had any physical attraction to them – and he started to engage in more stereotypical gay behaviors to prove to himself he was gay.

(Continued)

Table 5.1 (Continued)

What's the theme?	What is this theme about?	What does this theme look like, and how does it feel?
	People having sexual obsessions may have thoughts along the lines of "I notice I'm paying more attention to girls than guys – like, I like checking them out, and checking how cute they are. Is that because I'm gay?"	Tom also started replaying all the relationships he had had with women before, trying to remember how it felt to be with them, checking what type of feelings he had for them and whether he got turned on or not. He often got hooked on the thought, "What if I'm straight and I just have been denying it all this time?"
	Sometimes people stressed with this form of obsessions are terrified that, somehow, they're in denial of their real sexual orientation, and entertain thoughts such as "Maybe I'm just scared about coming out. Maybe one day I'll wake up and I'll have to come out of the closet."	The hardest part for Tom was that he really cared for his relationships, all of them; dealing with these sexual obsessions led him to isolate, avoid hanging out with the people he cared about, doubt himself, and waste hours and hours stuck in his head.
	Compulsive behaviors may include checking whether a sufferer feels more attracted to people of a different sexual orientation than they're usually attracted to; checking their desire to have sexual contact with the other person, (e.g., "Do I want to kiss her?"; "Do I want to have sex with them?"); testing their intentions when hanging out with others of a different sexual orientation; figuring out the physical sensations they experience; trying to find the meaning of having these thoughts; confessing their thoughts about their opposite sexual orientation as a way to validate and reassure themselves what they're not.	
	Avoidant behaviors usually include minimizing contact with people who are triggers and cutting down on watching TV shows or any social media related to people of the sexual orientation that is a trigger for them.	

Somatic or Soma-
tosensory OCD
See **Hyper-awareness**
OCD.

Suicidal and Self-
harm OCD

Suicidal or para-suicidal behaviors are usually associated with mood disorders such as depression or bipolar disorder and chronic emotion regulation problems.

However, because an overactive brain has the natural capacity to latch onto any thought, there are also people who experience intrusive thoughts about committing suicide or doing self-harm behaviors; these thoughts are very upsetting and stressful to them because they're far removed from their intentions.

The variety of suicidal and self-harm obsessions may vary from feeling terrified about getting depressed and committing suicide, jumping off a bridge, slitting wrists, intentionally losing control and crashing a car when driving, or even a fear of overdosing with medications, just to name a few.

Suicidal obsessions may appear in any form, like images of a person committing suicide or self-harm behaviors or thoughts of "What if . . .?" or "Do I want to . . .?" Sometimes a person's brain may link strong sensations in their body with wants or urges to engage in suicidal or para-suicidal behaviors. For instance, if a person is

For a moment, let's consider Thomas' experience with these obsessions and how they unfolded into his day-to-day life:

Thomas, an engineer in his mid-30s, was driving back from a long meeting at work and found himself appreciating the structure of the bridge he was driving on. While thinking of the amount of heavy work and calculations required to build it, he suddenly had the thought: "What if I jump off the bridge?" Thomas was perplexed at thinking that way, and then his mind continued: "Do I want to jump off the bridge? Does it mean I *want* to do this?"

Thomas started telling himself compulsively "I am not going to do that; I don't want to do that, but I can do so. Is there any part of me that wants to do so?" He then spent the rest of his commute listing all the events that happened recently that would indicate there was a part of him that wanted to die: a project didn't go well at work, his boss got fired, he didn't like his new boss, his wife was unhappy with the number of hours he worked, his friends complained that he didn't have much time for them, his parents had passed away the previous year, and his kids barely wanted to spent time with him now that they were teenagers.

(Continued)

Table 5.1 (Continued)

What's the theme?	What is this theme about?	What does this theme look like, and how does it feel?
	randomly walking in the street and feels a strong rush in their body, their brain may associate that strong rush with obsessions about wanting to die; then the person may report this association like "It feels as if I want to run to the car and kill myself." Talking about death, suicide, or self-harm has been another taboo topic for years. It's only recently that we've had more education and information about it. Yet there is not much information about intrusive thoughts surrounding this theme, so it can be extremely distressful for the OCD sufferer and also for a therapist who is not familiar with OCD. If a person reports suicidal thoughts, a clinician may conduct a risk assessment and even request hospitalization; this is necessary in some cases but can actually be counterproductive in others. When a person is dealing with obsessions focused on suicide, a risk assessment or exploring their feelings around it can inadvertently reinforce the OCD cycle because it leads to more compulsions and reassurance-seeking behaviors. And just to clarify, this doesn't mean that a person suffering with OCD cannot attempt suicide – they certainly can. The point is that when someone has a suicidal thought, we cannot automatically assume that a person wants to die.	After all that thinking, Thomas felt much more distressed at the idea that he may unconsciously have wanted to die – that he could commit suicide and may have wanted to do so; he also got petrified at the possibility of not being aware of his wants, which meant that "he may be decompensating and [was] not fully aware of the seriousness of what he [was] going through." When preparing dinner with his wife, Thomas asked her if she noticed him getting more stressed, upset, or feeling down about things lately . . . just to check the severity of his symptoms. She answered his questions but was a bit distracted because she was arranging dinner. This led Thomas to ask her again when they went to bed. But he still wasn't satisfied with how she responded, because she was tired, which meant she wasn't fully paying attention. The following day, Thomas asked similar questions, but still felt dissatisfied, because his wife was in a rush to drop off the children, which meant her responses weren't thoughtful enough. The chain of feeling unsettled with all of her responses about him wanting to harm himself became so bad that Thomas continued to ask the same questions, day after day, text after text, conversation after conversation. Thomas started researching symptoms of depression and signs of a suicide wish, and he contacted the suicide crisis line a couple of times. He had no idea he was dealing with OCD. His overreactive brain jumped onto every clue that indicated he had the potential to harm himself. It was a nightmare for him to leave his house, go to work, and take his brain with him.

This list could go on and on; however, one thing that emerges from it is that, it is impossible to capture all the themes of obsessions and compulsions that our brain could come up with; the reality is that our brain, as a content-generating and pattern-making machine, could latch onto anything and everything as obsessions and compulsions anytime, anywhere. Also, as you learned when reading through the different themes, there are overlaps between the different themes (e.g., harm OCD and pedophile OCD; existential OCD and pure OCD), and for some people, the theme of their obsessions has shifted over the course of their life.

The organization of OCD themes has certainly served a purpose – to recognize OCD and get access to services – but instead of being preoccupied with fitting your obsessions perfectly into a particular type of OCD or getting worried if a particular theme of obsessions has not been listed, I strongly invite you to focus on learning key and core principles to tackle any form of OCD as you move forward living your life.

These different types of OCD are just names, indicators, or tags for the one main theme of obsessions or compulsions – they don't mean that you have a different problem or a different struggle. Imagine if we have to add a new type of OCD every time there is a new obsession reported by a person; even if this obsession is frequent, it is quite impossible to continue adding and adding labels to the already long list in Table 5.1. What starts, augments, reinforces, and maintains any OCD is the same, regardless of the theme.

The list of themes is always going to be incomplete – trying to capture all the fears, worries, and anxieties that a reactive mind comes up with is like preparing to lose a marathon in which the mind is always going to be the winner. Table 5.1 is always going to fall behind!

Is the Theme of My Obsession Going to Change?

The brain has all the freedom to get hooked, consumed, and overly focused into everything and anything – from the most benign, exciting, and appealing topic to the most disturbing, horrifying, and disgusting one. *The theme of obsessions swings, morphs, and shifts, not because people have a new form of OCD but because their brain is latching onto new content.* So the answer to this question, is maybe yes, maybe not. The theme of obsessions could swing, morph, and shift, not because people have a new form of OCD but because their brain is latching onto new content.

A former client of mine once shared the following with me: "I had a dream about being a pedophile, transgender, and racist toward others." The brain is limitless, boundless, and has an infinite capacity to create content and patterns as it pleases. All the ACT and ERP skills presented in this book apply to you and to anyone dealing with any type of OCD episode, yesterday, today, and tomorrow!

Let's get started. How about doing an inventory of all the themes you have covered so far when dealing with obsessions?

Exercise: Inventory of Obsessions Your Mind Has Come Up With

The line in the center represents your lifeline, so you can start from the bottom and move up until you reach your current age group.

In your sixties and seventies, what are those sticky pesky obsessions that you're dealing with?

Moving to your fifties, what were those intrusive thoughts that were hard to let go of?

In your fifties, what were those intrusive thoughts that were hard to let go?

Looking at your forties, what bizarre thoughts showed up?

In your mid-thirties, what obsessions did your mind come up with?

What dark thoughts do you recall from your early twenties?

What disturbing thoughts came up when you were a teen?

What obsessions showed up when you were a kid?

What's your reaction when you look at this lifeline and map the single theme or themes of obsession that your mind may have generated? Now we can see why our brain is a content-generator machine that comes up with all types of ideas, concepts, hypotheses, comparison thoughts, and a stream of endless possibilities of content. These range from kind of bothersome to really disturbing ones, and, even though you don't want them, you don't love them, and you don't like them; it's what a brain does.

Takeaways to share

OUR MINDS ARE COACHABLE TRAINABLE AND SHAPEABLE

MIND SCHOOL GRADUATION

Figure 5.1 The brain is shapeable.

Congratulations, you just finished the first part of this workbook! Hope you can appreciate that you did a good job in learning core psychological concepts that, although a bit technical, are part of the foundation of the work the lies ahead to get you back on track in your life.

Here is a recap of what was covered in Part I:

- Obsessions are the norm and not the exception.

  Every single human being experiences at some point or another disturbing bizarre, weird, and dark, unwanted thoughts.

- Obsessions are not different than any other type of thoughts – they just happen to be extra sticky.

  As powerful and bossy as obsessions look and sound, and no matter what type of content they have – violent, moral, sexual, scrupulosity, harm, germs – they're just thoughts. And thoughts are just a string of letters, images, and words.

- Obsessions are not static but dynamic creations from your mind.

  Obsessions come in all types of colors, sizes, shapes, textures. And if your brain started with one particular type of obsession, it doesn't mean that that will always be the case; there is no switch that turns the brain on and off or switch that sets limits for it. Our brain is limitless when coming up with all types of content, including obsessions.

  Your obsessions may vary from fears of contracting an illness, doubts about if your partner is the right partner, doubts about making the best of your life, fears about committing suicide, doubts about whether you want to attack someone, or fears about making mistakes, to name a few.

- Our brain is a content-generating and pattern-making machine.

  Among the many amazing qualities of our brain, there are two that are especially important to know when it comes to OCD: The brain is constantly generating content, and it's constantly relating everything to everything.
  Our brain is designed to come up with all types of content, hypotheses, predictions, theories, past thoughts, fantasies, stories about others, narratives about ourselves, dreams, and so on. Non-stopping, it's always coming up with something.
  Our brain is also constantly relating, associating, linking, connecting – creating all types of patterns – no matter where you're at, who you're with, or where you're coming from. These thinking patterns, taken too seriously as absolute truth, push you to organize your behaviors in ways that can be helpful or unhelpful to you. When dealing with obsessions, questions like, "Is this thought true and accurate?" are not as important as "Is acting on this thought helpful in the long term or not?"

- There are four things that make it really hard for you to let go of obsessions:
  - You have a reactive brain.

    Even though it's uncomfortable, your brain is prone to overreact, overrespond, overprotect you, and overprepare you when anticipating any possibility of a threat – obsessions count as a threat for you brain, although that's a fake signal – an obsession is a thought, and thoughts are letters, images, and words put together.

  - You don't like the fear, anxiety, or any yucky feelings that come with obsessions.

    We don't have control of what we feel, how much we feel, or how intense our feelings are, but when having an overreactive brain, your emotions also get amplified and magnified, and naturally, you do what you can to get rid of those feelings and bring them down.

  - You're taking your thoughts too seriously and as absolute truths.

    As much as we want, we don't have control of what shows up in our mind; our mind is constantly coming up with all types of content like hypotheses, theories, past thoughts, revengeful thoughts, fantasies, and so on. Our mind doesn't take a break and is active 24/7. There are thoughts that are important, relevant, and helpful to you, but the majority of them are useless and pure noise – obsessions are bizarre noise.

  - Your brain is a pattern-making and content-generating machine.

    Your brain is constantly connecting everything with everything regardless when it happened, how it happened, and where it happened. Our brains are continuously creating thinking patterns that also organize behavioral patterns.

- The literature has referred to different types of OCD over the years – harm, existential, scrupulosity, relationship, contamination, hyperawareness, just-so/-right, metaphysical, meta, moral, pedophile, perfectionistic, pure, religious, responsibility, and suicidal OCD – but all those names, categories, or types are just because of the theme of obsessions or the theme of the compulsions; all the skills you're learning in this workbook apply to all of them.

- Dealing with OCD means that your brain – as a pattern-making machine – is playing it safe!

  Your brain is always doing its job to make sure you don't get hurt, you don't struggle. So, when having obsessions, your brain quickly perceives a threat – a fake threat – and demands that you play-it-safe. Then there are a couple of things that happen:

- You come up with thinking patterns, called mental compulsions, to respond to those annoying obsessions such as figuring out, arguing, solving, and so on (you will learn more about them in the next section).
- You develop observable patterns named public compulsions – tapping, rubbing, checking, and more – to neutralize those sticky obsessions.
- You develop avoidance patterns – you stop doing what you care about, what is fun and enjoyable, what you need to be doing, and instead, organize your behavior around avoiding obsessions.

- Our brains are shapeable, and you can overcome OCD!

  As impossible as it sounds, an overreactive brain is shapeable, coachable, and trainable, and you can learn research-based ways to tame those obsessions and get your life back!

Life Tracker

At the end of every section, you're going to find a "life tracker" exercise; this is definitely not a rigorous questionnaire but an exercise for you to pause, check how you are handling your obsessions, and check how you're living your life as you learn new ACT and ERP skills.

Reflect on how you have been living your life and mark an "X" where it corresponds.

Having obsessions as thoughts your mind comes up with	Seeing obsessions as problems to be solved
Approaching life as it is	Avoiding life because of obsessions
Taking action toward what you care about	Organizing your life around obsessions
Holding your thoughts lightly	Going 100% along with what your mind tells you
Checking what really works in your life	Doing stuff in automatic pilot mode
Making room for uncomfortable internal experiences	Pushing them down as much as possible

PART II

What Would ACT Do for You?

Welcome to part II! If you made it this far, I know that you're open, ready, and dedicated to stop OCD episodes from taking more time out of your life!

This section will explain to you how Acceptance and Commitment Therapy (ACT), combined with Exposure Response Prevention (ERP), will help you to tame those dark obsessions that your overreactive brain shouts at you.

All change in our life requires some combination of unlearning unhelpful behaviors, deconstructing old points of view, learnings new skills, making new choices, and making things real by "doing." ACT will show you how to do so!

What Is This Thing Called "ACT"?

First things first, let me start by clarifying what Acceptance and Commitment Therapy (ACT) is and is not.

ACT is a behavior therapy. Pause for a second and ask yourself what "behavior therapy" means to you. Then jot those thoughts down:

_____

_____

_____

_____

_____

I ask this question because "behavior therapy" can be a loaded term for some people.

Most people understand it as a therapy approach that focuses on action, goals, or steps. There are some opinions that behavior therapy doesn't take into consideration feelings, is robotic, ignores the relationship between client and therapist, dismisses family history, and focuses excessively on collecting data. Also, there is an idea that behavior therapists can be like robots and do robotic things with clients. (Oh boy, did I capture all those misconceptions, or do you have a new one?)

Here is a big clarification. There is no question that ACT, as a behavior therapy, invites you to take action in your day-to-day living, but there are specific characteristics that make ACT unique and different than any other behavioral approach:

- ACT doesn't just ask you to take any action or random actions. Before asking you to take any action, ACT asks you to check the big-picture stuff about what sort of person you want to be, invites you to get in touch with what gives you meaning, challenges you to figure out what you want to stand up for, and then encourages you to take action based on what truly matters to you. Pretty neat, right?

- ACT teaches you to make room for the yucky stuff – disturbing obsessions, fears, and worries – that shows up under your skin, and instead of pretending they are not there or putting all your efforts into getting rid of them, you learn to put all your energy into moving with your feet, hands, and mouth toward what matters to you.

Let's put OCD episodes aside for a second and bear with me for a moment while I elaborate more on what ACT is about.

To start, think about this. How often does your mind come up with a variation of a story that you're not good enough, you don't know what you're doing, or you're not attractive enough? How often do you feel overwhelmed by life circumstances to the point that you feel like screaming? Have those stories ever disappeared from your mind? Have those feelings stopped coming your way?

You may have managed to distract yourself from them by watching TV, listing your areas of success, or maybe even asking others about your accomplishments, but until the day you die, those narratives, those overwhelming feelings, those unbearable moments of panic, are likely to show up.

ACT doesn't teach you to act as if those stories are not there, to power through those annoying emotions, or to fake it until you make it. ACT, at its core, teaches you to develop a new relationship with your mind and with all those painful thoughts, memories, stories, overwhelming feelings, and challenging sensations that come your way so you can live with vitality, fulfillment, and purpose.

You may be wondering, "Does that mean I'll always have obsessions showing up, and I can't change that?" You're asking a very important question – one that my clients and students ask me often – and my honest response is to invite you to check your experience in order to answer that question yourself. Check for yourself, what has happened each time you hoped to get rid of your obsessions and went out of your way neutralizing them with compulsions, organized your day around them, and made sure to not approach anything that would trigger them? Did your life get better? Did the obsessions go away?

For me, I can tell you that the thoughts about not being a good daughter, not being caring enough with my family, or being too passionate about what I do, don't just disappear. Quite the opposite: they've appeared while writing this workbook, when walking on the street, even when spending time with my family (whom I deeply care about). Wherever I go, there they are. But learning to have them – instead of the story having me – has made a humongous difference in my life.

My mind, your mind, and everyone else's mind has a life of its own. It creates thinking patterns all the time, and while these patterns can be extremely handy most of the time, they can also amplify our struggles 100 times, like a Bluetooth speaker – especially if you have an overreactive brain. But hold on: this doesn't mean that our minds will constantly be running the show or that if you're dealing with obsessions, it's a lost cause.

We can all learn to have a new relationship with our mind, one in which our mind doesn't boss us around and tell us what to do or not to do. A relationship in which we just watch all the activity that goes on and on in our minds, including the stinky thoughts and the infamous feelings that come along – and we still do the stuff that matters to us. This new relationship with your mind is doable, achievable, and workable, and here is something important, amazing things will happen when you put into action all the ACT skills you will learn to simply live your life!

Now that you have a sense of what ACT can do for you, let me briefly tell you about its scientific background. ACT was developed by a group of psychologists (Steven C. Hayes, Kelly Wilson, and Kirk Strosahl) in the mid-1980s, and since then it has become one of the most prolific and quickly disseminated approaches in clinical psychology, with more than 350 randomized clinical trials – the gold standard of research – in less than 30 years. The clinical applications of ACT are too long to list here, but they range from specific psychological struggles (OCD being one of them) to mental health prevention, behavioral medicine, education, organizational culture, resilience, sports, and so on.

ACT has been applied to other domains besides clinical psychology because it's based on functional contextualism, and as such it seeks to understand human behavior as it happens in a given situation or historical context, taking into consideration our learning history, biological variables, developmental milestones, and so on. Functional contextualism and ACT principles, therefore, can be applied to every single situation beyond clinical settings. That's because every single human being is constantly interacting in a given context, 24/7, no exceptions!

At its core, ACT aims to promote a rich, meaningful, and purposeful life by fostering flexible responding to all experiences we encounter – including uncomfortable, annoying, and unpleasant stories, thoughts, doubts, feelings, and upsetting obsessions – regardless of anyone's age, skin color, gender, socioeconomic upbringing, relationship status, or religious beliefs. Amazing, right?

7

What About ACT and Exposure?

Let's talk about Exposure and Response Prevention (ERP). *Exposure* is the frontline treatment for tackling OCD and anxiety (Samantaray et al., 2018). In lay terms, exposure is the process of facing whatever situation, person, sensation, image, or thought you're scared of. Exposure applied to obsessions means learning to face the content of your obsessions. *Response prevention* is all about preventing compulsions or rituals from happening.

The first model to explain how exposure works was the habituation or desensitization model. It posits that, for exposure to work and be successful, a person's level of anxiety needs to decrease within an exposure session and between-sessions. For example, a person scared of taking an elevator would do an exposure whereby they stay in an elevator and take it back and forth until their anxiety levels are reduced to 40 percent of what they were when they started.

Over the years, most exposure treatments and books written about ERP have been based on this model. However, despite its success, there were still a significant number of clients who didn't respond to it, had a relapse, and/or dropped out of treatment prematurely (Craske et al., 2014).

Craske et al. (2008) studied what drives change – mechanisms of change – when facilitating exposure-based interventions. Her studies led to two breakthroughs: (1) the understanding that a person feeling less anxious is not what makes exposure treatments effective and (2) the development of the *inhibitory learning model* as a new frame to understand how exposure actually works and to reconcile with the fact that our brain doesn't work by removing experiences but by adding them.

Here is a key feature of the inhibitory learning model proposed by Craske: when a person experiences a chronic avoidance or anxious response to a particular stimulus, it's because they have learned a threat-based association between an aversive stimulus and a particular response. For exposure treatment to be effective, it's not about how much or how little anxiety a person experiences when approaching that aversive stimulus; it's more about how a person approaches that stimulus. When a person approaches what he's afraid of by noticing the emotion, removing safety crutches, and mixing the ways of approaching, that process will lead to the formation of a new relation called a new safe-association. With multiple experiences in different locations and in different ways, that new safe-association blocks the activation of the old learning, which is how exposure works, and that's the reason for the name of this model as the inhibitory mode (in which the new association inhibits the old association).

On a theoretical level, ACT capitalizes on the research derived from the inhibitory learning model. On a practical level, *ACT is already an exposure treatment* because, by nature, the whole model invites you to get in touch with what you're scared of, anxious about, or nervous about, regardless of whether you're dealing with OCD, phobias, social anxiety, depression, and so on.

Even though ACT is an exposure model upfront and all the way, certain struggles, like dealing with OCD episodes, require targeted interventions – and that's how ACT blends with ERP. Within ACT, exposure response prevention is a process of "organized contact with *repertoire-narrowing* stimuli for the purpose of *increasing response flexibility*" (Harris, 2019; emphasis added).

Basically, when dealing with disturbing thoughts in a targeted manner that blends ACT and ERP principles, you develop skills to make room for those obsessions while taking step after step towards the life you want to live.

As you can see, another uniqueness of ACT is that exposure practices are the means – not the goal – of treatment toward a fulfilling, purposeful, and rich life.

8

What Lies Ahead?

When I started writing this book, I was finishing an online class on how to find the rhythm for creative projects. For four weeks, I fine-tuned some ideas for a writing project and exchanged opinions with more than 150 creative minds. I was mesmerized by reading the posts of the participants, because for the first time I was a member of a creative community. I was exposed to interesting literature in creativity and productivity and witnessed firsthand how these creative minds pour their souls into translating words into visual images and many other ways to show information. I was the only nonartist participant in the group.

This online class confirmed my appreciation for designs that are beautiful, functional, and simplify the way we interact with our work environment. To make the best of this course, I blocked 3 hours a week for it in my schedule. Was I able to do follow through with spending those 3 weekly hours in the class? Here is my honest answer: no.

You may be pondering what this story has to do with this workbook. Here is its pertinence: you're starting a new route of change, one in which you're not held back by those obsessions or fearful moments; one in which you design the life you want to live and start living it.

This workbook offers you simple, short, actionable ACT and ERP skills that will help you to get your life back on track, so you can learn to have intrusive thoughts and still keep moving with your day-to-day life. This is doable, if you're willing to get out of your comfort zone and put into action what you're learning. So here are three questions for you:

1. Are you willing to put aside 1 hour every week to read a chapter *and* give yourself 5 to 6 days to put into action the skills you're learning here?
2. Are you willing to be open, try the exercises in this book, see how they go for you, and follow the recommended pace for each section?
3. What are you willing to put on hold while you work through this workbook and get your life back on track?

To make a real difference in your daily life, you need to make a commitment to yourself, work with this workbook wholeheartedly, openly put the research-based skills you will learn into action, and start a habit of making a bold move toward the life you want to live.

What This Workbook *Won't* Do for You

As much effort as I have put into this workbook, and as committed as you are to working on it, let's you and I be on the same page about what this workbook *won't* do for you.

This Workbook Won't Ask You to Focus on Your Past

Exploring your upbringing, how you grew up, where you grew up, and dissecting and reaching an understanding about your different past experiences is important and part of becoming aware of the context in which you became the person you are today. This workbook is focused on how obsessions are currently affecting your life and teaching you the skills you need to get unstuck and move forward in life.

This Workbook Won't Ask You to Do Weird Things

Learning ACT and ERP skills doesn't mean you're going to be asked to do weird things that I wouldn't do or that most people wouldn't do. It won't ask you to do things that are far out there and against your values or what you care about, either. Teaching you to face those intrusive obsessions is always done in the context of your personal values and in giving you all the room to choose what and how much you're willing to get out of your safety zone to get your life back on track. If an obsession is sticky, you will read and learn about different exposures to work with it.

This Workbook Won't Make Your Obsessions Go Away

As you move along in this workbook, you will learn that obsessions – as annoying, disturbing, and bizarre as they may be – are experienced by almost every person on the planet. Actually, all those efforts to get rid of them, neutralize them, or push them down strengthens them, and as a result, you move from having an obsession to having an OCD episode and from having an OCD episode to having an OCD problem in your life.

In this workbook, you will learn ACT and ERP skills to handle those obsessions as they show up in your day-to-day life – not by putting your energy into eliminating them but by getting better at having them.

This Workbook Won't Give You an Instant Solution

Have you ever tried instant coffee or instant oatmeal? Or have you cooked instant rice? These items share their "instant" qualities. And this book is not one of them!

Working on this workbook is similar to learning any other skill. ACT and ERP require practice – not a perfect practice, but a consistent, intentional, and committed one!

Last, if you're dealing with other struggles – such as trauma, depression, substance abuse, perfectionism, emotion regulation, trichotillomania, skin picking, worry, or eating disorders – take a look at the website www.actbeyondocd.com for special considerations. There you will find key points to see how this workbook can help you and whether you need extra support, as well.

I put a lot of thought, effort, and care into translating how I work with my clients into a workbook format that can teach you focused, specific, tailored, and empirically based skills to put you back into living a fulfilling, loving, and gratifying life.

While this workbook is not a replacement for treatment, everything you need to know to make a wise move in your life is here!

Takeaways to share

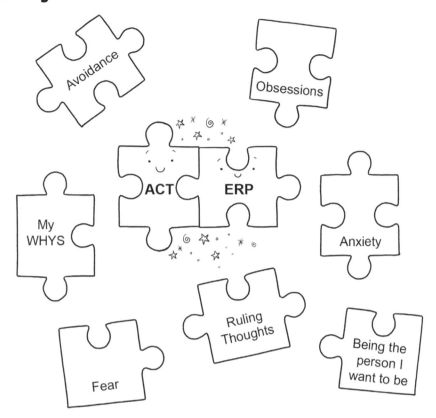

Figure 8.1 ACT & ERP puzzle.

Hey! Here you are, done with the second part of this workbook; it takes courage to be in your shoes and walk hour after hour with a reactive brain that throws hundreds of thoughts at you and goes quickly into a threat mode at any given moment.

When obsessions shift into OCD episodes, you experience a sense of prolonged fear, distress, and overwhelming reactions because your brain insists on perceiving and reacting in threat mode, even though there is no real threat, just obsessions jumping up and down. But if you continue to use the tools you have been using up to now, you may be feeding into OCD episodes; then before you know it, they start happening more and more often and, in more places, to the point that they dominate your life.

In this first section you learned about ACT, that ACT and ERP blend together, what you will learn in this workbook, and what this workbook won't be helpful for. You were asked to answer three key questions:

1. Are you willing to give 1 hour every week to reading a chapter, and are you willing to give yourself 5–6 days to put into action the skills you're learning here?
2. Are you willing to be open, try the exercises in this book, see how they go for you, and follow the recommended pace for each section?
3. What are you willing to put on hold while you work through this workbook and get your life back on track?

No one can answer those questions for you, and there's no one better than YOU to do so!

Life Tracker

As you move forward in this workbook, I hope you can see that every single skill and all of them together aim at getting you into living the life you want to live, all the way!

Reflect on how you have been living your life and mark an "X" where it corresponds.

Having obsessions as thoughts your mind comes up with	Seeing obsessions as problems to be solved
Approaching life as it is	Avoiding life because of obsessions
Taking action toward what you care about	Organizing your life around obsessions
Holding your thoughts lightly	Going 100% along with what your mind tells you
Checking what really works in your life	Doing stuff in automatic pilot mode
Making room for uncomfortable internal experiences	Pushing them down as much as possible

PART III

The Trilogy That Makes Your Life Miserable

No one enjoys the arrival of obsessions – they're hard to dismiss from your mind, they're distracting, they get you overfocused and anxious, and, just like drivers on the freeway that rubberneck to see an accident, they take you away from what's happening in front of you and slow you down or delay or block you from what you really want to be doing.

Despite obsessions being common and part of every person's experience, there is no script, class, or lecture on how to deal with them that is taught in school. Unless you received formal training in clinical psychology or a related field, you won't learn how to handle those disturbing moments that show up in your mind at all.

In Part III of this workbook, you will step back from being in the midst of an OCD episode and dig deeply into what keeps them from happening. This is super-important; otherwise, how would you know what to do different when your brain goes into a massive overreaction of threat, fear, and panic?

What Are the Compulsions You're Doing?

If you're reading this workbook, it's because you found yourself dealing with repetitive, unwanted, repulsive, or shocking obsessions that come along with an "Oh no, watch out" reaction when they pop up in your mind. And naturally, because obsessions come along with tons of fear, dread, and scary feelings, you do everything you can to suppress those overwhelming feelings. A common response to obsessions is to do compulsions.

Compulsions are reactive behavioral patterns or actions that your brain pushes you to make with the purpose of minimizing, reducing, or neutralizing the overwhelming discomfort that comes along with obsessions. And because of how they respond to obsessions, compulsions are considered a form of avoidant behavior, which you will learn more about in the next chapter. Because compulsions quickly morph into a behavioral pattern that takes on a life of their own, it's helpful for you to understand how they work.

Let's think about what compulsions look like. Some are private or covert, meaning no one sees them except you (e.g., counting silently in your head, repeating sentences, overanalyzing), and others are public or overt, so everyone can see them (e.g., switching lights on and off, touching objects, blinking).

If we think about how compulsions are organized, some are ritualized, meaning that they follow a strict order of steps you take, while others are non-ritualized, meaning you do steps until they feel right to you. In this workbook, the term "compulsions" includes both types.

Let's think for a moment about Robert, Darrah, and Jeff and how they handle their fears.

Robert struggles with a fear of being a pedophile. He loves his daughter very much, and when playing in the park with her he had this thought: "Am I looking at her as if I like her? Do I feel attracted to her?" Since having this thought, when going to pick up his daughter from school, he now performs a ritualized compulsion: telling himself, "God knows I have a good heart, God knows that I won't hurt her, God knows my heart." Robert usually repeats these phrases three times and then proceeds to spend time with his daughter, until the thought "I like spending time with my kid – does it mean I'm a pedophile?" shows up again. Then he follows the same private compulsion, and the chain continues throughout the day.

Darrah is afraid of people stealing her knowledge. When walking next to people who stare at her for whatever reason, she tells herself, "I'm getting my knowledge back" (a private compulsion) and makes a fist with both of her hands (a public compulsion).

Jeff has an obsession of "not performing at the best of his mental capacities" that gets activated every time he is completing a research project at work. With this compulsion, Jeff mentally reviews multiple times the way he said things, the words he used, and how people responded to his comments as attempts to get an exact idea of how he performed.

As you learned in Chapter 5 ("Are There Different Types of OCD?"), some of the OCD themes are based on the form of the compulsions – checking, just right, washing, and so on – and others on the content of the obsessions – religious, contamination, and so on.

Abramowitz, Taylor, and McKay (2009) describes five types of compulsive rituals: checking, decontamination, repeating routine actions, ordering or arranging, and mental reviewing. Hershfield and Corboy (2017) add other compulsions to this list: cleaning your environment, thought neutralization, and memory hoarding.

As OCD episodes vary from individual to individual, so do compulsions, and the themes of miscellaneous compulsions may grow as well. However, if we put classifications aside and instead consider the form of obsessions and compulsions, we can see that, more than by differences, all types of OCD are prompted and maintained by the same processes: an intrusive, disturbing, or unwanted thought that pops up with significant distress and a strong compulsion to get rid of the stress or minimize it in the short term; relationships, work, fun, and other life areas are negatively affected by this cycle in the long term.

A common form of overt compulsion is reassurance seeking, which is about asking others for confirmation that a particular outcome driven by an obsession didn't occur or won't occur or that you are free of danger.

Continuing with Robert, Darrah, and Jeff, this is what it looks like when they go into reassurance-seeking mode:

- Robert asks his wife, "Have I been a good father to our kid? I have never done anything inappropriate, right?"
- Darrah asks her sister questions along the lines of "When a person has all her knowledge intact, this person recalls events, and remembers words properly, right? Do I sound like a regular person?"
- Jeff asks people at work whether they would have come to the same decision he did about a particular topic.

Exercise: What Are Your Public Compulsions?

What are the public or overt behaviors you do when having annoying obsessions?

So far, so good right?

But what happens when your brain fires intrusive thoughts and you do the best you can to handle them by relying on what you think you have control over – your thinking? Let's take a look.

Mental Compulsions

Private compulsions are less easily identifiable than public ones primarily because they're so well hidden. However, even if they're talked about aloud (e.g., "Did I do anything that put my daughter in danger when she was a baby?"), they can look like regular forms of thinking to any person. However, they are compulsions because they perpetuate the cycle of OCD episodes.

Our brain is designed to analyze, explain, make sense, create coherence, and search for meaning. No wonder the popular expression of "I think, therefore I am" became so popular. But when having a reactive brain that excels in creating content and coming up with thinking patterns, it's easy to get lost in compulsively thinking over and over, compulsively going into answer seeking, and compulsively searching for the "right feeling."

Mental compulsions are mental actions that vary from simple to complex; they're equally as distressing as public compulsions, can be triggered by any type of obsession, and serve the purpose of getting rid of the fear, terror, and dreadful feelings, even just for a little bit.

Figure 9.1 shows the most common forms of mental compulsions.

Let's take a look in detail at each one of these compulsions and see what they look like in a person's life (Table 9.1).

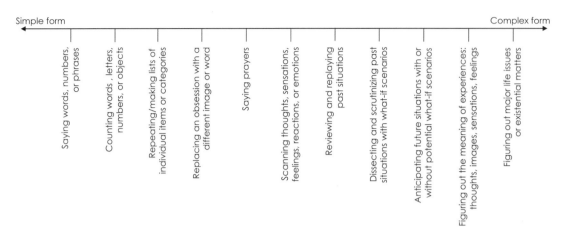

Figure 9.1 Mental compulsions continuum.

Table 9.1 List of mental compulsions

Mental compulsion	What is it?	What does it look like?
Saying words, numbers, or phrases	With this form of mental compulsion, the content of the words, phrases, and numbers doesn't matter: sometimes they're sensical, sometimes they're not.	Eric gets caught up in an obsessive thought of becoming an evil character in a movie. To neutralize this obsession, he tells himself, "I'm taking my power back; this is not real." Other times, he tells himself only the word "power." Lourdes struggles with the intrusion of contracting AIDS and gets easily triggered after touching a person's hand. She compulsively counts numbers in her head, like bingo balls, until she ends on an even number, which feels right to her. To minimize her anxiety about making mistakes, Lisa tells herself "Knock it out of the ballpark" when she gets caught up in the fear of making errors.
Counting words, letters, numbers, or objects	This compulsion involves counting. This can be counting letters, words, numbers, the first letter of a word, the times a bodily function happens, or anything the brain decides to latch onto.	Charlie has a fear of mixing bad energies with good energies and attracting bad things to him. When having a bad vibe about a person, he "counts" all the experiences with positive vibes to make sure they are even (not odd).

Mental compulsion	What is it?	What does it look like?
Repeating/making lists of individual items or categories	This compulsion is all about mentally creating lists of anything and everything, with the purpose of getting rid of obsessions (temporarily). Another form of this compulsion is making lists of categories: good vibes, bad vibes, good prayers for home, bad prayers at work, good prayers at school, and so on.	Sidney creates a mental list of specific dates in the year for birthdays and important family events, and the "right books to read" that are associated with good energy. If any of those dates or books don't have a good feeling, he cannot read them or will have to start repeating the list until it feels right to start a new one, with new dates or new book titles. Tax is afraid of being a bad person for not defending his sister from being bullied at school. He compulsively makes lists of all the people that have offended her and says, "You're bad," and quickly feels better, as if he is taking action.
Replacing an obsession with a different image or word	To neutralize an unwanted or scary obsession, the compulsion is to replace it with a positive image, feeling or word. You may try to neutralize "bad, negative" thoughts with the same number of "good" ones. The purpose is to reduce the anxiety that comes with the yucky obsession.	Fletcher is hooked on the obsession that his partner will cheat on him. When feeling petrified by this obsessive thought, he quickly thinks of and replaces it with a positive encounter he has had, recently or in the past.
Saying prayers	discomfort that comes with a blasphemous obsession, because both feel awful. Private mental compulsions include praying for forgiveness, saying prayers until they feel right or reach a lucky number, and making amendments with God.	Hayley has obsessions about her sexual orientation: "Don't you like her? Are you gay?" She's scared that if she doesn't try to deny those thoughts, it proves she's a lesbian. As a result, when triggered, she intentionally thinks about all the guys she likes and feels attracted to, prays, and specifically says, "God, you know, it's not me."

(Continued)

Table 9.1 (Continued)

Mental compulsion	What is it?	What does it look like?
	Saying prayers as part of living your faith is quite different than saying them to remove anxiety from your obsession. A challenge with this compulsion is that it's hard for people to distinguish between the natural discomfort that comes from not following your religious principles and the	Phillip identifies as Christian and is petrified at the possibility of attacking his relatives because of violent images he saw when watching a movie with them. When Philip gets hooked on this obsession, he quickly says this prayer: "God exists, God knows I'm a good person, God knows I wouldn't do that."
Scanning thoughts, sensations, feelings, reactions, or emotions	To reduce your anxiety, you check the quality of all your private experiences and make sure they are the "right way." This compulsion could also apply to checking your obsessions: "Am I obsessing? Do I have an obsession? Is this an obsession?" Sometimes people may check for particular thoughts to make sure that the "thought is under control," so they don't do anything inappropriate or inconsistent with their character.	Let's continue with Hayley from the previous example. When having a groinal reaction, she checks if that reaction is appropriate or not. "Is it strong? Did I like it?" Based on her responses, she feels reassured or engages in other compulsions.
Reviewing and replaying past situations	Some people refer to this form of compulsion as rumination, and sure, that makes sense, because you're dissecting past events. But this type of mental compulsion differs because you're reviewing past events to answer a question, to make sure you didn't do anything relating to the obsession you're dealing with, and to get rid of the fear, nervousness, and distress that comes with the obsession	Geoff is tortured by obsessions about "hitting people when driving without realizing it." So he avoids crowded streets, driving at night, and driving around school zones, stadiums, and major shopping areas. After driving, Geoff mentally reviews how he drove around pedestrians in the streets of a city: "I drove slowly on the right side of the street, saw a woman with a red sweater, looked at the light, checked both sides of the road before continuing driving . . ." and so on.

Mental compulsion	What is it?	What does it look like?
	(e.g., mentally saying, "I think I actually wanted this, I think I said this").	Kim feels terrified when buying into the obsession of doing something immoral (e.g., cheating on college tasks). When triggered, she ends up mentally checking how she behaved during a test or an academic task: "Did my eyes land on another person's work? Was I looking only at my work? When I asked my classmate to hand me the book, did I do anything else?"
	If people are in the process of recalling a past situation and they get interrupted, have a wrong feeling when doing this compulsion, or perceive that they didn't reply to the situation correctly, they may take the obsession as being the truth.	
	When holding the obsession as fact (e.g., assuming that you did make sexual moves toward your children and having an urge to turn yourself in to the police), people may quickly engage in other types of compulsions and also end up questioning their character, intentions, and values (e.g., "Did I have an ulterior motive to do that? Did I mean to do that?").	
Dissecting and scrutinizing past situations with potential what-if scenarios	Dissecting past situations as a compulsion can also include revisiting them with what-if situations by checking over and over how you would have handled yourself in each one of those scenarios in order to neutralize the obsessions.	Geoff sometimes replays how he drove; this makes him feels better afterward. Other times, replaying his driving doesn't feel right enough, and so he dissects it bit by bit: "Did I stop the car when I saw that pedestrian? Did I look in the rearview mirror? Did I see those teenagers on the other side of the street before driving?"
	As with any form of compulsion, you keep dissecting past events and scrutinizing every potential scenario until your anxiety gets relieved. It's possible that you may feel reassured after checking how you would have handled	Other times, Geoff takes this mental reviewing one step further by imagining how he would have handled other driving situations.

(Continued)

Table 9.1 (Continued)

Mental compulsion	What is it?	What does it look like?
	three scenarios (versus unlimited ones), but you may feel worse if you aren't able to validate past scenarios right away, and so you continue waiting and waiting or start another compulsion.	*Situation 1:* "If the teenagers didn't make it to the other side of the street, I'd know by now, because everyone would be screaming on the streets and I would have heard that." *Situation 2:* "If I didn't look at both sides of the street before driving and I hit someone, it would show up in the news or in the police reports. I need to check their website to make sure I didn't cause harm and didn't endanger anyone today." And that's what Geoff did. He checked the police website for more than a week. He also paid attention to the news and even asked his sister to drive with him in that area in case there was any sign of an accident. Geoff felt like he was losing his mind while living a chain of compulsions.
Anticipating future situations with or without potential what-if scenarios	There is a difference between considering how your future may look (e.g., preparing for a trip, planning your wedding, getting pregnant, and so on) versus foreseeing or predicting the future, with the aim that an obsession doesn't occur or to prove it wrong. When relying on this form of private compulsion, you may mentally do two things: (1) Go into prediction mode of a future scenario to reassure yourself of a particular outcome, usually a positive one.	When Frederik takes his mind very seriously, he gets terrified at the obsession of contracting MS. To make sure he's not putting himself at risk by dismissing this possibility and then regretting having MS, he spends hours researching the best MS doctors in the area and thinking about what he needs to tell the doctor to make sure he explains his symptoms correctly and targets them. Frederik also struggles with sexual obsessions involving children. To minimize the dread that comes with this obsession, he mentally imagines different

Mental compulsion	What is it?	What does it look like?
	(2) Take it a step further, and attempt to identify potential scenarios that may show up and how you may respond to each one of them while still trying to get reassured.	types of scenarios with his nephews when celebrating Thanksgiving as a way to anticipate whether he may be aroused or not.
Figuring out the meaning of internal experiences such as thoughts, images, sensations, and feelings	This is another common form of mental compulsion, and as its name indicates, it's all about mentally solving, concluding, and answering to the content of an obsession. In my opinion, any form of figuring out an obsession usually comes with "mentally scanning" your experiences, too.	Jaime gets caught up with obsessions about committing suicide. When feeling low or having a change in her mood, Jaime often reviews how she feels throughout the day. She ponders whether those feelings are similar or different than the day before and checks the potential reasons why she may feel the way she does. She does all these things to make sure she's not at risk of committing suicide.
Figuring out major life issues or existential matters	Any form of reflections, contemplations, or deliberations about life matters can easily be a mental compulsion, because they're done with the purpose of neutralizing a pesky obsession, regardless of its content – religion, sexuality, the meaning of life, life after death, etc.	Walter is reading a story on Facebook about a man's diagnosis of pancreatic cancer. He suddenly gets hooked on the obsession "What if that's me? I can have pancreatic cancer." Walter can't let go of this thought and finds himself pondering endlessly about aging, dying, and the afterlife: "What happens after you die? Where do we go? Do we have life afterwards? Do we know? Do we feel love? is it over? And, if this life is over, how is it to feel 'nothingness'?"

The types of mental compulsions are limitless. This list is not a definitive one, and you can be doing one, many, or a combination of them.

Now that you're familiar with all forms of compulsions, private and public, check which ones you're doing. Let's take a stock of the compulsions you've been doing in the last 30 days (Table 9.2).

The Trilogy That Makes Your Life Miserable

Excerice 9.1 Inventory of compulsions that keep you stuck

What are public and mental compulsions you do that keep you stuck?	How often did you do these compulsions?				
	Not at all	Sometimes	Often	Very often	Most of the time

Little by little, step by step, you will get better and better at catching them. Getting familiar with all the behaviors you do and how you handle an obsession is a key skill!

If you had to describe the long-term consequences of these compulsive behaviors in your life, what would you say they are?

_____

_____

_____

_____

_____

Compulsions are tricky, because at times doing them may feel as though you're doing something super productive, like when you answer ten emails in your inbox. However, if you zoom out and look at the bigger picture, as you did when you imagined some long-term impacts of your compulsions, you can see that you're actually missing opportunities to connect, have fun, enjoy your day, and do the stuff that you actually care about.

10

Don't Forget About Avoidant Behaviors!

Let me start by clarifying right away that "avoidance" is not a dirty, evil, or bad word. It's just a behavior to pay attention to as it shows up in your day-to-day life.

To be honest, when working on this workbook, there were moments in which I was stressed about conveying an idea, confused about the words I was using, or unsure about the metaphors I was thinking about. Then, next thing I knew, I was cleaning the kitchen (even though I had just cleaned it that morning), watering my beloved plants, texting a friend, or reading a book. Let's be real: from time to time, we all engage in avoidant behaviors. Avoidant behaviors are natural, we all do them, and that's not necessarily a bad, right, or OK thing to do. It just is.

When dealing with annoying emotional states, any human being can engage in avoidant behaviors: distracting oneself by watching Netflix, drinking too many Manhattans, exercising for mega hours, window shopping, browsing on Amazon, planning vacations, searching for the next fountain pen, and so on. As long as those avoidant behaviors are used in moderation from time to time, don't take you farther away from what's truly important in your life, and don't impact your day-to-day activities negatively, by all means keep using them.

The challenge is when those avoidant strategies get on your way of showing up to the people you love in the way that is important to you, hinder you from connecting with others, take you away from what's happening in the moment, or become an automatic response when you're in distress. So, the key is to always check how those avoidant behaviors are working for you.

To start, list the most common avoidance strategies you use that take you away from the life you want to have:

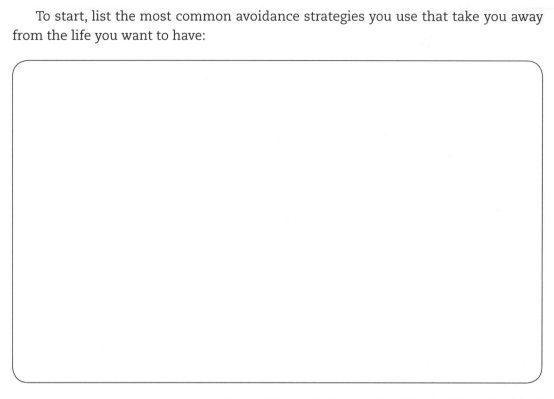

You may have notice by now that within ACT, the labels of "good," "bad," "right," "wrong," or even "healthy," "unhealthy," are not relevant when looking at any behaviors, including avoidant ones. But what's really relevant is the impact, effect, and workability that avoidant behaviors have in your life. As you continue progressing through this workbook, you will become more familiar with the concept of *workability*. For now, your task is to check how avoidant behaviors affect the quality of your life.

For instance, Rudolph was dealing with an obsession of getting contaminated and avoided touching the mail if it had been touched by a suspicious-looking mail carrier or paying for groceries to a cashier who didn't look healthy. He also refused to park his car next to a neighbor's car after learning a member of their family was sick. Monitoring all those potential triggers was time-consuming for Rudolph, made him more hypervigilant to new triggers, led him to feel agitate most of the time, and instead of going out with his friends and having fun, he spent his time mentally checking all these triggers.

When considering OCD, anxiety disorders, and other struggles like depression, procrastination, or perfectionism (to name a few), avoidance is like the gasoline that keeps them going. Avoidant behaviors perpetuate, reinforce, and strengthen all these disorders, organizing them into a rigid pattern of behavior that takes a person off-track, away from the person they want to be and the life they want to have.

This chapter focuses explicitly on behavioral patterns of avoidance that maintain an OCD episode and make your life difficult.

Let's list all the important life events, activities, challenges, or people that you have opted out of, quit, escaped, or withdrawn from because you were dealing with OCD episodes in Table 10.1.

Exercise 10.1 Inventory of meaningful activities that you are avoiding

What are the meaningful, important, and fun activities, events, or tasks you have opted out of because of OCD episodes?

What is the cost of opting out too much, too quickly, and too often? What things that are important to you do you avoid?

_____

_____

_____

_____

What came up for you when completing this inventory?

To have an amazing life – a life you're proud of – learning to notice whether your avoiding behaviors are expanding or reducing your life is a life skill.

Imagine for a moment that you wake up, do what you care about, do what you need to do, and return home fulfilled, no matter what your mind came up with, what you felt, or what you sensed in your body. What would that be like? This workbook will give you the skills to have moments like that, one after another, day after day.

Living a fulfilling life won't be 100 percent perfect, but it will be much better than living a life ruled by anxiety, fears, worries, and obsessions.

11

Do You Know Your Ruling-Thoughts?

When I was a kid and teen, my mom made sure that every year I learned and practiced a new sport, even though I wasn't so athletic. So, I got enrolled in swimming, basketball, volleyball, running, you name it. Sometimes it was a lot of fun, other times it was just okay, and other times, developed a collection of bruises. It was only when I realized how much I enjoyed swimming that I got a kick out of it for years. What about you? Did you grow up practicing sports? Are you still doing so?

When learning to play a sport, it's necessary to follow certain rules of the game. Whatever the sport is, there are certain behaviors that are acceptable, encouraged, and required and others that are totally disallowed because they're against the rules.

When dealing with bizarre, repetitive, or unrelenting thoughts, it's quite likely that you have organized your behavior around what you can or cannot do when obsessions show up, as if you're holding onto rules about the obsessions themselves – rules about fear, panic, worry, anxiety, and so on.

You can start recognizing these ruling-thoughts by key words or phrases that are attached to them, such as "should," "have to," "must," "ought," "right," "wrong," "always," "never," "can't because . . .," "won't until . . .," "shouldn't unless . . . ." Other times, rules are hidden by words along the lines of "Every time it's like this, this is just how it is" or conditions like "I can't do this until . . . unless this happens." If you step back, you will notice that these rules are everywhere; even though they don't always show up when dealing with an OCD episode, they are governing your day-to-day life in other ways. These ruling-thoughts are another thinking pattern your brain has organized, as it usually does.

What follows is a description of the most common ones that clients dealing with OCD get hooked on.

Ruling-Thought: "I Can't Handle It!"

When I ask my clients what gets in their way of tackling OCD, I usually get a response along the lines of "I can't handle this fear about harming my kid," "It will be too much to sit with my obsession about getting leukemia," "It will be awful to deal with my fear of dying," "It will be too much for me."

What about you? Has your mind come up with the same kind of thoughts at some point? The academic literature calls this process "underestimating your ability to cope," and it is basically your brain assessing if you can handle the anxiety that comes along with your obsessions.

But here is the challenge. As you read before, an overreactive brain is constantly on edge and searching for threat. It's not your fault. It's just that, when having an obsession – whether because of your reactive brain, your learning history, or a combination of both – it amplifies things and quickly makes predictions about what you can and cannot handle; it generates any version of the thought "I can't handle this." And if at some point in the past you let that thought dictate your behavior, then that response got reinforced to the point that, the more you obeyed it, took it as the absolute truth, the more you learned to hold onto it with white knuckles.

Give some examples from your daily life in which you notice the thought "I can't handle it" or something along those lines.

_____

_____

_____

_____

Ruling-Thought: "I Need to Know for Real"

Marisa has an obsessive thought about harming her daughter. When she gets hooked on this thought, she goes into detective mode and, as a detective trying to figure out what's *really* happening, she spends hours replaying in her mind the way that she holds her daughter, as a compulsion, just to make sure she isn't doing anything inappropriate. Other times, she asks her mom, "Did you see me doing something different when playing with my daughter?" And even when her mom responds, or if Marisa perceives a different tone of voice, or her mom doesn't look her straight in the eye, Marisa asks the question again until it feels right and she feels relieved that she hasn't done anything that would prove she's going to harm her child.

Marisa's behaviors show how she's fused with this ruling-thought about "I need to know for sure," which consequently feeds into a chain of asking for reassurance and doing other compulsions.

Getting hooked on this rule makes it very challenging for Marisa to learn to live in a world where she doesn't know how things could go, how things will be, how some things just are. There are things that we just won't know. For example, "Am I 100 percent sure that I won't die young?" "Can I be 100 percent sure that I won't ever harm another person?" "Can I 100 percent know that my partner loves me?" We might like to answer "Yes" to these questions and others, but the fact is we can't, because we cannot predict the future or know what's coming next, or even what our mind is going to throw at us in the next minute.

Yet organizing our behavior around *seeking absolute certainty*, as Marisa does, makes it very challenging to keep moving along, since it's time consuming, leads to more checking behaviors, feeds into an OCD episode, and is mentally exhausting. In the end, all those certainty-seeking behaviors withdraw so much time from the precious bank account of life.

Let me clarify: I'm not saying that we should stop scientific progress, because by nature, science evolves when we search for answers to questions about the world around us that we don't know. I'm referring exclusively to the unhelpful role of ruling-thoughts when dealing with obsessions, as well as its negative impact on your day-to-day life.

No number of certainty-seeking behaviors will prevent the outcome you're afraid of. As much as you hope to know *for real* that an obsession won't happen or that it is not true, certainty is just not possible at all times. Let's look what happens when, as a requirement for your well-being, you get consumed by hoping to know for sure.

What situations come into your mind when you are totally hooked on the thought "I need to know for sure"?

Ruling-Thought: "If My Obsessions Are Repetitive, That Means They're Important"

Let's go over Richard's OCD episode. When Richard, who identifies as gay, finds himself starring at a woman's genital areas, his mind yells at him, "Do I like women? Am I a hetero? Am I bi?" When hanging out with females, he makes a point of monitoring where his sight falls multiple times and pays attention to his reaction every single time. For Richard, having repetitive thoughts about his sexual identity means that those thoughts are super-important, 100 percent true, and therefore he concludes that he may have a different sexual orientation; when thinking that way, Richard spent hours feeling confused, doubtful, and stressed about it.

Up for an exercise? If you're up for it, think about something happening to the book you're holding in your hands within the next 24 hours. It doesn't necessarily have to be something tragic, but how about imagining something happening to it? Anything. See how it goes and jot down your response.

In Chapter 4, "Why Are Obsessions So Hard to Let Go of?" you learned that a thought is a thought. Even the most bizarre, dreadful, and scary thoughts are really a chain of letters or an image from the content generator of your mind. And let's face it, not even the best magician could make things happen just through thinking!

Here is my invitation for you to keep in mind as you move forward in this workbook and in your life: Holding a thought as an absolute truth – including thoughts that pop up hundreds of times in your mind – could easily drive behaviors that are totally inconsistent with where you want to go and take you south instead. A repetitive thought, it's a repetitive thought, not a cause of your behavior.

Ruling-Thought: "I Have to Do Something About This Obsession, Right Now!"

When Jack was driving to my office on a wintery and rainy day, he saw a woman at the intersection of one of the streets he was driving through, and he instantly had the thought about possibly hitting her without realizing it. He felt a knot in his chest so intensely and overwhelmingly, and right away he started checking the rear and side mirrors repeatedly. He even drove back to that corner multiple times to make sure there wasn't a body lying in the street. Jack didn't read this workbook, so he didn't know that when those intrusive obsessions show up in his mind, they're thoughts that he can hold lightly, thoughts that he doesn't have to respond to or act on so quickly.

There are problems that require being solved – for instance, when you lose wi-fi connection and you're writing, when you have a flat tire, when you have to give feedback at work and are concerned about how to do so, and so many other everyday situations. Then there is stuff that pops up in our mind that appears to be problems that have be solved right away – images coming at the speed of light, random hypotheses, reminders about things you have to get done – but most of them can wait. It's like your content-generating machine is coming up with fake-news, fake-problems, false alarms. Obsessions are a form of fake-news, fake-problems, and false alarms.

Getting hooked on the ruling-thought of "If I have an obsession, I have to do something about it right now, right here" is distracting and time consuming. But because your brain is working really hard to protect you from a potential threat – although there is no actual threat from having a disturbing thought – that protective response makes intrusions hard to have, given the fear, distress, and anxiety that come along with them.

Imagine for a moment a field of grass, full of sunlight and open space. Notice all the blades of grass quivering in the wind. Notice the hundreds, thousands, and maybe billions of blades of grass. Your mind is just as extensive as this field of grass, and all those blades of grass are like all the thoughts you have, including the obsessions. Sometimes, your overworking brain anticipates danger, but that doesn't mean that you have to do something about it at that moment or even later. A thought is just a thought.

Looking at last week, what OCD-related moment comes into your mind when you got trapped by the ruling-thought "I have to do something about this obsession, right now, right here"?

———————————————————————————

———————————————————————————

———————————————————————————

———————————————————————————

Ruling-Thought: "Because I Think About It, It Means I Want to Do So!"

Lily has been dealing with obsessions about stealing ideas from others or taking advantage of them. She gets triggered when having conversations with her friends about school projects, when discussing politics, or even chatting about a book. When she has these fears, Lily makes a point of squeezing both her hands twice, breathes fast four times, and then says to her friends, "You know, I mean to say this . . ." or "I actually mean this . . .," as a form of clarifying or overexplaining her opinions and self-reassuring that she's not stealing others' thoughts.

Like Lily, you may be getting caught on thoughts along the lines of "If I have those thoughts, it means I want to do all those things. Otherwise I wouldn't be having them." Do you relate to this theme of thoughts? Most of my clients do, because we have been told that everything we think is real, that things are exactly as we think about them, that we should respond to thinking with more thinking, and that we're defined by our thoughts.

Thoughts can be very powerful, and even though they seem so real, they're not reality. Please highlight this sentence: thoughts are not reality. Most of the time, thoughts can actually be an illusion of what's going on that takes us out of touch with what's really happening.

Think about it. Obsessions don't come with a happy, bubbly, or excited feeling. Far from it: they're hard to have, hard to acknowledge, and totally unwelcome. That's not a coincidence. Things that we want usually come with that sense of wanting, wishing, hoping for, and even desiring.

No matter how repetitive an obsession is, no matter how many times it shows up, no matter how upsetting it is, it has nothing to do with your wants, wishes, and desires.

When it comes to practicing your ability to choose your behaviors, all you have is the present moment.

Ruling-Thought: "I Need to Make Sure I Don't Have Weird Thoughts!"

Up for a quick mini-exercise? Read the directions for this exercise, set a timer for 1 minute for each direction, then put this book down and follow the directions.

First, do your best not to think about your toes for 1 minute. Yup, you read that right! For 60 seconds, put all your effort into not thinking about your toes. Second direction: for 1 minute, make sure you don't think about anything related to your toes, like socks, shoes, blisters, pedicures, nail polish, and so on. And third, the last part of this exercise, for 1 minute erase any memory, image, or thought related to your toes and, really, please do your best to make any image related to your toes disappear.

What happened when you completed this exercise? When I did it myself, all I had in my mind were my toes: having a manicure, the socks with polka dots, the sandals I like to wear during the summer, and so on. What about you? Many of my clients, when completing the exercise, they look at me and say, "Dr. Z, this is ridiculous. Images of my toes keep coming up, even when I try to think of something completely different."

When dealing with obsessions, a popular response from my clients, and maybe you, too, is that they do everything they can in their power not to have weird thoughts. My clients try replacing those intrusions with positive images, positive thoughts, telling themselves nice things, reassuring themselves, and so on. And yet here is a reality: you don't have control of what shows up in your mind, when it shows up, or how it shows up. Neither do I. But we can choose how to relate to those obsessions, how to respond to those thoughts, how to deal with them, even when they're a string of letters assembled together that come with repugnant and disgusting content.

What are the obsessions that get you hooked on this ruling-thought: "I need to make sure I don't have any weird thoughts"?

_____

_____

_____

_____

Ruling-Thought: "I Know My Obsessions Are Real!"

Up for another brief exercise? What about imagining for a couple of moments that there is an earthquake in your area that destroys your neighborhood. Imagine this earthquake in as much detail as possible. Picture your home falling to pieces, your neighbors' property destroyed to the ground, people running in the street, cars smashed by wind, the dust covering the air, and the sounds of people screaming. Isn't that a petrifying and scary image? And what happened around you when you imagined it? Is imagining the earthquake the same as actually being in the middle of one?

Let me ask you about another scenario. Are you into watching scary movies? What was the last horror film you watched? How was it for you to watch it? Were you entertained? What were your internal reactions to it? Was there any moment when you experienced fear? Maybe yes, maybe no.

Feeling fearful, alarmed, or afraid is natural – it's part of being alive. As frightening as it sounds to go through an earthquake, thinking about it doesn't make it happen, and the same applies to obsessions. Having obsessive thoughts, images, and urges – whatever they are and no matter how dangerous they seem, even when they happen hundreds of times – doesn't make them happen, because there's a difference between what happens in your mind versus what happens in reality. Getting hooked on a ruling-thought adds more misery, distress, and struggle to your day-to-day living.

There are things that are dangerous, for sure, and naturally the wonderful machine of our brain tries to prevent anything bad from happening to us. Therefore, at any sign of potential danger, whether it is an accurate perception or not, current or past, our brain organizes our behavior to respond to the threat.

But, and here is the big *but*, our brain is far from being a perfect device, and it actually makes discrimination mistakes – because it doesn't distinguish past associations from what's actually happening in a given moment. Think about it. Do obsessions come charged with an atomic bomb when they show up in your mind? What's to protect you from an obsession? Our mind plays tricks, no exceptions! What happens to your daily routine when you organize your behaviors like a firefighter when seeing obsessions?

Looking at your experience, when was the last time you took the ruling-thought "my obsessions are so scary that I 'know' they're true" as absolutely real?

_____

_____

_____

_____

Ruling-Thought: "I'm Weird Because I Have Weird Thoughts"

Let's pause for a moment. Check in with yourself: besides obsessions, how often does your mind come up with revengeful, jealous, possessive thoughts or images?

For hundreds of years, generation after generation, we have received all sorts of messages, including from many books, about how we shouldn't have weird, negative, or bad thoughts. Some popular figures have even built their careers on this topic. Along the way, the message that something is "defective, broken, or off" is also sent when a person has strange thoughts.

Instead of automatically accepting as truth all those messages that we grew up with, ACT asks us to step back look at our experience – particularly when having weird or disturbing thoughts – with open eyes and as real as it gets.

Let's do a mini-exercise. For the next couple of minutes, look back at different times in your life and do your best to recall, then jot down, any weird, strange, or uncanny images or thoughts you had.

When you were a kid:

_____

_____

_____

When you were a teen:

_____

_____

_____

In your early twenties:

_____

_____

_____

In your mid-thirties:

_____

_____

_____

In your mid-forties:

_____

_____

_____

Any reactions? Now, come back to the present day. What does your mind tell you to do when you have strange thoughts?

_____

_____

_____

If your mind is like mine, quite likely all those attempts to replace negative thoughts with positive ones may have lasted for a couple of moments, hours in some cases. But then next thing you notice, another weird thought pops up.

The reality is that our mind comes up with all types of thoughts: comfortable, fun, silly, pleasurable, as well as all sorts of negative ones. Your reactive brain will interpret a lot of thoughts, images, and sensations as a threat and then will try to quickly organize a defense response that is time consuming and takes you into a battle with your mind.

This is where ACT pushes the envelope, because with a solid scientific basis behind it, it demonstrates that how we have been thinking about thinking over the years is inaccurate. We cannot control our mind, we cannot ask our mind not to have creepy thoughts, and having a thought, including a bizarre one, has nothing to do with who we are.

Ruling-Thought: "Thinking Is Always Helpful"

For 1 minute, watch what your mind does: set a timer and just watch what your mind chats about. What's the chitchat that happens? After listening to the background sounds, does it make sense that every single thought needs to be responded to and taken seriously? Do you have to respond to every single thought? Do you have to fuel a conversation with each one of those thoughts and random images? Our mind usually has hundreds of inner monologues going on – too many during the day and too many to address.

We have been taught for years that any type of thinking needs to be addressed with more thinking, as if it's the only way to handle thinking. I don't mean to be a thinking renegade, because of course, there are problems that require thinking (e.g., when you're buying a property, deciding on a vacation, choosing a book to read, planning your weekend, and so on). In fact, let's look at this notion. As a mini-exercise, how about listing the situations in which you found yourself last week whereby doing what you were thinking was super handy and helped you to be the person you want to be (Table 11.1)?

Exercise 11.1 Stock of situations in which you were doing what you thought was helpful

> Jot down five different situations you encountered last week in which "thinking" took you in the direction you wanted your life to go in.
>
> *For example:*
> *When driving to the office, I had a flat tire, so I had to quickly think/remember how to change the tire and do it.*
>
> 1.
>
> 2.
>
> 3.
>
> 4.
>
> 5.

As handy as thinking can be at times, there are thousands of other situations in which thoughts are pure noise, background sound, or ongoing chitchat that your mind comes up with. And if you act on them, things get a bit rocky for you, as if instead of moving north you end up moving south. Think about last week and consider those moments when thinking wasn't so handy for you (Table 11.2).

Exercise 11.2 Stock of situations in which you were doing what you thought wasn't helpful

> Jot down five different situations you encountered last week in which "thinking" took you in the totally opposite direction you want to take your life.
>
> *For example:*
> *When going on a date, I had the thought, "She's not going to like me either way, so why try?" and I ended up not asking her many questions at dinner.*
>
> 1.
>
> 2.
>
> 3.
>
> 4.
>
> 5.

Is there any other ruling-thought you may have noticed that, even though it may not show up in the midst of an OCD episode, you hold onto? Having these ruling-thoughts and holding onto them is not problematic per se, but when you hold onto them rigidly, inflexibly, and as the source of behavior that is inconsistent with how you want to live your life, that's when they become problematic.

Ruling-Thought: "Because I Think So, It Makes Me So"

Your mind quite likely has come up with torrents of thoughts about who you are as a person, what your character is about, and what your essence is.

For instance, if you're having aggressive or sexual obsessions toward yourself or others, you may have been listening to narratives in your mind about who you are – for example, "I'm a pervert/a bad person/a potential killer/an ungrateful son." And, even if you're dealing with other forms of obsessions, you may still be attached to the ruling-thought "Because I think so, it makes me so." It's as if your mind quickly comes up with a self-description: "I'm _____." Sometimes, your mind may come up with an entire story, a narrative of who you are because of those disturbing thoughts. It is as if your mind is listing evidence to convince you that you're this or that. Isn't it annoying that our mind does that?

Isn't it annoying that this content-generating and pattern-making machine of ours not only wrongly reacts by announcing danger when an obsession pops up but also elaborates, explains, and even enlarges those thoughts about our character as if those thoughts are the absolute truth? Think about it. Does having a disturbing thought, or many disturbing ones, define our character? Is our persona defined by what we think, feel, or sense in our body? Or are we defined by how we behave, the actions we take, the words we say, and the moves we make?

There is a distinction between who you are and the pesky obsessions you're struggling with. There is a distinction between having a thought and being the thought. Here is a brief exercise to elaborate on this point.

Read the following directions and then complete the exercise. For a moment, close your eyes and bring into your mind a sweet memory you experienced about something special happening to you in the last month. Make sure it's a memory of a situation that you were part of, so you can see yourself as part of the image. Recall that sweet memory as vividly as possible: visualize who was part of that moment, remember what words were said, see if you can remember the smells or background noise in that moment, and hold it in your mind for a couple moments.

Next, open your eyes and answer these questions: Did you see yourself as part of that sweet memory? If you were part of the sweet memory, who was watching it? Ponder on this for a moment before carrying on reading.

Here is a take-home message to keep in mind as you progress in overcoming OCD episodes. A memory is a memory. It is not you. In the same way, a thought is a thought, an obsession is an obsession, a feeling is a feeling, and a sensation is a sensation. None of those things is you; those things are stuff you *have*, not stuff you *are*. Do you see the difference? I may sound a bit crazy right now if this is the first time you're reading about this distinction, so bear with me. You are learning how to watch your mind's busy activity for what it is, and you're also learning how to detach from it.

As clunky as it sounds, as you continue reading and practicing the exercises in this workbook, you will become more familiar with this idea and have direct experience of it. For now, my intention is to encourage you to ask yourself, "What are the effects of holding onto the stories about who I am due to obsessions popping into my mind?" Does your life expand or contract?

And you may be wondering, as my clients usually are when we do this exercise and discuss this rule, "If we are not our thoughts, feelings, and sensations, who are we?" Here is a short response: You're more like the sky, having different types of clouds; the foundation of the house that has different types of furniture; or the book that has different letters, ideas, and chapters inside it.

Looking at your experience, what are the stories your mind told you about your character or who you are because of obsessions?

_____

_____

_____

Ruling-Thought: "Not Doing Anything About It Is the Same As Causing It"

Are you open to doing another mini-experiment? Do you remember a time when you were a kid when you hoped for something to happen, like you crossed your fingers and hoped your parents would take you to the movie theater? And if your parents did take you to the movies, you may have concluded, "Because I crossed my fingers, I'm at the movie theater!"

Imagine if, by the randomness of life, that happened hundreds of times. Would it make sense that, as an adult, you would still hold onto the belief that if you crossed your fingers your wishes would come true, even though hundreds of times the outcome was far from your wish? Is that much different from taking your obsessions as written in stone and then, because you don't do anything to neutralize, get rid of, or minimize them, you are responsible for something bad happening?

The tricky part of thoughts along the lines of "If I don't do anything about it, it makes me responsible" is those thoughts naturally occur with your reactive brain. If you recall from Chapter 4, "Why Are Obsessions So Hard to Let Go of?" your brain is – evolutionarily speaking – designed to identify threats wherever you look, and on top of that, when perceiving a threat, it also comes up with all types of thoughts. Let's think for a moment of Julie, who one night noticed that, when holding her 2-year-old child, she had a sensation in her groin area. Her brain quickly shouted at her, "Have I become a pedophile? I felt aroused. That means I like children. What if I abuse my child? I felt it!" Instead of holding thoughts like "It's natural to have reactions in your groin," Julie didn't know what to do. She didn't know how to share with her husband what happened, she was terrified of calling a doctor out of fear the doctor would call child protective services on her, so she opted for avoiding holding her child or being alone with her, and she constantly monitored when she had a tingling sensation in her groin. And she tried to figure out what could have possibly caused it. For Julie, considering the option of not avoiding her kid or going back to holding her meant that she would be putting the child in danger, because she was holding onto this belief that "not doing anything about it is the same as causing it," even though those beliefs were thoughts arising from a reactive brain.

Looking back at all those OCD episodes you encountered, how was it for you to get hooked on the ruling-thought that "not doing anything about it is the same as causing it" is the only truth?

_____

_____

_____

If you find yourself holding onto the ruling-thought that "not doing anything is the same as causing it," take a deep breath and answer the following question for yourself. If you do exactly what that the ruling-thought tells you to do, what's it in the service of?

Is there any other ruling-thought you would like to add to this list? Think about all those beliefs you are adhering to about the way things should be, how you should feel, how you should behave, how you should manage obsessions, or how you should handle all the discomfort that comes in life because of obsessions.

_____

_____

_____

Now . . .

What About Checking the Rules You Get Hooked on?

Do any of the above ruling-thoughts relate to your behavior? Jot down the rules that you adhere to and how often you do so in Table 11.3. Remember that completing this workbook is only for you, so just do your best to check for yourself how often you get hooked on any of these rules!

Exercise 11.3 What are the ruling-thoughts you're holding onto?

The ruling-thoughts I'm holding onto and the behaviors associated with them	How often I get hooked on these ruling-thoughts				
	Not at all	Sometimes	Often	Very often	Most of the time
I can't handle it!					
I need to know, for real.					
My obsessions are repetitive, that means they are important.					
I have to do something about this obsession, right now!					
Because I think about it, it means I want to do so!					
I need to make sure I don't have weird thoughts.					
I know my obsessions are real!					
I'm weird because I have weird thoughts.					
Thinking is always helpful.					
Because I think so, it makes me so.					
Not doing anything about it is the same as causing it.					

There are things that we have, e.g., our jobs, what we wear, what we eat, and so on, and yet they don't reflect us; there is stuff that we do, e.g., paying bills, eating, exercising, and so on, and yet, they don't tell the whole story of who we are; there is all types of feelings, sensations, images, and thoughts we experience all the time, and yet, they are not us. The same is true with all types of obsessions we have – as annoying, sticky, and repetitive they are, they don't define us.

The reality is that the content-generating and pattern-making machine of our mind comes up with all types of content and creates all types of patterns. So, learning to step back and look at them for what they are – just thoughts – will help you not to be bossed around by them any longer.

Our busy brains can get overly focused on anything that could potentially could hurt us, such as obsessions. Coaching ourselves to recognize our thought patterns for what they are – and not what they say they are – stops us from becoming prisoners of our mind. And the amazing news is that our mind is coachable, shapeable, and flexible.

So how about this? Every time you get hooked onto a ruling-thought – either because you're dealing with an OCD episode or just going about with your day – instead of behaving in autopilot mode, you notice it, acknowledge it, and then say something along the lines of "Here is a ruling-thought. Here it comes. My brain is coming up with lots of ways to protect me." If you're a bit playful, you could even call it a silly name: "Here is Mr. Ruler, the unbreakable."

This suggestion may sound too simple, and yet coaching our brain doesn't have to be complicated all the time; in fact, labeling our thoughts is a powerful skill that help us to step back and build our capacity to choose our responses when feeling overwhelmed. A client who used to get hooked almost every hour on the thought "I need to know, for sure" decided to call this thought "wondering rules," and instead of continuing to search for more information, to get a false sense of safety, she noticed it, named it, and then refocused her energy on whatever was in front of her. Give it a try!

Takeaways to share

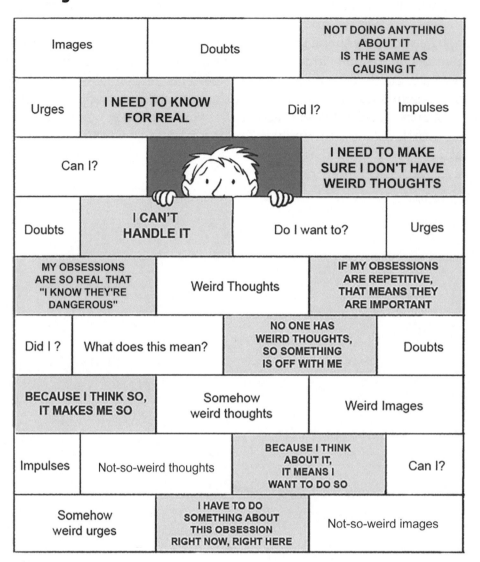

Figure 11.1 Ruling thoughts

Learning to watch what your mind does is a key skill to live the amazing, fulfilling and rich life you deserve! Here are the key takeaway points from this part:

- Our brains are designed to protect us from dangerous, uncomfortable, and painful situations at all times, even when we're sleeping. Whether those dangerous signals are stuff happening in our surroundings or are internal experiences we're having, that doesn't matter for the brain, our brain will jump in a fraction of seconds to make sure we don't get hurt. If you have an overactive brain, it means that your brain is jumping and jumping up and down, left and right, almost all the time.
- When the content-generating and pattern-generating machine of your brain throws out all types of bizarre thoughts and you perceive them as a threat, of course you're going to do anything in your power to neutralize them, like avoidant behaviors, compulsions, and coming up with ruling-thoughts to keep yourself safe. It's understandable.

- Behaving compulsively, avoiding triggering situations, and holding on with white knuckles to ruling-thoughts about how what you can or cannot do when feeling scared, what obsessions mean, or how you should handle a compulsion are very common responses when dealing with an overreactive brain that generates hundreds of obsessions. It's not your fault; it just happens that your brain is working extra hard to protect you.

- The most common ruling-thoughts you need to pay attention and check how they work in your day-to-day life are:

  - I can't handle it!
  - I need to know, for real
  - If my obsessions are repetitive, that means they're important
  - I have to do something about this obsession, right now!
  - Because I think about it, it means I want to do so!
  - I'm weird, because I have weird thoughts
  - I know my obsessions are real
  - Thinking is always helpful
  - Because I think so, it makes me so
  - Not doing anything about it is the same as causing it

- When noticing any of those ruling-thoughts you can give them a name and start labeling them. You could say to yourself things like "here comes Roger, the ruler" or any other name that helps you to catch them as they come your way.

Life Tracker

Reflect on how you have been living your life and mark an "X" where it corresponds.

Having obsessions as thoughts your mind comes up with	Seeing obsessions as problems to be solved
Approaching life as it is	Avoiding life because of obsessions
Taking action toward what you care about	Organizing your life around obsessions
Holding your thoughts lightly	Going 100% along with what your mind tells you
Checking what really works in your life	Doing stuff in automatic pilot mode
Making room for uncomfortable internal experiences	Pushing them down as much as possible

PART IV

Facts and Fantasy About Getting Rid of Obsessions

In Part III, you unpacked the most common actions that start and maintain an OCD episode, make you miss opportunities you want to have, take you in the opposite direction of where you want to go, and add more misery to your life. By the end of it, hopefully you had a clear understanding of all the things you do outside your head, inside your head, beliefs you are holding with white knuckles, and all the random or important stuff you avoid in order to manage all those bizarre obsessions that show up in your mind.

As you worked through Part III, you may have noticed that even by simply paying attention to your thinking patterns you can learn to have them as they are – content that your mind generates over and over – and that, but itself is a first step toward overcoming OCD. You will continue learning more skills to unhook from those disturbing obsessions, decrease those reactive moves that your brain pushes you to do, and do more of the stuff you care about.

Now, with the end goal of getting your life back on track, in Part IV you will take a peek at how all those things are working in your life.

Let me shift gears a bit and ask something different. Bear with me for a moment. Have you ever had a relationship in which you found your partner cute, fun, smart, sexy, you loved their sense of humor, their personality, and yet you knew it wasn't going to work between the two of you? And if so, what did you do? Did you break up right away? Did you go to therapy to check what was happening with you? Did you chat with your friends about it? Did you Google online for "How to tell if he's the one"? Did you try to make changes, adjustments, act as if nothing bothered you, and stayed stuck for a bit?

If your answer is "Yes" to any of those questions, welcome to the club. Don't we all do things like that in our life at some point? Whether it's because of relationships, work situations, how we handle our hurts, and so on, at times we all try to fit a square peg inside a round hole.

By the end of this section, you will see how this relates to how you handle OCD episodes.

12

How Do Ruling-Thoughts, Compulsions and Avoidant Behaviors Work?

When obsessions pop up, naturally, your over-protective brain pushes you to pay attention to them, to make a reactive move, and to take them as a serious threat – even though in reality, obsessions are fake-news. But the more OCD episodes you deal with, the more you organize your behavior around them. So let's take a peek at how these behavioral patterns are functioning in your life!

For You to Do

Let's start by doing a mini-inventory of the three most common *ruling-thoughts* you hold onto, the three most frequent *compulsions* you do, and the three most common situations you *avoid*. Jot them down inside each hexagon in Figure 12.1!

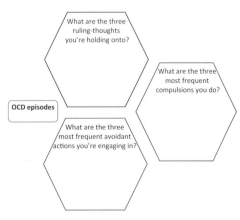

Figure 12.1 What are the three frequent ruling-thoughts, compulsions and avoidant behaviors that are affecting your life?

Now, take a peek at how these rules, compulsions, and avoidant behaviors are currently affecting your day-to-day living, as if you're stepping back from the top of a mountain and looking from afar at what has been happening to your life. Jot down a short response inside after each question (Figure 12.2).

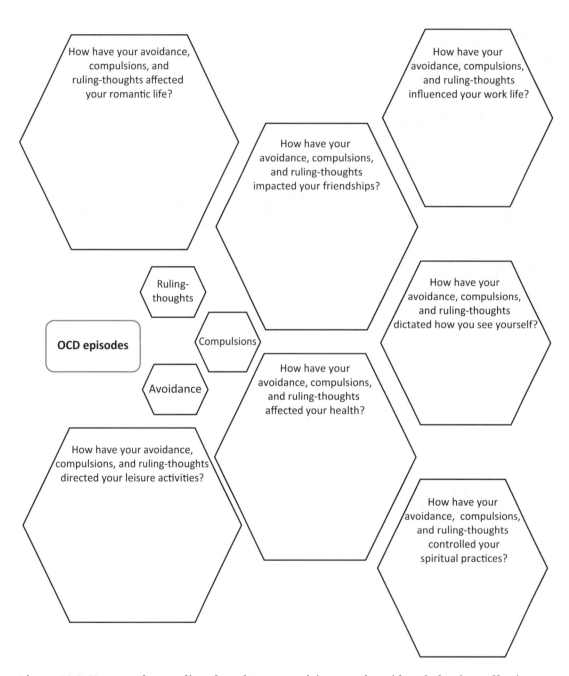

Figure 12.2 How are those ruling-thoughts, compulsions, and avoidant behaviors affecting your life?

If you zoom out one more time, can you recognize the long-term impact of all those problem-solving strategies when you have a compulsion in your life? Can you picture how it may look in 10 years' time if nothing changes and the content generator of your mind keeps dictating over and over what to do and what not to do?

Figure 12.3 What's the long-term impact of those ruling-thoughts, compulsions, and avoidant behaviors in your life?.

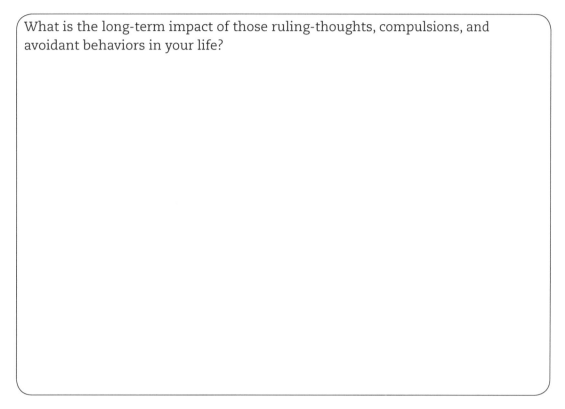

What is the long-term impact of those ruling-thoughts, compulsions, and avoidant behaviors in your life?

What were your reactions when checking what happens to your day-to-day life when you do everything you can to get rid of, suppress, and deny those obsessions?

How Are you Relating to Yourself These Days?

Dealing with OCD episodes, trying to control the obsession-problem with reactive moves, is also dealing with the fact that all those responses affect how you relate to yourself. You have been doing the most intuitive thing, which is to fight back those disturbing thoughts and try to control them with your behavior, and while you may already know that the most popular responses haven't been helpful, let's still take a peek at how OCD has affected the way you relate to yourself and the story that may have arisen because of it.

For You to Do

To start, here are some questions for you to ponder.

How have all those efforts to eliminate obsessions affected the relationship you have with yourself?

_____

_____

_____

How has using any of those strategies to get rid of the obsession-problem gotten in the way of doing things that are important to you?

_____

_____

_____

Do you feel connected with the people you care about?

_____

_____

_____

How do see yourself these days?

_____

_____

_____

Are you being the person you want to be?

_____

_____

_____

How often do you criticize, put down, and punish yourself?

_____

_____

_____

Quite often, when working with my clients, I get questions along the lines of the following:

- Am I the only one dealing with this?
- Have you seen any other person with OCD with this type of obsession?
- Am I the first person with this type of OCD?
- How do people live with this obsession?

Other times, my clients hold onto beliefs or stories about themselves such as "I'm messed up; no one would love me because of my OCD; no one would want to do stuff with me because I'm an anxious ball."

When those stories appear, you may start to defend them, try to prove them wrong, or even try to come up with a positive thought to neutralize them. I totally get that those stories come with a lot of pain, but as distressing as they are, paradoxically, the more you debate, push, and fight them, the more you get hooked and consumed by them. I'm not saying that the hurt you go through when having those narratives is not real or that your pain should be minimized. I'm just inviting you to check if fighting them, really works. The truth is that we all carry a criticizing voice that can be quite harsh, judgmental, critical of everything we do, and it can take over our day many times. We get caught up in our inner critics as we become our own bully.

If you are hooked on any variation of that criticizing story, here is my response to you. It's not your fault, you didn't plan it this way, it's another activity that our mind does, coming up with narratives, stories, themes about who we are and who we are not. Is our mind our enemy? No, it's not. It just happens that, in order to survive, an inner critic voice kept our ancestors on check so they didn't get kicked out of the tribe and die on their own. The challenge is that times have changed, our environment has changed, we're no longer surrounded by dinosaurs, wild animals, or terrible weather conditions. We certainly have other types of worries, but they're not as immediately fatal as the ones that the cave dwellers encountered. And as you can imagine, your brain has quickly organized a thinking-pattern about these stories, maybe adding proof that the story is true, creating more biases for you, and demanding that you take it seriously.

In this workbook, "self-criticism," "stories," or "narratives" are just terms to capture all those thoughts that your mind generates about who you are as a person. This is not to say that they don't hurt or that I don't acknowledge the pain that comes with them. I just want to highlight that, as negative as the story is about yourself, it's a narrative that gets amplified, augmented, and intensified by your reactive brain.

While our mind is fulfilling its core job of protecting us, that story of "being not good enough, broken, or defective," if taken as the absolute reality, rather than helping us, can be quite harmful, because instead of pushing us to do things that we care about, it usually organizes our behavior to disconnect, hide, avoid, and disengage from living the life we really want to live.

As you move on with this workbook, you will learn to view that story – the bully, the inner critic – as it is: simply a chain of letters and words put together. Our minds have the capacity to be harsh, critical, and bossy at times, that's an ordinary capacity. But, we also have the capacity to be kind, gentle, and caring when listening to those messages, that's an extraordinary capacity. In Chapter 23, "Hold Your Mind Lightly!" and Chapter 45, "Soften up With Self-Compassion" –you will discover skills to handle them.

There is no one better than you to make a shift – from living in isolation and punishing yourself to reconnecting with yourself and the person you want to be!

14

What's Really in Your Control?

1. What would you do if you bought a t-shirt that didn't fit you? You could return it, give it to someone else, or donate it, right?
2. What would you do if a person smoking a cigarette is standing next to you and the smell bothers you? You would probably move away.
3. What do you do when the radio station plays a song you hate? Don't you change the channel?
4. If you turn on the TV, and there is one of those Latino telenovelas that you don't like much, you quite likely switch channels, right?
5. If you go to a restaurant and the menu only offers vegan food, of course you stay, and you try at least five dishes from it, right? OK, I may be the only one staying in the restaurant, and you will probably look at the menu and plan your way out of it – or, if you're adventurous and curious, you may stay.

There are many things around you that you have control of, can regulate how much or how little you get of them, and can even stop them right away.

For You to Do

Jot down the things that you directly had control of today.

> Think about today. Don't worry about the time of the day, but just jot down the things, situations, activities, you had direct control of.

How was it to list all the things you have direct control of? How did it feel to jot those things down? Here is the other side of the coin. No matter how fast technology is moving forward in this information area – e.g., machine learning, robotics, virtual reality, artificial intelligence, and so on – we don't have a switch for our mind. I know it would be nice if Amazon would sell one. I'd buy one for myself, for sure, and a couple of them "just in case." But that's far from reality.

We have a mind that has a life of its own, and left to its own devices, it inundates our brain with hundreds of hypotheses, theories, doubtful thoughts, worries, angry thoughts, "what-if" scenarios, stories, reasons to not go dancing, convincing lists of why it's so good to eat dark chocolate, memories about trips we took, wishful thoughts about how things could be different at times, and thoughts in which we compare ourselves with others – and your mind (like my mind) also comes with intrusive obsessions.

As much as you have control of many things, there are thousands of things you don't have control over. And that's the tricky part, because you are so used to fixing, changing, getting rid of, and controlling certain things that spontaneously, you try to do the same with those obsessions. But, you don't have switch to stop the content-generating machine of your mind to come up with obsessions; and all those efforts to solve the obsession-problem actually makes them worse and keep you stuck. Every time you go into solving the obsession-problem, it's like rubbing salt in the wound.

Don't listen to me. Look at the outcomes of all those ruling-thoughts, compulsions and avoidant behaviors. What does your experience tell you? Look at what happens when you get caught up in those stories about yourself that your mind comes up with? How do you relate to yourself? Have any of those strategies ever worked to make your life better and keep you on track?

You're not broken and you're not defective. You're just off track from the life you want to live, spending too much time on the obsession's track in your mind and trying to solve a problem with strategies that make them worse.

Having obsessions is manageable, even if you have been struggling with them for a long time. It's time for you to get back on track in your life, and this workbook will show you new ways of relating to those pesky intrusive thoughts. By now, you get it: the content-generator machine of your mind has a life of its own. Obsessions are not a choice, but your behavior is a choice.

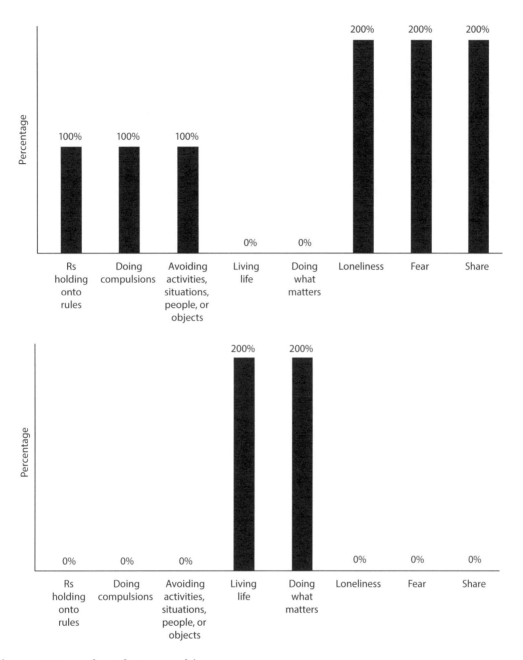

Figures 14.1a and 14.1b Bar graphic.

15

What About Dropping Those "Getting Rid of Obsessions" Strategies?

If you're like one of my clients, it's quite likely you have done your best and put a lot of effort to get rid of the obsessions-problems that the content-generating and pattern-making machines of your mind have been coming up with, which makes sense all the way.

And yet, in all the previous chapters you have seen how holding rigidly and with white knuckles onto ruling-thoughts about handling obsessions, needing to know for real whether the content of an obsession is possible or not, making sure you don't have a weird thought – and doing all types of compulsions and avoidant behaviors actually makes things worse for you and makes it difficult to move forward with your day-to-day activities.

Check for yourself. What has had a higher price in your life: the presence of obsessions, or the frantic energy you have spent making them stop? It's like all those responses were trying to calm a fire, but instead they were adding gasoline to it.

If doing compulsions and avoidant behaviors holding with white knuckles to ruling-thoughts and seeing obsessions as problems that have to be solved doesn't work in the long-term, could it be that those approaches are actually the problem?

I don't ask this to be obnoxious, but actually from a place of caring. What if the very act of doing compulsions and avoidance adhering to ruling-thoughts and targeting obsessions as evils that have to be exterminated is creating so much misery in your life?

Obsessions happen. They're not your choice, and this simple truth is inescapable. It applies to you, to me, and to every human being on earth. No one is exempt from having annoying, unwanted, and bizarre obsessions, but that doesn't mean you have to live your life stuck with them, full of fear, and let those obsessions run the show like a tyrannical dictator in your life.

For You to Do

There are two things you need to do:

1. Drop the fight, resistance, and pushback with either your public or private behaviors when those intrusive thoughts show up.
2. Accept they're showing up.

Acceptance is letting and allowing whatever obsession shows up to be there without trying to change, question, or get rid of it.

Image that someone you care about gave you a half-jalapeno and asked you to try it. You agree, place the half-jalapeno in your mouth, and taste it. What would your face look like when trying it? Now, imagine that you try the half-jalapeno again, but this time, if you notice any frowning or tension around your mouth or eyes, you relax your face. Acceptance is the second scenario, the one where you choose to feel what's to be felt without powering through.

When dealing with OCD, acceptance is about learning to have in your mind whatever obsessions the content-generator machine of your mind comes up with, to feel whatever you need to feel, and to sense whatever sensation shows up in your body.

The first step in putting acceptance into action is noticing when you're fighting the obsessions in any way, like judging them as bad things, judging yourself for having them, judging the situation, doing compulsions or avoiding a situation, a person, an activity, or a place.

It's time to end the battle against obsessions, discontinue all those efforts to make them go away, and stop exhausting all the solutions you have tried to solve the obsession-problem. It's time for you to develop a new relationship with those disturbing obsessions and a new relationship with your mind.

Takeaways to share

Figure 15.1 Deck of cards

When urges to do compulsions and avoidance hit, it's hard, incredibly hard, to not give into them; even if I offer you a million dollars if you don't do a compulsion or avoid a triggering situation right now, as tempting as it sounds, it's hard not to engage in old behaviors. And yet here is what psychological science has demonstrated over and over again when we need to change our behavior: (a) doing what matters is much more powerful than getting paid, (b) learning specialized skills is necessary, and (c) behaving progress markers keeps us moving in the direction we want to go in. This workbook is organized into those three main ideas, all the way!

It's your turn to make a shift from being off track, from making reactive moves based on what your brain pushes you to do and get your life back. And to get your life back on track, you're going to need to develop a new relationship with your mind, too.

Learning to be in a romantic relationship that is full of love, caring, tenderness, and commitment requires to learn other skills: how to choose a partner, how to handle our hurts and our partner's hurts, and basically how to show up for the relationship when there are disagreements, fights, and upsetting moments. Not an easy thing to do at all, but because we care, we commit to do so, we learn skill after skill, even though it feels impossible at times.

Living the life you want to live requires that you step back, watch what you're doing, and see how it is working in your life; this part was all about that! Here are the key take-home messages from it:

- When feeling scared or having disturbing thoughts or bizarre images coming at the speed of the light into your mind, of course you're going to do what you can in your power to get rid of them immediately. Who wouldn't? And yet compulsions, avoidance, and holding with white knuckles to ruling-thoughts add unhappiness into your life.
- Compulsions can be public and private behaviors or behaviors that are inside and outside your head with the exclusive purpose of minimizing, getting rid of, and neutralizing obsessions.

- Mental compulsions can vary in form from the simple to the most complex one: saying words, counting words or letters, repeating phrases, repeating lists, repeating prayers, reviewing past situations, reviewing past situations with what-if scenarios, anticipating future situations, anticipating future situations with what-if possibilities, figuring out the meaning of thoughts, feelings, or sensations, and figuring out life issues.

  A way to differentiate thinking strategies from mental compulsions is not based on how they look like but based on how their work, the setting in which they happen, and their impact in your daily living.

- Checking the effects of avoidant behaviors, compulsive actions, and holding onto ruling-thoughts is key to getting your life back on track. Important clarification: Checking the consequences of any behavior – compulsive behaviors, avoidant behaviors, or doing what you usually do because of a ruling-thought – doesn't mean checking whether that obsession or that ruling-thought is true or false; it means making a choice to step back for a moment and asking yourself if doing that particular behavior, doing that particular action, or taking that particular step is going to help you to show up in life as you want to show up? You can ask yourself questions like: is doing that "X behavior" helping me to be the person I want to be? If I take that "X action," am I the friend I want to be?

- Obsessions are not a choice, they just happen.
  Letting obsessions be, dropping all those strategies to get rid of them, discontinuing any fighting tactic you have against them, while it's not an easy or exciting thing to do, is the first step to get your life back on track. Doing nothing when those obsessions show up is key!

- Trying to control obsessions is a fantasy!
  As annoying, disturbing, and bizarre obsessions are, trying to control them, get rid of them, fight back is pure fantasy!

- OCD episodes continue happening because of reactive moves: compulsions, avoidance behaviors, and doing anything that comes along with ruling-thoughts.

Life Tracker

Reflect on how you have been living your life and mark an "X" where it corresponds.

Having obsessions as thoughts your mind comes up with	Seeing obsessions as problems to be solved
Approaching life as it is	Avoiding life because of obsessions
Taking action toward what you care about	Organizing your life around obsessions
Holding your thoughts lightly	Going 100% along with what your mind tells you
Checking what really works in your life	Doing stuff in automatic pilot mode
Making room for uncomfortable internal experiences	Pushing them down as much as possible

PART V

Learning to Date Your Mind

One Sunday evening, my friend called me and said, "Come for dinner!" I didn't have anything going on that night, so I put my hair up, grabbed my keys, and drove to her place. I parked the car, walked to her apartment, and found that the door was unlocked, so I let myself in. She was watching a video from Match.com, an online dating company, and was furiously taking notes on her notepad. She heard me walk in and said, "I'm almost done, I'm learning how to date." A couple of minutes later, we sat to eat a delicious vegan meal, and I heard about all the dating tips she learned, like specific questions to ask to learn whether a partner is a good fit, what to say and what to avoid saying if you're not interested in your date, or even figuring out when to switch from texting to meeting face-to-face with a potential romantic partner. I also got to hear how discouraged she felt from her dating experiences the last couple of months and how she realized that she needed to learn new skills to relate to potential romantic partners in a different way.

This is a sweet memory and reminds me that when we don't know something, we search for information, ask about it, and learn all the necessary skills to make things better.

Imagine for a second that your mind is like a potential romantic partner for you. Now answer these questions: "When having obsessions, how have you been dating your mind? How have you been treating that partner of yours who accompanies you wherever you go? Have you been annoyed at your partner for throwing disturbing obsessions at you?" Take a couple of moments to reflect before jumping in to respond.

Step back for a moment and think of a moment when you tried to control or manage another person's behavior in a romantic relationship. What was the outcome of telling that person what to do and what to think? Did it help the relationship to grow?

When dating comes with a forceful, pushy, and controlling agenda toward a partner, the outcome is not ideal. And the same applies to your relationship with your mind.

I get that you did the best you could; I know it's very stressful to be dealing with unwanted intrusive thoughts, and you've put your avoidant behaviors, compulsions, and ruling-thoughts in motion. But quite likely, it was all done with a single purpose: to control your date – to control your mind – from coming up with more bizarre thoughts and taking you spiraling down with them. In Part IV, you took a detailed look at the impact of all these behaviors on your life.

Here is my invitation for you moving forward. What about learning to date your mind without pushing, forcing, or even coercing it when it comes up with unsolicited content such as obsessions?

I'm not asking you to love, approve, or even like all the content that this "date" comes up with. I'm not suggesting that you don't do anything about those uncomfortable obsessions that come your way. How about, instead of fighting against your mind with controlling gloves as if you're a boxer, you learn to date it with kindness, making room for all the stuff that it comes up with, checking the workability of those urges to take action, getting out of the content of thoughts, looking at thoughts as stuff your mind comes up with rather than as stuff that you always have to listen to, and making a choice to keep engaging with life as it's happening in those moments?

The chapters in this section will show you how you can start dating your mind as it is, as it comes, with all the sweet, ugly, and good stuff included!

Let's get you moving!

16

Let Your Mind Do Its Own Minding

Let's do an exercise. Make a mark on this page, close this book, and if you have a timer, set it for 5 minutes, then just watch what your mind comes up with as if you're watching a movie. What was the stuff that your mind came up with during those 5 minutes? When I completed this exercise, my mind came up with thoughts about how much I love cashews, an image of taking the train to San Francisco, a memory of a dinner with a friend, a worry about making sure I'm backing up this writing, and so on.

If you recall from Chapter 4, "Why Are Obsessions So Hard to Let Go of?" you learned that your mind does its own minding, its own thinking, and it generates content patterns 24/7 a week, no exceptions. As much you dislike, hate, and even get mad at those sticky obsessions, you don't have control over when they show up, how often they show up, or in what form or with what content. They just show up – images of exposing your private parts in public, fears of contracting AIDS, and obsessive thoughts about not knowing whether you made the *right* decision about choosing a partner.

Given all the thinking-content and thinking-patterns that show up in your mind, do you really think all of it is true, accurate, and reasonable, all the time?

Nobody's mind has the absolute truth all the time, nor is it 100 percent correct all the time or paying attention 24/7 to what needs to be paid attention to. In fact, throughout our day, our minds have thousands of thoughts, images, words, sentences, and all types of theories, hypotheses, worries, doubts, and so on, that go up and down, left and right. And when I say "thousands of . . ." I absolutely mean it – there really are thousands of them.

Sometimes our content-generating machine comes up with very helpful content. For example, when I was planning a trip to the OCD conference this year, it was handy to think about different dates for the trip, hotel arrangements, dinners I wanted to attend, and people I wanted to see. But most of the time, our mind comes up with nonsensical content, and we spend tons of time in our head and not living our life. We're already spending hundreds more hours in our head than our ancestors did because we have access to all types of sources of information: Google to search for everything, YouTube to figure out how to install a picture frame, as well as books, documentaries, and more. It's only natural that we end up confusing thinking with reality.

Dating Tip: Thank You, Mind

Whenever your over-protective brain comes up with an avalanche of fearful thoughts, doubts, obsessions, or worries, see if you can acknowledge the hard-working job your brain is doing in that moment by saying, "Thank you, brain; thank you, mind; thanks, reactive brain."

Practicing these skills won't make the obsessions go away, but it will help you with catching the urge to respond to every single thought that shows up in your mind.

You can apply this checking skill anytime, anywhere!

17

Fall Out of Blind Love With Your Mind!

- Have you ever watched a movie about a character who is consumed with love for another person?
- Have you been in relationships in which you cannot function unless you were with that person?

Here is a different set of questions for you:

- Have you ever counted how many hours you spend paying attention to your mind?
- Do you experience mental fatigue because of all the thinking and thinking and minding and minding you have been doing?
- Did you feel that at times your mind may be erratic as it jumps from one theme to another?

If you answered "Yes" to any of these questions, it's likely that you have been preoccupied with your mind too much and too often. Think about it. Is it possible – as people in the 1960s wrote about love addiction – that you're facing a mind addiction? Or a thinking addiction?

There is a time and place to pay attention to your mind and make the best of your thoughts, hypotheses, ideas, and even your worries, but that's not *all the time*. Imagine if we had to respond to every single thought that popped up in our mind. Imagine how it would be if you had to dwell on every single image that emerged in your head. This may sound contradictory to every single message you have heard about the power of the mind, such as the power of mind over mood, but check your own experience. What would happen if you took every single thought to be serious, important, and urgent?

I'm not suggesting you ignore your mind at all times, because that wouldn't be pragmatic or realistic in your day-to-day life, but I'm seriously inviting you to reassess your relationship with your mind. Are you fixating on it, similar to what we do when we fall in love? Is the price you're paying worth it, all the time?

Although it's important and necessary to pay attention to our mind, your mind will be fine without you, and you too will be okay as you learn to develop a new relationship with it.

Dating Tip: Do I Have to Respond to This Thought?

Imagine for a moment that the content-generating and pattern-making machine of your mind is like a YouTube channel announcing news all the time. When listening to it, ask yourself: "Do I really have to respond to this thought?"

You don't need to wait for an OCD episode to put this skill into action. And although this may sound like a simple step, training your brain to shift the focus of your attention from the inside to the outside world (where life is actually happening!) is a core skill and a step toward designing the life you want to have.

Give it a try!

18

Get Out of the Content of Your Mind!

When was the last time you were chatting with your friend, and in the midst of the conversation you couldn't remember a word and ended up spending hours searching for it in your mind for the rest of the day? Have you ever watched a movie and were so captured by the story that you forgot the next conference call you had for work? Did you ever go on a date, and while talking to your date, your mind imagined how the second date might look like with this person?

Chances are that you have experienced one, two, or all of these situations, and in those moments. We all have experiences like that, when we're fully consumed, engaged, and absorbed by the stuff that our mind comes up with. It's hard not to, but learning to date your mind means that you need to learn to differentiate when it's useful, helpful, and important to get absorbed in it and when it's not.

Look back at the last month and recall all those moments when you were fully present with the content that was floating in your mind and it was fun, effortless, and even easy to do so.

Exercise: List of Situations in Which You Were Fully "Engaged" With Your Mind

Think about last month, and recall all those moments when you were fully present with the content that was floating in your mind and it was fun and effortless.

Let's zoom out one more time and recall moments in which you were fully engaged in your mind at a not-so-ideal time, got distracted from the present, and had to deal with not-so-good outcomes. Here is a personal example. When writing this chapter, my mind came up with the image of Sidney, my kitty, and next thing I knew, I started thinking, "Did I get his favorite treats this week? Where is he right now? Did he eat? Did he play enough today?" And after 20 minutes, I looked at the screen, and I had a single paragraph written for this chapter. You see, what happened in that moment is that I was fully absorbed with the image of my kitty and dismissed, ignored, the task I had in front of me: writing this chapter.

Here is the irony of this story. I actually love writing so much; it's part of my commitment to disseminate research-based and impactful skills. If I care so much about writing, how did it happen that I got consumed by other thoughts? Here is a short response: I got hooked on the content of my mind!

What about you? When was the last time you got consumed by thoughts in your mind and it wasn't so helpful to you or the people around you? Jot down your responses in the next exercise.

Exercise: List of Situations in Which It Was Not Helpful to Get Hooked on Your Mind

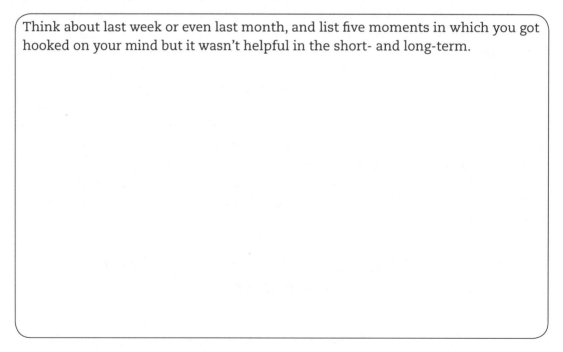

Think about last week or even last month, and list five moments in which you got hooked on your mind but it wasn't helpful in the short- and long-term.

What about taking a peek at moments when you got consumed by your obsession, OCD episodes, or any OCD-related stuff?

Exercise: List of Situations in Which You Were Absorbed in OCD-Related Stuff

Think about last week or even last month, and list five moments in which you got hooked and consumed on OCD related stuff.

How did it go? Did you notice how our mind can take us into so many directions without us realizing? Here's a mini-tip to help you continue learning to relate to your mind in a way that guides you to create a life that is worth living!

Dating Tip: Chessboard Image

Given that your mind is a content-generating machine and is constantly creating thoughts, and you know that getting into the content just makes things worse for you, what about trying something new? Imagine for a moment that your mind is like a chessboard. A chessboard has many pieces – thoughts, images, memories, judgments, and all types of content – but the chessboard is neither good or bad, it just is. Imagine that all those obsessions your mind comes up with are like the pieces of the chessboard that you can watch, see, observe, and notice.

Getting out of the content of your mind will help you to develop a new relationship with it, and instead of living in your head, you can go back to being present with what's happening in front of you!

19

Stay "In the Moment," Not in Your Head!

I want to check this recommendation from Amazon about this book – oops, how many reviews does this book have? What? Who is this author? Did I send the email to Mark? I'll do it quickly; I have 5 more minutes to do so. Did I place my order for tissue paper on Amazon? I have to get back to it. I'm wondering what's happening with the prices on flights to Europe? . . . I forgot to clean the shelf – it will take me 2 minutes to do so. What's this stain?

You just read here what my mind goes through when I'm sitting in front of the laptop. The reality is that our minds wander in all directions, up and down, left and right. Not one time, but hundreds of times.

Because obsessions take you away from the present, deprive you from enjoy what's happening in front of you, or learning from the day-to-day tribulations we go through, this chapter is about bringing yourself back into the present!

Staying in the moment seems very challenging to do when your mind is continually throwing hundreds of mental distractions or bizarre content at you and thousands of stimulating things happening outside your skin at the same time. And yet what's the alternative? If you continue to stay in your head 24/7, what happens to the errands you have to run? Do you do the fun stuff you want to do? Does your life get better? You cannot choose the obsessions that come into your mind and you cannot stop them from happening, but "analyzing, dissecting, understanding, or trying to figure them out" will just make things more challenging for you.

Learning to create a new relationship with your reactive brain means learning to let all types of thoughts – obsessions included – come and go without getting hooked on them.

Dating Tip: Five Deep Breaths and Grounding

When a painful obsession pops into your awareness and you have an urge to get lost in your mind, that's the time to bring yourself back to the now, to the present, to what's happening in front of you.

The first thing to do is to pause, take five deep slow breaths, focus on the rise and fall of your ribcage, notice the sensations of the air as it flows in and out of your body, and do your best to switch the focus of your attention to your surroundings. Notice five things you see, four things you hear, three things you smell, and two things you can touch, and you can even move your tongue to notice any taste in your mouth.

If you're talking to a person and you find yourself paying attention to the ongoing stream of thoughts your mind is generating, then intentionally take a deep breath and put all your effort into focusing on what this person is saying; notice how they move their lips, their pitch, their tone of voice, and so on.

I know this can be hard at first, but if you end up lost in the whirlwind of obsession, you know what happens next: a full-blown OCD episode and a downward spiral of compulsions, avoidance, and ruling-thoughts being reinforced. Practicing staying in the moment is something you can do whenever possible; it won't make the obsession go away, but it will help you to develop a new relationship with your mind in which you're not being bossed around by it.

Give it a try!

Keep in Mind the F of Thinking, Not What It Looks Like!

Your mind will never stop telling you "blah blah blah" or, as my aunt says in Spanish, "cha cha cha." You know by now how your mind has a life of its own and how it doesn't stop relating and relating, connecting and connecting, and generating and generating thousands and thousands of bits of content, anytime, anywhere. Whether you live in Europe, Asia, South America, Oceania, or Central America, our minds do it all the time. You also know by now that obsessions are another type of content that your mind comes up with and that your brain perceives as a potential threat, so it quickly organizes your body to go into combat mode, prepares a massive attack, and relies on classic go-to strategies: holding onto ruling-thoughts, and doing compulsions and avoidant actions all the way!

Imagine for a moment what happens when a person gets hooked on all the obsessions a brain generates. What happens when a person gets consumed with obsessions about causing harm to others, fears about not being happy, intrusions about insulting others, images about losing control and going crazy, unwanted thoughts about writing obscenities, doubtful obsessions about sexual identity, and so many more. Check your own experience. What happens when you get caught in all those sticky obsessions?

One of my clients said it nicely: "It's a nightmare!"

Our mind's ability to give meaning to all our experiences, relate one thing to another, and identify what could possibly go wrong is a quality that has been super-helpful to our survival. However, when dealing with obsessions, taking them too seriously and as absolute truths, you may end up fused, hooked, and trapped with whatever content your mind is coming up with.

Quite often, you may ask yourself whether or not the stuff that shows up in your mind is correct, accurate, or real. But when dealing with obsessions, checking their content or theme will just get you hooked on them and start a downward spiral of compulsions.

Do you see why it's ultra-important to date your mind in a different way? That's why, keeping in mind the *function* – consequence, impact, effect – of your thoughts is much more important than the content or thought or how it looks like.

Dating Tip: Broadcasting Useful or Not?

Using ACT skills, instead of checking what the obsession is about, you can check the impact that getting hooked on that obsession has in your life. Very different, right?

Imagine for a moment that your brain is broadcasting news, then check two things.

- If the radio is broadcasting something useful, tune into it!
- If the radio is broadcasting something unhelpful, tune your attention to what you're doing in the moment.

21

Make Room for Disturbing Content in Your Mind!

Before writing this chapter, I went for a quick run. I usually run for 20–30 minutes after a half-hour of procrastination. As much as I love running, I tell myself all types of reasons why I should delay my run, like "Maybe you should finish this chapter first," "It is late," There may be a lot of people in the gym," "Who will do the laundry?" The reality is, running keeps me healthy: my body relaxes, my mind gets clear, and I feel totally refreshed. But when running, my mind doesn't come with flowers and butterflies all the time; it also comes with thoughts like "I feel tired, stop, it's too long," and so on. I feel like giving up and stopping so many times.

Have you had moments like that? Moments when, even though you're doing what you want to do, your mind comes up with thoughts that could easily stop you?

As we are reminded in these well-cited lines, "We cannot control the wind, we can only adjust the sails." We cannot stop the mind doing its minding, our body sensing what it senses, and feeling what we feel, but we can intentionally and purposefully make room for all those uncomfortable thoughts, sensations, feelings, urges, and weird obsessions that come along.

Making room for what we don't like that happens under our skin is not giving up on having those experiences. It's simply acknowledging that those annoying experiences – including disturbing, bizarre, and pesky obsessions – come and go wherever we go, and they will show up when we are doing what matters to us.

For example, Martina loves to have a full night's sleep and take a nap at times, but dealing with the obsession of "not knowing when she will die" pushed her to keep herself awake as long as possible, drink many cups of coffee and green tea during the day, and exercising late at night in order to keep herself awake. If Martina is to live the life she wants to live and get her life back on track, she will need to learn to make room for thoughts like "How will I be able to notice that I'm dead if I'm already dead?" or "How will I have a perspective or conscience if I'm dead?" or "If I can't notice that I'm dead. Will it always feel like I'm alive or immortal?" – as well as the fear that comes along with those obsessions.

Making room for those bizarre obsessions comes with two bedfellows: acceptance and willingness. Let's briefly investigate them both.

You read about acceptance in Chapter 15 "What About Dropping Those 'Getting Rid of Obsessions' Strategies?" Throughout this workbook, you will come across acceptance as a skill in different sections. It's a key concept in ACT and ERP for overcoming OCD episodes and getting your life back on track.

Acceptance is allowing, acknowledging, or making room for experiencing things as they are, whether they are happening outside of you or within you and whether they're comfortable or not. Just to clarify a popular misconception: acceptance is not giving up, resigning, losing hope that things could be different, or being a doormat. It's actually opening the door to experiences as they come. In this workbook, we use acceptance as a posture or attitude you take with purpose, and willingness goes hand and hand with it, because it's about choosing to face a difficult situation as it is, with acceptance. *Think of willingness as choosing to face an obsession and acceptance as a posture or attitude you take to make room for it, have it, hold it, and allow it to be, instead of adopting a fighting-it-back posture!*

Dating Tip: Weather Metaphor

For this tip, I want to invite you to participate in a brief visualization exercise. Read the directions first, and then practice visualizing.

Imagine for a moment that you're lying on your back in the middle of a field of grass looking at the sky. You see clouds of all different sizes and shapes as they move one after another. You see the weather changing as the day passes by . . . and as you see everything changing in the sky, the sky remains the same, the sky doesn't change . . . and like clouds in the sky or the weather, thoughts, feelings, obsessions, and all types of mind noise, disturbing or not, pass by . . . and you're more like the sky, expanding in all directions, without restrictions, without borders, without a beginning and without an end.

When you feel overwhelmed because of disturbing content, close your eyes and remember this exercise. Don't underestimate the impact of these skills for learning to hold your mind lightly. They may look simple on the outside, but you may be shocked when you put them into action in your life. Try them out!

22

Watch Out for Fake-Acceptance!

Have you ever been at a dinner where they served a tofu dish that didn't look good and tasted a bit bad, but you had no other choice than to eat it? And every bite you took, your mind said, "This is awful. How is it possible I'm eating this. Eurgh, I hate this"? Well, I kind of dislike tofu myself, too, so I totally relate to that experience (as a sidenote: I actually think tofu is overrated).

But seriously, have you ever had to eat something you didn't like much or was tasteless? How did you do it? Do you remember what was going on inside your head? Maybe on the outside no one noticed, but under your skin was quite different.

Sometimes my clients confuse acceptance with fake-acceptance. Let me tell you the difference between these two ideas, so you can learn real skills, not pseudo-ones.

– In Chapters 15 and 21, "What About Dropping Those 'Getting Rid of Obsessions' Strategies?" and "Make Room for Disturbing Content in Your Mind," you learned that acceptance is about acknowledging that those annoying experiences come and go, back and forth, left and right, and it's also an attitude you take on to make room for, have, hold, and allow those disturbing, bizarre, and pesky obsessions to be exactly as they are.

– Acceptance is not about liking everything you feel, think, or sense in your body. Instead, it is learning to take it as it is without judging, criticizing, complaining, or condemning it – for example, "I'm noticing this tingling sensation in my stomach," "I'm having a thought 'This is bad,'" "My heart is beating fast."

– On the other side of the coin, fake-acceptance has a lot to do with having an obsession and getting hooked on judgments and criticizing thoughts like "Why do I have to go through this? I hate this! I can't take it any longer. Why do I have to have this thought?" This is not to say that you need to be at peace when having an obsession – it's natural to have those reactions – but acceptance is nonjudgmentally acknowledging an experience as good or bad, healthy or unhealthy, old or new.

Let's do a mini-exercise. Describe five moments in which you were in fake-acceptance mode. Remember that when you judge, criticize, evaluate an internal experience you have as good (whether it's a thought, image, memory, or urge), that's a clue that you are not fully accepting things as they are.

_____

_____

_____

Acceptance of obsessions can be tricky for some of my clients, because their mind comes up with a thought along the lines of "If I accept this obsession, that means I'm okay with it, but I'm not." Is your mind doing anything like that? If so, please go back to Chapter 11, "Do You Know Your Ruling-Thoughts?"

Acceptance of an obsession is beginning to stay present with what's happening under your skin, right there, as it is. Learning to accept your obsessions without becoming them or acting on them is like being here in in-the-moment-land, before rushing there to action-land.

You can choose to have an obsession, to feel a feeling, to sense a sensation as they come, with the discomfort that comes with it. You don't have to like or love your obsessions, and you don't have to choose to feel them while forcing yourself and gritting your teeth, either.

Dating Tip: Three Questions

Check the following cues for yourself and with yourself:

- _Are you powering through the moments when obsessions show up?_
  Practicing acceptance is not "powering through." If you find yourself having the attitude to just do it, rush through, and press on the accelerator when you have an obsession, that may be an indication that you're not fully making room for it. Think about when you press down the accelerator in a car. Are you having that attitude toward your obsessions? Do you have a hostile attitude toward them, like "Come on, come on, I'm ready to fight you?" Do you really have to fight with your scary brain? That doesn't mean that you have to have a stance of cuddling with the obsessions, either. Rather, it is making room for them as a choice, with an openness to have them and be with them as they are: bizarre thoughts that show up that come with uneasy feelings.
- _Are you telling yourself that you want to get past the obsessions as soon as possible?_
  It makes sense that you want OCD episodes to be behind you, of course. They are hard to have and can be very time-consuming, but allowing obsessions to appear with everything they come with, with different rhythms, is a skill you can practice. You don't have control of the speed at which those obsessions show up in your mind, but as a new behavior you can practice letting them come and go at the pace they please.
- _Does any part of you still hold onto the thought "I want to be able to control what I feel"?_
  Do you find yourself having some wishful thoughts like "I just want this to be over," "I want to get in charge of what shows up in my mind," "I seriously need

to get a better grasp of these thoughts"? Who doesn't want that at times? Who doesn't want to have a switch that controls what we feel? But we don't, and here is something important for you to keep in mind: if you pause for a moment right now and step back and think about it, what happens in your life when you continue to hold onto those kinds of thoughts? Has it ever helped you to handle OCD episodes? Is it helping now?

These are just some clues to noticing the difference between "making room for obsessions" and fighting them and hoping for them to go away. On the outside, this may look like you're practicing acceptance and willingness, but watch out, because you may be tricking yourself.

Before finishing this chapter, keep in mind that by encouraging you to be willing to take things from an acceptance posture, as you give it a try, I'm asking you to open up to every aspect of your experience as it is when those annoying obsessions show up, entirely as they are and with all they come with. You see, in making room for them, you actually gain freedom to do what matters to you!

Hold Your Mind Lightly!

Dealing with OCD episodes is not easy at all. In my opinion, it's actually very courageous to be walking in your shoes and carrying a reactive brain.

If your mind is like my mind and my clients' mind, it's probable that your mind compares how you're doing in regard to others, criticizes you for having the obsessions that show up in your mind – as if it was your fault – comes up with stories about what a bad person you are when doing compulsions, and judges you more so if you're trying not to do compulsions. And on top of all that, it shouts at you thoughts along the lines of "I'm broken, no one will love me, I'm a mess, I'm a disaster."

Do you recognize all those criticisms your mind comes up with about yourself? My clients usually tell me how challenging is to listen to their mind all the time; it's already challenging when they have a disturbing obsession, and it's extra-hard if they're hooked onto those self-criticisms.

In Chapters 4 and 11, "Why Are Obsessions So Hard to Let Go of" and "Do You Know Your Ruling-Thoughts?" you familiarized yourself with your mind as a content-generator and pattern-making machine and how it not only generates obsessions but also stories about your character, and some of those narratives are quite painful.

We all do things we regret at times or say things we wish we hadn't, yet going into harsh criticism mode is one way to handle our flaws. But does it really take you close to the person you want to be?

As you continue to build the skills to get your life back on track, you will notice that taking your mind as a source of truth all the time – without checking the context, the situation, or what's important to you – just makes things worse. That's why learning to develop a new dating relationship with your mind is key to get your life back on track.

Looking back at your experience, what are the stories or comparison thoughts your mind comes up with about yourself?

_____

_____

_____

Wouldn't it be nice if you learned to respond to those criticisms as you respond to the people you care about when they're dealing with a difficult situation? Think for a moment. When was the last time one of your friends, your partner, your kids, or even a coworker approached you and shared how bad they feel about themselves? What did you do? What did you say? How did you handle it? Did you turn your back and walk away? Did you agree with those self-criticisms and add some more? Quite likely not, because when we care for someone we do the best we can to let them know that we're there for them, right? We all want the same thing: to know that there is someone there for us who gets us, sees us, cares for us, appreciates us, and makes room for us to be next to them with whatever feeling we're having.

However, because for so many years we have received hundreds of messages about having to be happy, upbeat, and enthusiastic at all times, we have also learned to hide our struggles and forgotten how to respond to them. For instance, when someone asks a routine question like "How are you doing?" what do we say? Most of us say, "I'm doing okay. I'm doing fine, thanks," and move on or ask another question, even though we're actually far from being okay and we're hurting, we're upset, disappointed, or frustrated. Have you noticed how much we actually don't say what's really going on with us, and we've played that game for hundreds of years? I'm not saying here that you should tell everyone what's really going on with you, but just check for yourself how much you might be hiding your struggles and difficulties, sugar-coating things, or downplaying things, even from the people you care about.

And what happens when you respond to your hurts with censure, disapproval, or discontent? Does it really help to criticize yourself because of an OCD episode or because you have a reactive brain? Does putting yourself down help you to be the person you want to be? Don't listen to me; just reflect on your experience for a moment.

Dating Tip: Soft Touch and Soft Responding

Here is a tip for you to continue developing a new relationship with your mind. How about rather than criticizing, complaining, and even getting mad with your imperfect mind when it tells you that you messed up or how you're ruining your life, you start holding it softly?

By holding it softly, I mean acknowledging your mind's imperfections, making room for them, and even thanking it for working so hard when pointing your mistakes. Your mind is not your enemy – it's just doing what it's supposed to be doing after hundreds of years of rehearsing over and over those strategies.

Think for a moment of a person you admire, your best friend, or your coach. What would they say to you? Can you bring them into your mind and respond to your hurts as they would? Can you say kind, caring, and gentle statements when you notice your mind is coming up with those criticizing thoughts? Words like "Thank you. I know you're working hard, and let's go gentle," or "I'm hurting right now, so let's be caring, please" will help.

And if it's not your thing to coach your mind in that way, take a deep breath, notice any type of bodily reaction you are having, then place one of your hands in that area of your body, take a deep breath, and acknowledge that you're hurting, that you're upset.

Give these skills a try!

24

Always Check What Works!

Writing about workability is one of my favorite themes in ACT!

Moving onward, "workability" is a key word for you, so please make sure that you get a tattoo with it. Just kidding, although it wouldn't hurt to take the idea of "workability" to heart in any way you can.

Leaving my silly jokes aside, as you have noticed in this workbook, we're not talking about you checking whether your obsessions are true or false, good or bad, or right or wrong. You're actually often invited and asked to check whether or not the way you respond, handle, and deal with an obsession is workable!

In Chapter 20, "Keep in Mind the F of Thinking, Not What It Looks Like," you learned about the problems of getting caught up in the content of an obsession and how important is to check if it's helpful (or not) to respond to it. In this chapter, we'll delve deeper into this idea. What does it mean to check whether your handling of an obsession is workable or not?

Everything you do – whether it's inside or outside your head, publicly or privately – is a behavior, and it can be a move away or a move toward the things that truly matter to you. Let's have a look at two scenarios to make sense of this concept.

- Scenario 1: When writing, my mind comes up with thoughts along the lines of "You don't know what you're doing, your writing is not good enough, no one is going to read your book." If I get hooked on those thoughts and do what they tell me to do, I'll stop writing right away, come up with excuses to not write, or distract myself with fun stuff. But any of those behaviors – in that situation – will take me far away from living according to my value of sharing and spreading the word about research-based skills that can be impactful in a person's life.
- Scenario 2: When my partner is getting ready to travel and asks me to spend time with him before his trip, I pause my writing. I do stop writing because, in that moment, I put my value of connecting with the people I love first. Here, not writing is a behavior that takes me toward my relationship value.

Do you see the difference? The same behavior, "stopping writing," can be a move toward or away from the stuff that we care about based on the situation, the context, or the setting you're in.

Checking the workability of your behaviors is best thought of as checking if you're living your life with direction, meaning, and vitality and focusing on the results of your behaviors (not the content of your mind). In other words, checking the workability of your actions is checking their impact, effect, and consequences in a particular situation.

Here is how this relates to you. Obsessions happen, obsessions are not a choice. However, when having urges to do a compulsion – thinking over and over about things you did in the past, checking whether your feelings of attraction for your partner are the same as yesterday, squeezing your hands and telling yourself "You're okay, they're okay," checking the quality of your breathing, disinfecting your cell phone, or counting money multiple times to make sure you didn't make a mistake – that's when you put this dating tip into action. You ask yourself: Is doing a compulsion working in the service of my values? Is doing a compulsion helpful in the long-run?

When dealing with the content-generating and pattern-making machine of your mind, there is no winning an argument. But there is winning in your life when not giving in to a compulsion.

So checking the workability of acting or not acting on an obsession is what truly gives you the power to live life as you want to live it.

Dating Tip: Checking What Works!

Instead of answering thinking with more thinking, responding to obsessions with compulsions as your go-to reaction, ask yourself any of these key questions:

– Is responding to this obsession helping me, in this moment, to be the person I want to be?
– Is responding to this obsession getting me closer to what's truly important to me?
– Is what I'm doing working to get me the sort of life I want to have in the long-term?
– Do those obsessions guide me toward having an amazing life?

If you answered "No" to any of these questions, then do your best to put into action all the skills you're learning in this workbook to stop those responses. And one last thing: I truly hope that even when you're done with this workbook, you never stop checking whether your actions are moves toward the stuff that matters to you or moves away.

Takeaways to share

Figure 24.1 Dating app.

Our ability to think is incredibly valuable and adds so much to our quality of life! We do need to come up with theories, hypotheses, dreams, and wishes, to create, dream, plan for the future, anticipate what could go wrong, and so on; and yet a lot of our thoughts are not helpful and are pure background noise. Imagine for a moment if someone plugs a device into our mind, translates it, and creates a podcast from it. What percentage of the content of the podcast would be of great use? Quite likely a pretty small one.

Learning to relate to our mind as the content-generating and pattern-making machine is essential to live your life, a purposeful life, and a life without obsessions controlling you. Obsessions are not a problem, but the way we respond to them, the way we relate to our mind: that's what creates misery in our life.

Think about this: musicians practice regularly; chefs cook their recipes often; writers write almost every day; so, when dealing with obsessions, you can intentionally apply all these dating tips every time you encounter a triggering situation.

Practicing all these dating tips will help you to develop three new frames:

(a) a new relationship with your mind, one in which your brain doesn't bully you around, boss you around, or dictate your actions.

(b) A new relationship with your obsessions, one in which you learn to notice, watch, and observe all the obsessions your mind comes up, regardless of their content, how often they come, or how bizarre they are.

(c) A new relationship with fear-based reactions in a way that you learn to handle any fear, obsession, worry, and anxiety that comes your way as life unfolds.

I personally think that facing our fears – doing exposure exercises – in the service of our values help us to get unstuck from OCD and anxiety struggles; but learning to navigate our fears effectively in this imperfect, unpredictable, and uncertain life is a life skill that goes beyond exposures and one that ACT offers us.

Here is a list of the dating tips you learned in this part:

- Let your mind do its own minding.
- Fall out of love with your mind.
- Get out of the content of your mind.
- Stay "in the moment," not in your head.
- Remember the F of thinking, not what it looks like!
- Make room for disturbing content in your mind
- Watch out for fake-acceptance
- Hold your mind lightly!
- Always check what works!

Keep learning, keep trying, and keep moving toward designing and living the life you want to live! You got this!

Life Tracker

Reflect on how you have been living your life and mark an "X" where it corresponds.

Having obsessions as thoughts your mind comes up with	Seeing obsessions as problems to be solved
Approaching life as it is	Avoiding life because of obsessions
Taking action toward what you care about	Organizing your life around obsessions
Holding your thoughts lightly	Going 100% along with what your mind tells you
Checking what really works in your life	Doing stuff in automatic pilot mode
Making room for uncomfortable internal experiences	Pushing them down as much as possible

PART VI

Shift, Shift, Shift . . . Shift Your Moves!

Are you familiar with the old, very old, song, "Shake, shake, shake your body?

I don't know your age, so you may or may not remember it, but if you have time, search for it on YouTube so you can hear the tune of it; if you're from a new generation, you may be more familiar with the song "Shake It Off," by Taylor Swift.

Instead of dancing and shaking your body when listening to that song, I invite you to make a 180-degree shift in your moves when dealing with obsessions.

In Part V, you got familiar with tips for dating your mind and fostering a new relationship with it. Now you are going to learn a super, ultra, duper, and core skill: defusion.

What is defusion? Defusion is an ACT term that basically means stepping back, separating, detaching from our thoughts and seeing them for what they are: a bunch of letters put together or pictures showing up in our mind. Defusion, in a nutshell, is about learning to watch your mind and what it does!

Within ACT we say that you get "fused" with your thoughts when you're holding them with white knuckles, buying into the content of them as the absolute truths, and getting bossed around by them – up and down, left and right. Defusion skills are the antidote to getting fused so you can continue learning to date your mind in a new way, being the person you want to be, and doing the stuff you care about.

In this section and throughout the rest of the workbook, when talking about defusion skills, I'm also going to use the terms "watching your mind" or "watch your mind" interchangeably.

Do you remember that in chapter "Why Are Obsessions So Hard to Let Go of?" I mentioned that your mind doesn't work by subtraction but by addition? Because of that it's never going to stop coming up with obsessions, and when buying into the content of them, it's like you get welded, fused, glued, hooked, and even cemented with that obsession. In those moments of fusion, your mind quickly picks up speed and energy – no different than a cascading chain reaction that fuels an atomic explosion – and pushes you to neutralize, get rid of, minimize, and control the obsession. That's when defusion skills are ultra-handy for you!

Learning defusion, learning to watch your mind, learning to watch your obsessions, and learning to watch the content of your obsessions will give you all the freedom you need from being trapped in your mind.

In the next chapters you will read about many different ways to watch your mind; here is my honest and upfront request for you: try them out, see which ones resonate with you more than others, create new ones, and most importantly, put them to work when needed!

Do not rush through this section! Take your time to learn and try these defusion skills out over and over, day by day, and hour by hour. In fact, when you're done reading this section, I urge you to take a 2- to 3-week break from this workbook and give yourself time to put into action all what you have learned.

You may be wondering why I'm suggesting this ridiculous idea of pausing reading this workbook; here is my response: trust me, it's not to upset you but to actually support your learning in getting your life back on track!

Over and over I have witnessed how my clients struggle not to cave in to the urge of solving the "obsession-problem;" at times, even with their best efforts, they ended up hammering the "obsession-problem" with reading hundreds of books, spending hours online to find the right solution, taking online surveys to check the severity of their symptoms, and even throwing themselves at what they're scared of to power through it.

The challenge with all those responses is that, even though they're coming from a place of wanting to overcome OCD episodes, they do make them worst. It's only when you learn to make room for disturbing thoughts as a choice, without fighting against them with old tools to get rid of them but responding to them with acceptance, willingness to experience the yucky stuff that comes along, and take actions toward what you care about, that you get your life back on track.

Let's shake those obsessions and let's make a shift!

25

Watching Your Mind

I know it can be time consuming to read these chapters, take notes, complete the exercises, deal with obsessions, and move along with your day. Kudos to you, and my sincere appreciation for all the effort you're putting into getting your life back on track!

Hope you can clearly see that obsessions are the norm and not the exception for any human being, and even though they're annoying, they're not the problem: what leads to an OCD episode and makes your life miserable is attaching rigidly to a ruling-thought, doing compulsions, and avoiding people, situations, or places. You learned that obsessions are hard to let go because your mind is a content-generator and pattern-making machine that is over-working all the time to protect you, given that your amygdala does an incredible job shouting at your fake-news of danger. And you learned that creating a new relationship with your mind is key to have the life you want to have.

In this chapter, you're going to learn what to do when those bizarre obsessions show up in your mind, and when you're done with these pages, you can apply all the core skills anytime and anywhere, without any limitations. Let's zoom in!

Let's say that Russ has obsessive thoughts about harming his newly born child; in this chapter, Russ will learn to *watch the thought of* "What if I stab my child" instead of taking the thought of "What if I stab my child" as the truth, a sign of his personality, or an indication of hidden intentions. Do you see the difference? There is watching, defusing, and having a thought, versus acting on the thought, taking the thought too seriously, or becoming the thought. You will have plenty of opportunities to practice this skill and make it yours.

Defusion is not about getting rid of obsessions, eliminating them, making them disappear, or making sure they don't become true. And just to be crystal clear, while defusion is a skill, it's more than a technique; it's an extension of learning to watch your mind. Learning to watch your mind is learning to have those wacky thoughts and all types of content – thinking – that our mind is constantly coming up with; you already practice the skill of watching your mind in Part V, Learning to date your mind, when putting into action new dating tips to relate to your mind. Defusion and learning to watch your mind go hand-in-hand with each other; think of defusion as the skill to face an obsession and watching your mind as the posture or attitude you take to have it and allow it to be!

When practicing defusion skills, keep an eye for the following traps that may come your way:

- If the intrusive thoughts vanish or kind of go away, that's a plus, and let's appreciate that, but remember that there is no switch that turns your mind on and off to make those obsessions go away forever. It's not helpful to you to get hooked in fantasy land by believing that any of the ACT and ERP skills in this section or workbook will make your obsessions go away forever, since clinical research demonstrates totally the opposite – the more we try to suppress thoughts, the more often they pop up.

- If you notice that when practicing defusion skills you start feeling better, happily in that precise moment – not to be a party pooper, but that's an extra benefit, too. Of course, in the long run, living the life you want to live will come your way with many rewards, but if when practicing any of these skills to watch your obsessions you find yourself getting hooked on the "feeling better" mood, be careful . . . because that's a trap.

- If after practicing the defusion skills you somehow feel less anxious, that's great, and let's appreciate that moment without making it your goal when practicing this skill. Keep in mind that learning to watch your obsessions is not about feeling less anxious or less uncomfortable; it's about getting better at feeling all types of things, including anxiety, worry, or fear, and still moving forward in your day-to-day life with your feet, hands, and mouth.

- If your mind comes up with thoughts like "I suck at this; I'm not doing this right; I won't ever be able to do this watching thing . . ." notice those thoughts, don't argue against them, take a deep breath, acknowledge them, and say "I'm having judging thoughts," or "here comes Ms. Judgy Judy." Your mind is never going to stop doing its own minding, and responding to those harsh thoughts is a distraction in your learning.

Getting entangled with an obsession and doing what it pushes you to do holds you back in your relationships, work, school, spiritual life, and other areas of your life. Time to make a shift, your shift!

Maybe right now your mind protests by saying "but these obsessions are true; it's true that I could contract pancreatic cancer." The thing is that you and I can spend years and years arguing with your mind whether that thought is true or false today, tomorrow, or at any moment, but by doing that, guess what comes next? Life passes you by; you spent time arguing with a thought, and even if you win for a couple of moments, is only a matter of time before the same thought or a thought along the same lines will pop up again. Don't listen to me; check what happens when you get welded to these obsessions and you let them guide you. When holding to the obsessions tightly with white knuckles, does it help you to live the life you want to live? Does it help you to act like the person you want to be? Quite likely, no.

Let's jump to different skills to watch your mind and the stuff that comes with it! I'm going to ask for your permission to be a bit playful with these exercises, since some of them may seem a bit ridiculous, and yet they can be very powerful in dealing with obsessions.

Naming Your Obsessions

This defusion skill is the first step for all the other ones. Naming your obsessions may sound simplistic and almost insignificant, but you will be shocked how helpful it is when dealing with an OCD episode.

The name you choose doesn't have to be a serious and rigorous scientific name; you can choose a name that captures the theme of your obsessions like "break up thoughts, robbery thoughts," and so on. You can also name your obsessions with silly names, like "bachelorette Jane; Susan the cranky; Peter the perfectionist," etc. Are there are characters of movies or books that may remind you of your obsessions? You can also use those names to practicing naming your obsessions.

Timothy had obsessions about "things not feeling or looking right" when walking into certain rooms and spent hours rearranging items in different locations until they gave him a good feeling; he decided to call those obsessions the "unwise helper," because when triggered, his mind said "Hey, this doesn't feel right, so just keep rearranging until the room feels right," but he knew that the more he does a compulsions, the more OCD episodes he will struggle with, and the less time he will have to do what he really wants: cooking for his friends to connect or watching movies at home to relax.

Naming an obsession, as simple as it is, is like pressing a brake when you're driving on the freeway: it stops the car. In this case, it stops your reactive brain from running at a fast speed.

Try This

Think about one of your obsessions, and if you're dealing with different themes, choose a name for each one of them, so when they show up, instead of getting caught by them, you can recognize them, notice them, name them, and refocus on what's in front of you:

_____

_____

_____

Make It Yours

Time to put your creative juices in motion, and don't worry, you don't need to be artsy to do so. Here are some prompts to help you on coming up different names for those disturbing thoughts:

A serious one:_____

A silly one: _____

A scientific one: _____

A classic one: _____

A sassy one: _____

A tragic one: _____

Let's move on to the next skill.

Visualizing Your Obsessions

Every time one of those pesky obsessions pops up, whether it's a thought about getting contaminated, a violent image, a sexual thought, a worry about losing control and getting crazy, – imagine it, visualize it, and look at is as an object that you can watch!

In Figure 25.1, there is a list of ideas for you to practice watching your obsessions; there is a mixture of suggestions involving images of your obsessions moving and staying still, but all of them make the obsession a thing to look at. I suggest you try them all, check the ones you like, and make them yours.

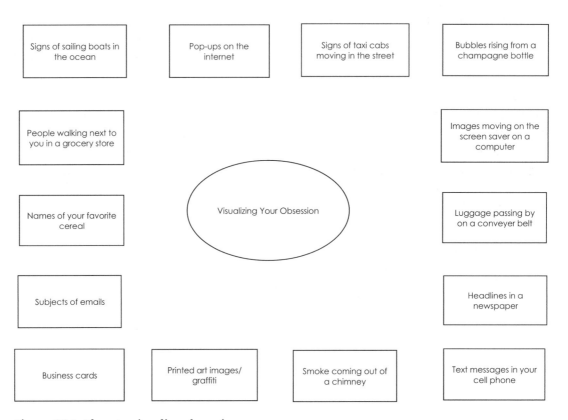

Figure 25.1 Ideas to visualize obsession.

Try This

Your turn. Pick one of the suggestions to visualize your obsessions, chose any of the obsessions you have been struggling the last week, and for a couple of moments visualize that obsession as such; feel free to try a couple of them to see which ones you relate more to.

It may feel weird, odd, and uncomfortable to try these skills, and yet, are you open to doing it? Do your best to try them out and check how it goes for you.

Make It Yours

What about coming up with your own defusion exercise based on pictures that are relevant to you? For instance, Russ, after delivering his child, was surrounded by diapers of all types; when having an obsession about not doing things right, he imagined the obsession as the label of a diaper and imagine it printed on the diaper. Here are the new brands of diapers he came up with: "Sucking at this; bad thoughts and bad smells go together; messing up all the way."

No matter how certain your mind is, a thought is just a thought, an obsession is just an obsession, and as bizarre as those obsessions are, obsessions are harmless; they're not your enemy, they're just a product of your pattern-making machine dealing with an overworking amygdala.

Saying Your Obsessions

Dealing with disturbing obsessions requires that you try different ways of "watching what your mind does" without getting absorbed in them. In, "Get Out of the Content of Your Mind!" you learned a new way of relating to all the stuff that your mind comes up with is getting out of your head and reengaging with what's happening in front of you.

Let's think of Tania for a moment: she was struggling with an obsessive thought about "living a life in an alternative reality;" to put this skill into practice, she wrote a song a about it to the tune of "The Mess Is Mine" from Vance Joy, modified the lyrics accordingly, recorded it on her phone, and listened to it when driving to work.

Petra was tortured about her fear about exhibiting her private parts, so she sang her obsessions to the tune of a popular lullaby in the United States, like "Baa, Baa, Black Sheep."

In Figure 25.2, you will see a list of potential ideas to say your obsessions; this list is by no means an exhaustive one, just a list of suggested ones.

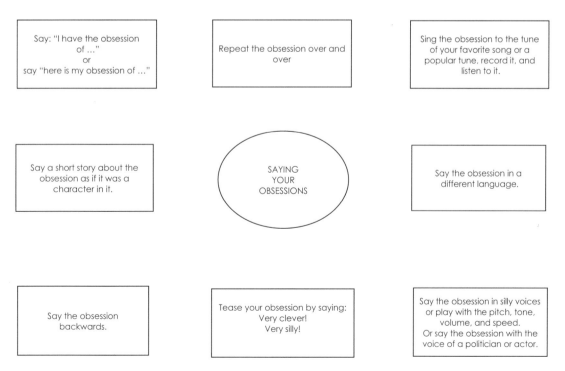

Figure 25.2 Ideas for saying your obsessions.

Try This

Choose one of the intrusive thoughts that the content-generator machine of your mind comes up with and complete the defusion exercises here. Give yourself a couple of minutes between each one of them, and notice your reactions. Don't forget that learning to watch your mind is not about thought-reduction or obsession-elimination, but it's about creating a distance, space, and a separation between you and the stuff that shows up. So I invite you to have less attachment to an outcome and more openness to the process of checking how it goes!

- Say, "here comes . . . ."
- Repeat that obsession for 30 seconds.
- Singing the theme of your obsession to the tune of "Happy Birthday"!

Make It Yours

There is nothing better than personalizing your skills, making them yours and making them relatable to your day-to-day life. I don't know if you're into karaoke, or poetry, or movies or have an accent, but I invite you to think about one of those activities that you like to do and get a kick of when doing it, and use it as a prompt for saying your obsessions. You can also think about your favorite singers, actors, or cartoon characters as an inspiration to say those annoying obsessions in their tone of voice or pitch, or singing them.

Over the years I witnessed that when teaching these skills, my clients said things like "I'm not creative at all, I'm not into singing . . . and so on," and with patience, they found different ways to verbalize, say, sing, recite, or even narrate the theme of their obsessions in very creative and unique ways.

To be honest, I never stop being surprised by my clients' hidden talents; not to say that they turn out to be professional singers, but they do have songs, authors, or comedians they like and are open to get out of their comfort zone to practice this skill; for instance, one of my clients loves Queen, and his favorite songs were "Somebody to Love" and "Bohemian Rhapsody." When he was practicing this defusion exercise, I heard him singing his obsession "I don't know if I say the truth or not" to the tune of it.

Which defusion exercise, saying your obsessions, would you like to try and make yours for this week?

Physicalizing Your Obsessions

This is one of my favorite defusion skills, maybe because, in general, I like to move my body and enjoy doing something physical.

Physicalizing that obsessions that your mind comes up with is another way of learning to watch your mind; you can use your body, belongings, and even some props.

Consider Peter, who was frightened about stabbing his partner: when putting this skill into action, he moved his index finger in the shape of a Z when the obsession showed up.

Alex was getting stuck with a relentless obsession of attracting bad luck to him; putting this skill into practice, he started making a gesture with his left hand as if he's catching the obsession and putting it in his pocket. Alex knew that obsessions come

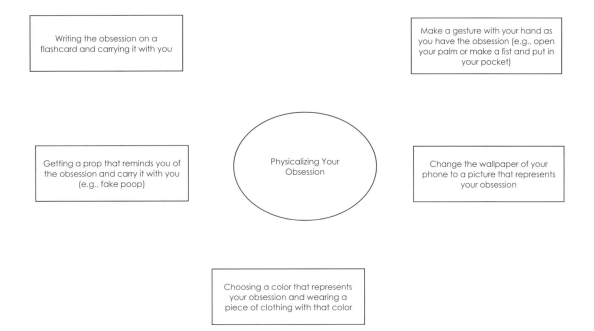

Figure 25.3 Ideas for physicalizing your obsessions.

and go, so instead of fighting them, he made the point to remind himself with this gesture that he can "have them."

In Figure 25.3, there are some ideas for you to check as a starting point to physicalizing your obsessions.

Try This

It may feel a bit nuts to physicalize your obsessions, but try it out anyway. There is learning with our mind and there is learning with our experience, and given that our mind plays tricks, isn't it better to learn by direct experiences?

Looking at the list of different physicalizing exercises you can do, which one do you commit to try this week? Choose one to start, jot it down here, and see it how it goes for you:

This week I commit to try this physicalizing exercise: _____

Make It Yours

And now it's your turn to customize this defusion skill and make it yours all the way! Physicalizing your obsessions doesn't have to be complicated, so you can start with a very simple gesture; watching your mind is more about fostering your capacity to unhook from obsessive thoughts that have been organizing your behavior and take you far away from the person you want to be and how you want to live your life.

Checking the Workability of Getting Hooked on Your Obsessions

Sometimes, my clients prefer other types of defusion exercises, such as checking the workability of their obsessions; although ACT is all about workability of your behaviors, all of them, when looking at obsessions, this is also a form of detaching, distancing, and creating a space between you, the disturbing obsessions, and your behaviors.

Try This

See in Figure 25.4 a list of questions you can ask yourself to check the impact of getting hooked on an obsession when getting triggered; keep in mind that none of these questions is intended to engage you in a debate about whether the content of the intrusive thoughts is true, false, accurate, or not, because that's a recipe for disaster. These questions have the goal of assisting you in checking how it works for you when getting fused with them.

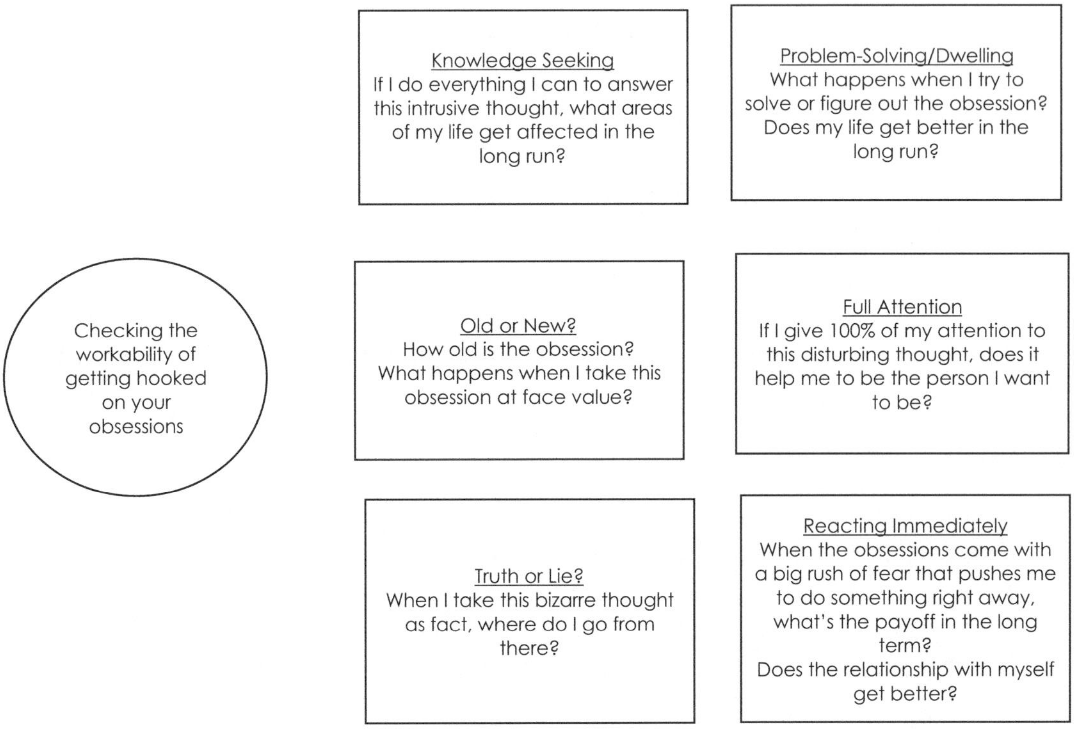

Knowledge Seeking
If I do everything I can to answer this intrusive thought, what areas of my life get affected in the long run?

Problem-Solving/Dwelling
What happens when I try to solve or figure out the obsession? Does my life get better in the long run?

Checking the workability of getting hooked on your obsessions

Old or New?
How old is the obsession? What happens when I take this obsession at face value?

Full Attention
If I give 100% of my attention to this disturbing thought, does it help me to be the person I want to be?

Truth or Lie?
When I take this bizarre thought as fact, where do I go from there?

Reacting Immediately
When the obsessions come with a big rush of fear that pushes me to do something right away, what's the payoff in the long term?
Does the relationship with myself get better?

Figure 25.4 Ideas for checking the workability of getting hooked on obsessions. Make it yours.

Is there any other question you could ask yourself to check the consequences of buying into an obsession? If so, jot it down here:

_____

And if not, which two questions did you like the most from the suggested ones, so you can practice checking the workability of getting hooked into your obsessions when dealing with a triggering moment?

Question 1: _____

Question 2: _____

Watch Out for the Trap "Watching the Obsession, Means I'm Okay With It"

At times, when going over defusion skills with my clients, if they're dealing with aggressive, sexual, harm, or suicidal obsessions, I usually hear questions along the lines of "But is saying the name of my obsession the same as approving it or liking it, or even making it happen because I'm not doing anything to prevent it?"

If your mind is coming up with any of thought along those lines, take a deep breath and take all those thoughts as what they are: thoughts coming from a reactive brain, and given the protective nature of your brain, it makes sense that your brain still takes every single thought as the absolute truth.

What could possibly happen if you buy into the thought? Would your day-to-day life get rich, meaningful, and purposeful if you listen to that thought? Quite likely no, so as you do with any other thought, you can name it as "Obsessions-on-the-go; or "Miss P, for perseverance," as suggestions; or you can simply thank your mind by saying to yourself, "Thank you, mind," since it's just trying to protect you from what it perceives as dangerous.

Building Your Practice of Watching Your Mind

When you get fused, caught, trapped, and dominated by a weird thought, it's like you're walking around with smoke in your mind, seeing everything through the smoke, and assuming that all the smoke is the truth. Tricky, right?

Because it's so easy to get fused, I strongly encourage you to practice a different defusion skill you learned every day and every time one of those disturbing thoughts show up in your mind; mix them up, combine them, and capitalize them the best you can.

One day you can practice visualizing obsession, the next day you can try a physicalizing exercise, the next one saying the obsession, and so on. All these defusion skills are flexible by nature; you don't need to use them in a particular order, and you can come with new ones as you continue to your journey of overcoming OCD episodes and getting your life back on track.

Remember that you're practicing watching your mind and watching, specifically, an obsessive thought when it shows up instead of getting trapped by it. See if you can catch when and where you're most likely to get lost in obsession land: is it when you're driving back home, at work, when eating lunch, sitting in your favorite chair, or hanging with your siblings? After watching the obsessions, do your best to get out of your head, notice where you are and what you're doing in that moment. With practice, you will learn to make a shift from being trapped in the smoke of your mind and get back into the present!

Every time you practice your "defusion skills" and choose to not act on the obsession, you're teaching your reactive brain that you're in charge, that you can decide how to live your life, that you can choose what to do, when to do it, and how to do it.

Give your best when practicing defusion, be patient, do your best to practice defusion as a choice you make, – not as a problem-solving technique, and most importantly, be consistent!

26
Riding the Wave of Fear, Anxiety, and Terrible Feelings

Read the statements below and circle any that resonate with you:

a. My obsessions come with strong emotions.
b. I have little control over the fear, anxiety, and distress that come with my obsessions.
c. When having strong fears, I feel like I have to act.
d. If I don't do anything when having an obsession, my feelings get worst.
e. All of the above.

Which items did you circle? Most of my clients circle option "e."

While all of us are at risk of being dominated by our emotions, those of us dealing with OCD episodes are particularly vulnerable, given that the brain is shouting, mobilizing, and working ultra-hard when it perceives a threat. It's not your fault; you just have an overworking brain. And as a result, a cascade of overwhelming emotions comes your way, trying to push you in one direction or another like a puppet, demanding that you do a compulsion or screaming at you to avoid a triggering situation, place, or person. It's not your fault.

In this chapter, you are going to learn a key skill to get better at feeling all those distressing feelings that come along with obsessions: *watching your emotions*.

In the previous chapter you learned different defusion skills to watch your mind and the obsessions that pop up; this time, I'm going to invite you to apply the same skill to your emotions. And trust me, as challenging as it seems, it's doable.

Here is the deal: imagine for a second that all your feelings of fear, distress, panic, and others are like water naturally running from a faucet. Now what would happen if instead of letting the water run its own course, you place your hands under it and block the faucet? Would the water run naturally and follow its course? Would the water splash all over the sink, your clothes, and the mirror?

If you're not sure what'll happen, try it – and be prepared to clean the mess that follows. Our emotions are just like water naturally falling from a faucet. When we try to stop their natural flow, they wind up going in a lot of different directions and making a mess. The reality is that we don't choose what we feel or how we feel, but we can choose to not make things worse for ourselves.

Getting your life back and overcoming OCD episodes requires that you put all your effort, energy, and dedication into the stuff that you care about, the stuff that truly matters to you.

Compulsions or avoidant behaviors are emotion management strategies that are time consuming, distracting, and can even give the impression that you're self-absorbed because you're overly focused on them. It's emotionally draining to constantly be at the mercy of your feelings all the time. Have you considered how much effort it takes in the long run to suppress those annoying emotions that come along with obsessions?

Lots of self-help books and articles you may have seen populating your social media feeds encourage that, when feeling overwhelmed with uncomfortable emotions, you do something nice for yourself, like going for a long hike, watching a silly movie, going to see a comedy, and so on. All those activities are fun, relaxing, and a great distraction. As with anything, there is a time and place for every behavior: if you distract yourself from uncomfortable emotions by being kind to yourself, and it helps you to show up as the person you want to be, please go ahead; however, if doing something nice for yourself is done to run away from facing the obsession and the discomfort that comes along in that moment of struggle, consider that you're just feeding into OCD episodes.

Try This

The skill of watching and labeling your emotions involves two micro-steps that you can easily remember as "2D." When you are experiencing an unpleasant emotion:

1. Describe to yourself what you feel and what you sense in your body. Start by taking five deep and slow breaths and focusing on how your body is breathing. Notice the movements of your chest, diaphragm, and abdomen as you inhale and exhale; notice the sensations in your nose, throat, shoulders, legs, and abdomen. As you do this, notice the prominent sensation, follow it with curiosity, notice if it's moving or staying in the same place. Notice any shape it may have, its size. Finally, give it a name. This is called *labeling* (it's similar to what you did when naming your obsessions).
2. Don't do what you usually do, for real.

    Let me break down these micro-steps:

    Matthew Lieberman and his team from the University of California, Los Angeles, confirmed that the simple process of labeling your emotions diminishes the overactivation of the brain; the ability to describe your emotions is very handy when having an obsession or starting to ride an OCD episode. Labeling your feelings is not about finding the perfect name but a name that helps you to distinguish the emotion and recognize it. It's more important that you describe what you're sensing in your body when feeling intense emotions (e.g., "I'm noticing tingling sensations, a rush of heat," and so on).

    Watching the emotions that come along with obsessions allows you to make room for them, acknowledge them, allow them to be there, accept them as they are, and begin to say what's happening under your skin (e.g., "I'm scared; my hands are getting sweaty; my hands are shaky," and so on).

Make It Yours

Learning the skill of "labeling your feelings" doesn't mean that you have do things robotically; it's totally the opposite. As with all the skills in this workbook, you will make best use of this skill by personalizing it. One way to do this is by recognizing the feelings that come along with your obsessions and giving them a unique name.

For example, when Harry noticed his suicidal obsessive thought about hanging himself, he said to himself, "Here is fear, here is terror," and he also described his heart beating fast. Instead of calling 911, taking a depression questionnaire, repeating to himself reasons to be alive, or analyzing his emotional well-being – all compulsions he usually did after having an obsessive thought – he took a deep breath and then described to himself, "Here is this knot in my stomach and the heavy sensation in my chest." Later on, he decided to name this feeling the "brick feeling" – it became one of his cues that he was heading to obsession land.

Your turn. Recall a recent OCD episode and, using the silhouette of the human figure here, make a mark where you felt bodily sensations, and then describe each one.

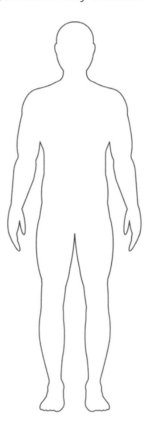

Figure 26.1 Human silhouette.

If you were to give a name to those sensations and feelings, what would that be?

_____

_____

This may sound a bit tedious, but noting the unique sensations that bother you when dealing with obsessions will take you closer to taming OCD episodes and living your life as you please!

Build Your Practice of Riding the Wave of Fear and Other Terrible Emotions

Labeling your emotions takes practice. And it's helpful to begin practicing when you're not having an OCD episode. That way, when an obsessive thought pops in your head, you'll know what to do.

Checking your emotions

Set an alarm on your cell phone twice a day to simply check in with yourself. When the alarm sounds, notice what you're sensing in your body, the intensity of the feeling, whether it's a comfortable sensation or not. Then give it a name. If you have trouble naming the feeling, simply describe to yourself the sensations you're noticing in your body in that moment. If you don't want to set a timer, you can practice this skill in any place and at any time (except when you're asleep, of course): waiting in life at the coffeeshop, waiting at a red light, watching the commercials before a movie, before starting your day, or practically anywhere.

Connecting with your body and connecting with your surroundings

If you experience emotions that are too overwhelming, remember to do your best not to fight it but to describe how it feels in your body. It all starts with acknowledging our internal experiences. If the emotion's intensity increases, you can use your body to (1) ground yourself and (2) reconnect with the outside. To ground yourself, you can press your fingers against each other, balance your body from one side to another, take slow deep breaths, or any other form of physical movement. To reconnect with your surroundings, you can use your senses to describe what's happening outside you, e.g., describe to yourself a smell and notice how it feels inhaling it; describe the shape of an object, describe a sound, and so on. Connecting with your body and connecting with your surroundings won't make the distressing emotion go away but it will help you to navigate through it more effectively and without sinking. And lastly, keep in mind that you may have to repeat these steps multiple times in a giving moment.

Give it a try, and keep practicing the skill of watching your emotions when the emotional wave shows up. From time to time, the reactive mind will tell you, "You can't do this; you can't handle your emotions; this doesn't make sense," and so on. If you get hooked on these thoughts, say to yourself, "That's my mind talking; that's my mind thinking," or you can label with single words like "thinking," "thought," "image." Then gently go back to focus on the act of breathing.

Watch Out for the Trap of "Powering Through Your Feelings"

If you find yourself powering through your feelings, gritting your teeth, and pushing yourself to have a certain emotion, watch out, because any of these responses is not watching your emotions but fighting against them.

When my clients tell me, "I tried to stay with the feeling, but it was too much, too overwhelming, and I just couldn't sit with it," I usually invite them to start practicing with a less-overwhelming sensation and sit with it for just 30 seconds. You don't have to like it, love it, or even enjoy it, but aiming to noticing the emotion, saying to yourself how it feels in your body, as hard as it may seem at first, gets easier with practice.

27

Acceptance Moves

For the past 14 years, I have been attending the annual conference of the Association of Contextual Behavioral Science for ACT practitioners. It's one of my favorite events of the year, and I love to blend my passion for ACT and traveling.

One year, the conference was going to be in Dublin, so I decided that it would be nice to spend a couple of days wandering the streets of London beforehand. This particular time was a special one for me because I was receiving a nomination as a fellow; as a woman and minority, coming from a working-class family in a third-world country, and creating a career in the United States, it meant a lot to know that my clinical work was being acknowledged.

I worked on my visa application to London, submitted it, and covered all fees in less than two weeks. I was supposed to receive an email with the shipping labels, but it never came. So for approximately three and a half months, I emailed the UK visa agency every other day, asked my administrative assistant to give me a hand, filed complaint after complaint electronically, searched for a phone number to contact someone because their website didn't list one, and repeatedly, I let them know that my flight was leaving on June 19.

I prepared for this conference months in advance, blocked out my work calendar, organized other activities around it, prepared a presentation with a colleague of mine for it, and searched some of the sightseeing in London and Dublin that I really wanted to see. Around mid-May, I finally received an email from the agency asking me to submit my passport through a paid courier service. They reassured me that they would send my passport back in time for my trip. I was a bit hesitant with this request given their record, thought about canceling my trip to London and going straight to Ireland, but given the content of their email, I decided to go along with their request.

My passport arrived one hour before my flight was leaving. I couldn't make it.

I tried everything I could to board the plane, but my passport was mailed from New York at 10 a.m., a day before the flight was leaving. I contacted the private courier, begged them to change the delivery address of the package so I could pick it up at an office close to the airport and go straight to take the plane. I contacted the airline company to reschedule the flight, explained what happened, and asked for a consideration given that I also bought flight protection. They couldn't refund my ticket and offered me another ticket for approximately $5,000.

I was shocked, hurt, disappointed, and extremely mad at this outcome. I did everything I was asked to do, went out of my way to do it promptly, and yet I couldn't be present at a gathering that meant so much to me, explore two cities that I've never seen, or hang out with dear friends and colleagues that I only see once a year.

I can assure you that I wasn't a fun person to be around those days.

Sometimes, bad things happen to us that are totally outside of our control. We don't want them, we don't love them, we dislike them, and we hope they never happen to us or the people we care about. And when they happen, we wrestle with them, fight against them, and at times feel defeated by them.

Obsessions are not pleasant experiences at all; their content can be cruel, disturbing, and horrendous and take your life into a downward spiral of rumination, worry, and fears. Obsessions cut into your sense of self and, unless you learn research-based skills, lead you into a life of suffering, disconnection, and loneliness.

You have learned to watch your mind. You have learned that your mind is a content-generating and pattern-making machine. You have learned that when obsessions show up, the first step is notice when you're getting lost in or absorbed with them. Then you learned to defuse from them by using your favorite defusion skills. And then you learned to ride the wave of those uncomfortable emotions by watching them as transitory experiences that come and go. Using these skills together will get you back into the present and snap you out of having an OCD episode.

Here is another skill you can use that prompts you to remember to watch your obsessions and all the feelings, sensations, and urges that come along: *making an acceptance move*.

You have read in different sections of this workbook that acceptance is a choice to make room for those disturbing and intrusive thoughts, fears, worries, and anxieties – and all the yucky stuff that comes along with those experiences.

Acceptance is a pretty powerful skill and yet is not easy to do, because it feels counterintuitive and quite uncomfortable. But if you look at any regular day you have, quite often you discover that you do need to accept, accept, and accept again hundreds of things that happen around us –running out of gas, a cloudy day, being in a waiting line at the grocery store for 25 minutes, being put on hold when calling the cell phone company, and much more.

An acceptance move is a sweet, soft, and gentle move to make room for those obsessions without fighting against them. The idea is to really open up to them so you can expand your day-to-day living.

Acceptance moves can include short acceptance prompts that you tell yourself, such as:

- I want to give my best in this moment to ride this wave.
- I want to do what I can to let this obsession come and go.
- Fighting this wave makes it worse.
- I'm going to let this one go.
- I want to get through this without fighting.

As Russ Harris, a well known ACT trainer, wrote,

[T]rue acceptance is not a thinking process; it's an attitude of openness, interest, and receptiveness, which originates with the observing self. Therefore, silently saying things such as the above examples will not make you truly accept . . . but what these words can do is act as a prompt: they can remind us and guide us to accept. (2019)

Here is what I find fascinating about acceptance skills at a brain level (apologies for my nerdiness): neuroaffective science of emotions has demonstrated that the skill of observing or detaching from the meaning of our stress-based responses – in plain terms, the skill of watching an overwhelming experience and then letting it go – is extremely handy and even faster than other skills in reducing the activation of our nervous system.

Basically, acceptance prompts – not stories about acceptance – actually use less brain resources, so our emotional system can slow down and allow the frontal lobe to kick in, and then we can choose how to handle a troublesome situation. Fascinating, right?

Here is a brief take-home message: acceptance-based moves are more efficient than emotion-based moves to overcome OCD episodes. Now less blah, blah, blah and more doing for you.

Try This

Here is what to do when encountering an OCD trigger: notice and watch the obsession, watch the emotion, and then use an acceptance prompt to remind yourself to fully make room for it – instead of fighting it, judging it, or acting on it. Here are some prompts for you to try:

- "It's not worth it to fight this obsession."
- "Not doing anything about this obsession will help it pass."
- "I dislike very much having this obsession, and I'm open to do what I can to accept it."

Remember that using an acceptance prompt is never with the purpose of making the obsession go away or eliminating the emotion; it's just a cue for you to check if you're fighting your experience instead of making room for it, and letting it be.

Make It Yours

Let's customize your acceptance prompts. How else can you remind yourself to practice an acceptance move? What's the short and sweet prompt you can use? Write your own here:

Again, practicing acceptance moves as prompts is never about getting rid of the struggle of the moment. It's about going through the struggle without making it worse. Wouldn't compulsive and avoidant behaviors make it worse in that moment?

Building Your Practice of Making Acceptance Moves

One way to build the muscle of acceptance moves is to go back to distressing situations you encountered either recently or a long time ago. This is not to torture you but to create more golden opportunities for you to practice this skill instead of waiting for OCD triggers to knock on your door.

Read the following directions and then practice this exercise. If you want, you can also record the directions on your cell phone and then listen to it.

"For the next couple of moments, focus your gaze on a single point in the room, or close your eyes and gently focus your attention on your breathing. [Pause for 2 to 3 minutes.]

"Next, bring into your mind a mildly upsetting memory you had last week. For a couple of moments recall this image as vividly as possible. Notice how it feels to have the emotions that come along with it. Notice the sensations that come along. Notice what shows up in your mind about this image or anything else.

"See if you can recognize the pull for acting, the pull for doing anything, the pull for making those reactive moves. In those moments, check with yourself to see if you're fighting, resisting, or trying to suppress the emotion. And if you find yourself doing so, take a deep breath; acknowledge the fight by saying to yourself, 'I'm fighting this emotion'; and then do your best to go back to paying attention to what's showing up in your experience.

"See if you can notice the life of this emotion, how it changes naturally and how maybe a new sensation comes its way. As you move forward with this exercise, practice one of your favorite acceptance prompts. Notice how it goes. Remember that putting into action acceptance prompts is not about getting rid of the emotions, thoughts, or sensations that come along, but to coach yourself to let go, to let the experience be, and to catch yourself if you're fighting against it.

"Continue noticing your experience for a couple of moments, and then take three to five deep breaths to finish this exercise."

You can practice this exercise as many times as you want, but once a day is ideal to start. You can visualize different types of emotionally charged situations: anger, fear, stress, etc. You have various opportunities to practice acceptance of different emotional states.

When practicing, notice how it feels to sit with, open up to, and get in contact with a feeling without doing anything. ACT skills are not about forcing you to be in discomfort but rather about learning to get better at having those yucky feelings that come your way as a personal choice and when it matters to you.

It's liberating to learn to live with the yucky stuff that shows up under your skin. It gives you the freedom to put your time, energy, and efforts into what you really care about instead of putting all your resources into fighting an internal battle.

Keeping an Eye on Your Shift Moves!

This workbook is all about getting you back into a life full of direction, meaning, and rich connections with others and yourself – a life that is fulfilling from the moment you open your eyes to the moment you fall asleep. And to get you back into that life, it's important for you to keep an eye on all the shifts you're making, from reactively responding to the obsessions that the content-generating and pattern-making machine of your brain comes up with to more skillful responses. Watching your mind, watching your emotions, and practicing acceptance moves are your shift moves, turn them up all the way!

In Chapter 6, "What Is This Thing Called 'ACT'?" I asked you to write down all the ideas and concerns you heard about behavior therapy. Had you ever heard the saying that "behavior therapists are full of logs?"

I honestly have been criticized so many times in my career for having logs, starting with my non-behaviorally oriented peers and ending with my students, who think that completing logs is "extra work" for clients. But here's the deal: more than completing logs, it's the tracking of your behaviors that I care about the most.

Let me unpack what I mean by tracking.

Dan Ariely, a professor of psychology and behavioral economics at Duke University, has studied for years what keeps people motivated and engaged; how people make decisions; how, despite having factual data in front of us, we still make nonsensical choices; and many other matters of our day-to-day life. Despite all the messages that pop psychology tells us about pleasure, fun, and desire for money being the motivators of our behaviors, Ariely shows over and over that actually doing what matters *and keeping track of those behaviors* are big motivators for us to continue making changes

But here's the clincher: tracking or logging a behavior just to do it, or because your therapist tells you, or because it's encouraged in this workbook won't be helpful. What is helpful is tracking steps that are meaningful to you – that's the key. The meaningful steps you take and keep track of every day – regardless of whether they're tiny, medium, or big – are the ones that help you to keep going.

Let's think for a moment of some writers whose work became popular because they took consistent steps, not rigidly but flexibly, and kept track of them:

J.K. Rowling, the author of *Harry Potter*, writes every day, usually from before 9 a.m. until noon. Stephen King, before becoming a famous writer, worked as a janitor for approximately seven years; he wrote every night for approximately three to four hours after having dinner with his family. Gretchen Rubin, author of *The Happiness Project*, writes from 15 minutes to an hour, usually every day, including on weekends, holidays, and vacations.

My invitation is for you to take consistent steps when dealing with obsessions, keep track of them, and make a habit of it.

Building Your Practice of Shift Moves

Putting into practice a new skill can be challenging, but doing it as often as possible and keeping track of every time you do so makes it easier and easier to do. It's like frequency nurtures frequency.

You don't have to practice your ACT skills to perfection, because that's not the purpose of this practice, but I do invite you to do your best to be consistent with all your efforts to watch your mind and your obsessions – and to track your efforts when putting your skills into action.

There are no rules about how to keep track of how you practice your watching, acceptance, and wave-riding skills. Simply use the log in Table 28.1 as a starting point and complete it at the end of every day.

You can also try different ways of tracking your practice of shift moves. For instance, you can just use one plain tally sheet per day. Or try switching tiny rocks from one pocket into another every time you practiced a skill. Or you might try the notes app on your cell phone.

What's really important is to make your tracking as visible as possible; otherwise, if your tracking is out of your sight, then it's out of your mind too. And if your tracking is out of your mind, your chances of building your practice and getting your life back get slimmer and slimmer.

Exercise 28.1 Shift moves log

Looking back at this past week, how would you say you did using your ACT skills?

	Mo	Tu	Wed	Th	Fr	Sat	Sun

Watching moves

Acceptance moves

Riding the waves

Takeaways to share

Figure 28.1 Shopping carts.

No matter what disturbing, annoying, or weird obsessions show up in your mind, what really matters is what you do with those obsessions, how you respond to them, and how you relate to them. Obsessions are not a choice, but your behavior is.

This part walked you through core skills to make a shift from reacting automatically to all the stuff that the content-generator and pattern-making machine of your mind comes up into building the life you want to live.

Here is a brief, very brief, summary of those skills:

– Watching your mind
You can visualize, say, or physicalize your wacky thoughts, or check the impact of getting hooked on any obsession that shows up in your mind.

You can start by using any of the suggested defusion exercises on Chapter 25, "Watching your Mind," or you can come with new ones and be as creative as you want; there are no rules and no limitations about defusion exercises. What's really important is that you customize all these defusion skills, make them yours, and practice them over and over!

– Riding the wave of emotions that come along with obsessions
Obsessions don't come alone; instead, they come with a cascade of overwhelming emotions –fear, worry, anxiety, stress – that makes it hard, really hard, to let them go.

Instead of fighting, suppressing, and trying to get rid of those feelings, you can watch them as visitors that come and go and as they rise and fall.

You were introduced to two micro-steps for riding any emotional wave:

• Describe to yourself what you feel and what you sense in your body; give it a name (it doesn't have to be a perfect name, but just a name that helps you to recognize the feeling).

• Don't do what you usually do (let me say it one more time, don't do what you usually do, for real)

– When feeling overwhelming emotions, take five deep and slow breaths and focus on how your body is breathing; notice the movements of your chest, diaphragm, and abdomen as you inhale and exhale; notice the sensations in your body and follow them with curiosity.

- Making acceptance moves
  It's easy to get busy fighting an obsession in your head or fighting an emotion in your body, so by using short acceptance prompts, you can coach yourself to make room for the yucky stuff that comes under your skin when dealing with OCD episodes.

  Examples of acceptance prompts are "fighting this wave makes it worse; I'm going to let this one go."
- Tracking all your shift moves
  Practicing all your skills – watching your mind, riding the wave, and acceptance moves – and keeping track of your practice are key to keeping your momentum going, optimizing your learning, and getting your life back on track, all the way!

  In the chapter "Keeping an Eye on Your Shift Moves," there is the "Shift moves log" that you can start using right away. But any other form of tracking is welcome: plain tally sheets, changing pennies from one glass into another one, or any other form of tracking that you can check at the end of the day or the week. Tracking is not to torture you, but to keep you going!

There you go! Please make all these skills yours and practice, practice, and practice again. Keep going!

Life Tracker

Reflect on how you have been living your life and mark an "X" where it corresponds.

Having obsessions as thoughts your mind comes up with	Seeing obsessions as problems to be solved
Approaching life as it is	Avoiding life because of obsessions
Taking action toward what you care about	Organizing your life around obsessions
Holding your thoughts lightly	Going 100% along with what your mind tells you
Checking what really works in your life	Doing stuff in automatic pilot mode
Making room for uncomfortable internal experiences	Pushing them down as much as possible

PART VII

Designing Your Life and Living Your Life

There so many things that we have to do endlessly hour by hour. When it comes to dealing with OCD, do you ever feel like you're in an endless battle to manage it, and as a result, other areas of your life are getting behind, ignored, or dismissed?

This section is a special one because it will help you to figure out how you want to live your life, what's truly important to you, and clarify the steps you need to take to live it. There will be questions, exercises, and more questions for you to reflect on the person you want to be, how you want to show up for the ones you love, how you want to show up for yourself when getting stuck with obsessions, what matters to you when thinking about your career, spirituality, religion, and any other area of your life. At the end of it, you will get a sense of how a well-designed life looks like for you.

Designing your life invites you to be curious, to have a bias to action, to develop a new relationship with your mind, and to unpack stories you have been telling yourself about obsessions, fears, thinking, and all the stuff that the content-generator and pattern-making machine of your mind comes up with.

What could happen when you do those things? What could happen when you start showing up for your life in alignment with what matters to you? What could happen when you make bold moves when dealing with obsessions?

Your life turns into a portfolio of experiences, adventures, silly moments, hardships, and frustrations, but in the end, it turns out as a life that is yours.

Living a life you love is possible, and you can start exactly where you are.

Figuring Out What Matters

Welcome to one of my favorite chapters of this workbook, and one that will hopefully make you shake your core in a good way!

Let me start by briefly sharing a personal story. I promise you, I'll keep it short!

When writing, my mind does its own job of coming up with all types of thoughts, like, "I can't believe you wrote that; that's not clear enough; you better watch the Avengers movie, aren't you hungry? Where is the timer? Is it time to pause now?" I usually do my best to continue writing while my mind keeps going on and on; at the end of the day, I'm excited to share a nice meal with family at home or with friends.

On one of those evenings, after having a great time catching up with friends and their 2-year-old, when getting ready to leave, the 2-year-old asked me to stay and play with her while she took her bath. Of course, I said yes to that sweet request; I couldn't and didn't want to say no to her.

I played all types of games with her in the bathtub, searched for toys that were dropped over and over, hung in there with her screams about not wanting shampoo on her hair, and got half of my clothing wet. I even got to change her into those large pajamas she loves to wear. At the end of the evening, I gave everyone a big hug and walked toward my car; it was such a sweet time of connecting – I loved it!

Here is what's also interesting: as soon as I closed the door of my friend's home, I ran to my car, drove to my place, parked my car, and ran quickly into my apartment – all because I was so eager to write a bit more of this workbook. I felt so alive typing and typing that I still remember how it felt!

Why would I do something like that? Why would I eagerly run to my laptop and write for a while after having such a sweet moment with a toddler? Why would I do something so singular when I absolutely valued connecting with the people I care about? Is there something wrong with me?

Here is why: Because I absolutely love creating content for the people I work with! Writing is one way of creating content. Writing has helped me to be a better therapist; it keeps me curious, reminds me to be humble, stretches my thinking in fascinating directions, connects me with very interesting people, and it puts into action my commitment to get people unstuck from any fear-based reaction they're struggling with.

Writing keeps me alive and keeps me going, and I honestly don't foresee a future without creating new resources because *that's HOW I want to show up for the people I work with: sharing research-based skills that get them unstuck.* I know that creating new resources is not the only thing that keeps me moving in life, but it's one important one that translate the stuff that matters to me into pragmatic actions.

The reality is that we all have things that keep us alive. We feel them, we treasure them, and we miss them if we're not living what matters to us. It just happens that, at times, given the business of our mind and the saturated world of our surroundings, we forget what makes us tick.

Are you living the life you want to live? Are you showing up as the person you want to be? This chapter is all about answering questions about HOW you want to show up to life. Your values are your HOWs.

I'll use the terms "HOWs," "values," and "life principles" interchangeably.

Let's dive in!

To Keep in Mind

There are hundreds of things we have to do every day, things we like, things we dislike, things that we're indifferent about, and so on. And since childhood, we've all received messages about what should be important for us. Do you remember all the messages you heard when growing up about the type of person you should be or what should matter to you? Do you recall how many advertisements circulated about things that should be important to you? What about all those movies sharing ideas about how you should be to others? Since birth, we've been bombarded with all types of ideas about what needs to be important for us.

Don't take me wrong, I don't think it's wrong at all to have aspirations about who we want to be and what's acceptable or not, to function as individuals and as a group. But I do think that we make ours many of the messages we've heard over our lifetime without ever checking what they mean, if they're truly important to us, or if we even relate to them.

Here is an example of what I mean: if you put a group of psychologists together in public and ask them what the biggest driving force is in their career, what do you think they would say? The clichéd response is usually "To help people." I'm sure many of us mean that, want that, and care about that, but why do we automatically respond without deeply checking our true *why* for helping people? Because of the socialization of language!

So, in this chapter, I'll invite you to beyond all those messages you have socialized with, and answering questions about what's deeply important to you, what you want to make your life about, be remembered for, and live by every day. In answering those questions, you will discover your HOWS, your life principles, your values, or qualities you want to embrace.

Hundreds of self-help books have been written about goals, values, life principles, and so on, but when you take a deep look at them, there are a few challenges:

- *A confusion between HOWs and goals*
  (e.g. "I want to be a mother")
  Goals are all the stuff that are related to values and that we check off as completed. But our values are not things that we fully complete; our values are ongoing life principles we want to live for. I cannot check "being caring" as something I do once and then forget about it, right? That makes "being caring" a value. Goals, on the other hand, are all the activities, actions, and specific steps I take toward my HOW of "caring" and can be checked off from a to-do list.

- *A misunderstanding of HOWS with feelings*
  Making a HOW of "wanting to be content" or "being happy" is very tricky because, as you learned in this workbook, we don't have control of our feelings, and emotions are very transitory experiences that come and go. There is, of course, nothing wrong with wanting to experience a particular feeling more than another, but organizing our life around it that's a different story because it may create quickly a trap for us. Hoping to have a particular feeling, it's like hoping to win the lottery: we're always waiting for it.

- *A mix-up between HOWs and wishes for others' behaviors*
  Sometimes, when having a conversation about values, I hear comments along the lines of "I want to be respected by others." Here is a clarification about those statements: It's natural to want to be seen, appreciated, and respected by others – and we certainly deserve it. But here is the caveat: we just don't have control of other people's reactions, behaviors, and feelings about us.

- *The assumption that values are nouns*
  Most self-help books refer to values as nouns (e.g., appreciation, love, etc.). But if we take them as they come, without a specific action, they are just beautiful words that vanish in the air. Values within ACT are described as "verbs" because they reflect ongoing action in our lives.

ACT takes the conversation about your HOWs to a different level; in ACT you are asked to choose who you want to be and how you want to show up in different areas of your life. And just to make it crystal clear, in ACT, values are life principles viewed as "verbs," as specific behavioral goals you can put into action every day. Quite different, right?

ACT doesn't offer you a perfect life that is free of struggle, free of obsessions, or exempt from anxiety, worries, and panic. But it does offer you a life worth living by teaching you how to sit with the yucky stuff that gets under your skin and still act toward what truly matters to you.

Let's start by . . .

Exploring Your HOWs

In this section you will find different exercises to explore your HOWs. Even if you believe that you already know what you really care about in this moment, I still invite you to complete these exercises. Be curious. Be open to the idea that some of your values might not actually be your own but rather passed on to you from a parent, spouse, boss, or doctrine.

I urge you to really spend some time reflecting on these exercises, because without realizing it, all of us can be living in automatic pilot mode unless we pause, check where we're headed, and decide what we want our life to be about. Viktor Frankl, in *Man's Search for Meaning*, narrates his discovery of what truly matters for him that helped him survive in a Nazi death camp:

> For the first time in my life I saw the truth as it is set into song by so many poets, proclaimed as the final wisdom by so many thinkers. The truth – that love, meaning, and connection are the ultimate and highest goal to which man can aspire. Then I grasped the meaning of the greatest secret that human poetry and human thought and belief have to impart: the salvation of man is through love and in love.

And if in this moment, your overreactive brain is telling you, "but I have OCD!" or "my life is about managing OCD," take this moment to answer these questions: what happens when you act on these thoughts? Do you do more or less with your life? What if learning to deal with obsessions is part of something that truly matters to you?

When feeling triggered, this is exactly the time for you to reconnect with your HOWs, because as challenging as it feels, your values will show, guide, and even escort you on the road of living your values! So, when these thoughts show up again, how would you name them? Here are some suggestions: "Ms. Doom and Gloom," "bad-news telenovela," or what about "the return of Mr. Fatale"?

Let's start with the first exercise!

Exercise 29.1 Values-exercise: Creating a mind map of an activity you're fully engaged in

Think about any activity that you were really, totally, utterly engaged with. Now create a mind map for it. A mind map is just a freestyle graphic that, in the middle, has the activity you were doing. Go ahead and jot down the activity now. Next, around the activity, in any order, write down related words and concepts one more time; next, repeat the same thing with those news words. Your mind map may have two to three layers around the main activity that you started working on. Don't worry about having the perfect mind map; this is a personal exercise to unpack your values, so doing it perfectly would be missing the point.

Reflection: HOW did you show up for this activity?
Think in terms of life principles, qualities, and values that were key for you when participating in the activity you chose.

Here is another exercise for you to get in contact with your personal values.

Exercise 29.2 Values-exercise: Stock of moments of purpose

Think about an activity in which you felt alive, full of purpose, and had a sense of meaning even though you were feeling a bit tired and fatigued, but you knew it was the thing to do because it was revitalizing. Now create a mind map about it.

Reflection: HOW did you show up for this activity?
Think in terms of life principles, qualities, and values that were key for you when participating in this activity.

Sometimes it's in our most challenging moments that we discover what we're made of. As you unpack your HOWS, move into the next activity that focuses on the moments of hurt because of OCD.

Exercise 29.3 Values-exercise: Identifying what you care about behind your hurts with obsessions

Think about a moment when your overworking brain came up with bizarre obsessions and you did your best to handle them by doing compulsive or avoidant behaviors. Next, think about the hurt that came with those obsessions. What are the activities you care about that get affected because of these obsessions?

Reflection: HOW would you like to show up when having obsessions?

Life is complicated. It brings all types of experiences into our day-to-day life, some of them more challenging than others and some tickling us with sweet moments. Tap into a sweet memory as an exploration of what you care about.

Exercise 29.4 Values-exercise: Identifying what you care about in a sweet memory

Recall a very sweet memory you had, either recently or in the past. Choose one that captures that preciousness of life. Do your best to bring that moment as vividly into your mind as possible, as if it were happening now in front of you. Savor the sweetness that comes with it as you engage in it, with what else comes with it. Make room for those feelings and then briefly write about it.

Reflection: When looking at this sweet memory, what was special about it? HOW did you show up for it?

Now that you have completed these exercises, take a look at all of them. Take your time. Reflect on how you were treating yourself and others, reflect on HOW you showed up to those moments, how you behaved. Recognize those personal qualities you want to embrace in your life.

In ACT, our values are described as *ongoing actions or verbs* because we take steps of all sizes – petite, small, medium, large, or extra-large – to live them, experience them, and put them into action. And every step you take towards what you truly care about is welcome! Examples of values as ongoing actions are: learning, loving, being caring, being supportive, and so on. There are no right or wrong values; there are just qualities you really want to be remembered for and to live for.

As you ponder on your HOWs, maybe you want to pause, put this workbook down, move around, sit a bit with the reflections that are showing up for you, roll your shoulders back and forth, take a moment to breathe. Take 5 minutes or longer, if you prefer, before continuing.

After reflecting on the previous questions and pausing for a bit, now identify your HOWs and jot them down.

My personal HOWs are: _____

_____

_____

_____

_____

_____

Kudos to you! You just finished identifying your personal values! That's a great starting point to continue overcoming OCD episodes and making the best of this life.

To Do

Now that you have a grasp of these values-exploration exercises, do the same for other areas in your life, because richer lives have many areas that we participate in. Look at your HOWS in the following domains: work/career, personal growth, relationships, spirituality, and health.

Figuring out your values in these other areas may take some time, so I encourage you to not rush through it. In fact, I urge you to pause and use this opportunity to check how you really want to live your life. There's no one better than you to do so!

You can break down your values-exploration exercises one per day, so it's not overwhelming and so that you have a chance to really reflect on them.

Obsessions often make it difficult for you to act on your core values. In fact, some of my clients get so busy managing these obsessions that they forget how much they care about other things in their life. They stop doing activities they usually feel engaged in, that make them feel alive and excited, or they feel too exhausted to do them because they have been fighting a battle with obsessions.

Let's think of Naomi for a moment. She was struggling with a fear of showing her private parts, and as a result, she avoided being in her house without wearing a belt and a fully buttoned sweater. When walking next to other female adults, she usually turned her body in the opposite direction, holding the front part of her clothes very tightly. If she wasn't sure whether she had exposed herself, she would ask her friends if her clothes looked normal; if her clothes looked mess up to them, that would prove that she had exposed her private parts.

Naomi only went out for 30–50 minutes with her friends. She stopped going to book club meetings (because they usually took 3–4 hours) and canceled her membership at the local pool as a precautionary measure.

When completing all the values-exploration exercises in this chapter, Naomi realized how much she appreciates connecting with others and being active. These are her HOWs. And she also realized how much her OCD was preventing her from living her HOWs.

Now, your turn to write down your values on the top part of your Values-Dashboard. In the next chapter, you will read more about how to complete the rest of it; so for now, it's more important to choose one area you want to focus on and its respective value.

Values-Dashboard

VALUES-DASHBOARD

Circle the area(s) you want to focus on this week

HEALTH • WORK • RELATIONSHIPS • SPIRITUALITY • PERSONAL GROWTH

What matters to you? What's the value you choose to focus on this week? Jot it down here.

What actions are you willing and committed to take this week toward that value? Be as specific as possible.	Mark an X when you complete that specific action.						
	Mon	Tue	Wed	Thu	Fri	Sat	Sun
1.							
2.							
3.							

At the end of the week, jot down any overall comments:

It's possible that obsessions have kept you in your head too much time while life was happening outside of you, and that thinking about your values is too much or too confusing. Here are my two tips for you: (1) patience with yourself; learning to live your values and getting unstuck from OCD is not about living perfectly but a day-to-day process; (2) if you have been dealing with obsessions that have created doubt of who you are, I invite you to be gentle with yourself and keep in mind, that you won't discover what's important to you by thinking and thinking about it but by trying, experiencing and experiencing again. Making a shift from living reactively because of OCD and calming the fires that come because of compulsions is not easy, and yet it's not impossible. It's doable. Just keep working through this workbook, put the skills into action – in particular all the skills to watch your mind – and you may be joyfully surprised at what you discover.

Getting in contact with what you care about, your HOWs, your values, is a first step to *design the life* you want to have. There is another key step *to live that life* you want to live and that's . . .

30

Living Your HOWs

Welcome to a super-cool chapter: putting your HOWs into action!

All the chapters up to this point have given you the foundation you need to make a shift from living reactively because of obsessions to creating a new relationship with your mind, your obsessions, the overwhelming feelings that come with them, and fundamentally, prepare you to move forward in your life as different fearful moments come your way.

In the previous chapter, you got in contact with your HOWs; now, putting your HOWs in action with your feet, hands, and mouth is the next step. Which brings us to the next skill to keep you moving: making commitments to yourself to live your HOWs.

To Keep in Mind

ACT is a therapy about change that pushes you to make a shift from living reactively when having obsessions to living purposefully, richly, and meaningfully.

There are two key things to remember as you move forward with your life as you want it to be:

1. Your HOWs are your direction, and
2. The goals or actions you envision are your destination.

Think about this: if your value is learning and you are into art, you might set a goal to take a Photoshop class or participate in a wood-working workshop. But after completing those classes, you would likely want to do something else to keep living your values of learning, right? Those other activities are your destination, your goals.

Making a commitment to both your HOWs and the action you'll take on those values takes a lot of courage, because your reactive and overprotective brain will give you 100 reasons why you shouldn't approach what you have been avoiding and why you shouldn't stop doing your compulsions. And yet I urge you to check the price of organizing your life around OCD. There's no one better than you to choose how to live your life!

Meryl Streep, a well-known American actress, was told that she was "too ugly" for the role as an unknown in a King Kong movie at the beginning of her career. In her words,

[T]his was a pivotal moment for me; this one rogue opinion could derail my dreams of becoming an actress or force me to pull myself up by the boot straps and believe in myself.

(https://www.eonline.com/news/883834/awkward-macklemore-unironically-references-a-fake-meryl-streep-quote-in-an-interview)

She continued to apply for many other roles; by now, she has received three Academy Awards and been nominated for a record 21.

Within ACT, when taking steps to live your values, that process is called *committed action*. At its core is a commitment you make with yourself. It's more like a personal choice and promise you make to take a specific action regardless of what shows up under your skin.

I intentionally didn't say anything about making the right, perfect, or logical choice, not because logic or reasoning doesn't matter, but because when we commit toward taking a specific action, the workability of the behavior is all that matters: is this behavior a move toward or away from my values?

In other chapters, you've become familiar with the notion of workability within ACT, but let's revisit it by considering Kirk's struggle for a moment.

Kirk was dealing with obsessions about being punished by God when noticing that a person besides his partner was an attractive individual and having sexual images about it. Kirk felt guilty and disturbed by his attraction, so he prayed for approximately 1 hour, or until it felt right, or until he was sure that God wouldn't punish him. Kirk really wanted to show up with loyalty in his monogamous relationship with his partner, and he also valued creating community with his friends. Despite having clarity in his HOWs, because of this intrusion Kirk didn't hang out with his friends or attend birthdays, dinners, or theater gatherings; he was scared that, out of the blue, he might look at a person and have thoughts about how hot they are.

As part of his personal commitment, Kirk decided to reconnect with his friends even though his mind might come up with all types of obsessions. Kirk called five friends and invited them for dinner even while his mind was throwing tantrums: "Are you sure you want to do that? Are you intentionally going to upset God? How are you going to control those impure thoughts?"

If Kirk responded to those obsessions, *logically and reasonably*, he might go back and forth many times analyzing, dissecting, and basically dwelling on his action, and he might not have even grabbed the phone to call his friends. The *workability* of Kirk's behavior of calling his friends is considered in the context of his values. What do you think is the impact of Kirk's behavior to call his friends? Was that a move toward or away from his personal values? A move toward, all the way!

The more that Kirk chooses to act on his HOWs and do what matters, even if it's a micro-step, the more likely he is to take more workable actions in other areas of his life. In essence, once you start showing up for life as you want to and you savor what comes with it, it's really hard to go back to a reactive life organized around obsessions.

To Do

Grab your Values-Dashboard from Chapter 29. For each area of your life, think about specific actions you can commit to take. Make sure that each step clearly specifies *when you will do it, for how long, with whom*, and so on. Don't worry if it seems like an action that's too small or too big – the most important thing is that you choose to commit to doing while also making room for the yucky stuff.

For instance, when writing this workbook, I made the commitment to write three chapters a week, and I designated Wednesday as my writing day. It wasn't perfect at all. But, every Wednesday for six months, I sat down on my desk, set the timer for three hours, and wrote and wrote with a cup of tea, kombucha, or a smoothie ready to go. My mind shouted at me all types of thoughts "This sucks! That example doesn't make sense. Are you seriously going to write that? You always make mistakes!" And in those moments, I knew that getting angry at those thoughts, criticizing myself more, dwelling on them would just take me away from writing. Instead, I sometimes imagined those unhelpful thoughts as headlines in the newspaper "Psychologist Writes for Hours, Nobody Reads Her Work." Other times, I imagined all those criticizing thoughts like little Smurfs, standing next to the laptop, shouting at time.

No matter where you are in your journey of overcoming OCD, what you do for living, where you live, your age, your gender, or ethnicity, my hope is that by living your HOWs, you discover other hidden treasures that inspire you, give you a sense of connection, and get you living meaningfully!

Living the life you're designing is absolutely possible, and it won't be handed to you on a silver platter. Quite often, you are going to be invited to make room for difficult feelings, pesky obsessions, and annoying sensations in your body; you're going to be challenged to unlearn compulsions and avoidant behaviors you were relying on in the past; and you're going to be asked to flexibly hold onto ruling-thoughts about fears, obsessions, worries, and anxieties lightly as you move forward. But the rewards of living the life you want to live are worth it all the way!

And as you live your HOWs with your feet, hands, and mouth, I also encourage you to keep . . .

31

Counting Your HOWs Moves

Tracking matters, period, and there is data supporting that, period again, as my *tia* says!

In one my first ACT workshops many years ago, I heard very loud and clearly that "talking about values without taking action is like saying beautiful words that are taken by the wind." So figuring out your HOWs is one step, doing your HOWs with your feet, hand, and mouth is another – and tracking them is another skill, all in the name of leaving behind reactive moves.

Keeping a vigilant eye on how we're living our life doesn't make our struggles go away, and it won't make a reactive brain never react to obsessions. But it will help us to track how we're responding in those moments and check if we're going into reactive mode or in the direction we want to go.

Trust me, I'm not suggesting that you count your HOWs to add a tedious task to your plate but to help you to continue freeing yourself from OCD episodes. Would you rather live a life organized by fear, anxiety, worry, and obsessions? Or would you rather live a life worth living? Living a life worth living requires keeping track of how you're living!

To Keep in Mind

Imagine for a moment: how would it be if instead of focusing on how many tasks you check off your to-do list, you focused on how many steps you take toward your HOWs? Quite different, right?

I'm not saying that you shouldn't do all the necessary things that we all have to do, like laundry, cooking, paying bills, and so on. I'm just saying that doing those tasks or managing obsessions is not everything – there is more for you to do and live for than just completing functional tasks.

To Do

In Chapter 29 you completed a Values-Dashboard that you can start using to log the steps you commit to take toward living a fulfilling life. I strongly encourage you to use this log to plan your week and then check it at the end of the week to see your progress (believe it or not, I do have mini-tracking sheet in the whiteboard in my office; I'm usually checking how I'm living my values in four areas).

Of course, feel free to use any other system you prefer to count your HOW moves. Whatever tracking method you choose, my invitation is for you *to make it as visible, physical, and tangible as possible so you can see yourself building momentum toward your values.* (Nerdy research says that these attributes of any tracking system are key to keeping us motivated.)

A tip for you: if you find yourself having anxious thoughts about tracking your values-based moves (e.g., "I have to get this done, I have to do it now!") or struggling tracking them (e.g., "What if I forget or don't do it perfectly?"), take a deep breath, pause, and go back to your HOWs behind the behavior. Are you tracking your values-based moves to get rid of any anxiety or fear, or to neutralize an obsession? Or are you keeping track of them to make the best of your time on this earth? Every behavior, and I mean it, *every behavior* could become a compulsion, and an overreactive brain can latch onto anything and everything, so keep your eyes open to it.

Exercise 31.1 Weekly Values-Dashboard

VALUES-DASHBOARD Circle the area(s) you want to focus on this week HEALTH • WORK • RELATIONSHIPS • SPIRITUALITY • PERSONAL GROWTH							
What matters to you? How do you want to show up? What's the value you choose to focus on this week? Jot it down here.							
What actions are you willing and committed to take this week toward living your HOWs? Be as specific as possible.	Mark an X when you complete that specific action.						
	Mon	Tue	Wed	Thu	Fri	Sat	Sun
1.							
2.							
3.							
At the end of the week, jot down any observations:							

32

Taking a Break

Have you ever pushed through a workday, event, or big chore to try to get as many things done as you could? If so, you're not alone. Almost every person I know gets hooked, at different times, on a course of doing more things and doing them faster and better. We all get ambitious about how much we can get done, the amount of time it will take, or what our body can handle.

For instance, when you first opened this workbook, did you feel an urge to rush through it, to read it as fast as possible, so you can get rid of the obsessions?

It makes sense. Whether you have been recently diagnosed with OCD or suspect you have OCD, or if you've been dealing with OCD for years and are desperate to refresh or learn new skills, naturally you want to read this book as quickly as possible so reap the benefits as soon as possible.

But from the beginning of this workbook, I've asked you to not rush and to make your work on these chapters about putting skills into practice slowly, day by day. Working through this workbook is one thing, but it's not enough alone to capitalize on the skills, just as reading a book on mechanics won't magically give you mechanic skills to fix your car. If you want to learn to fix your car, you must practice, practice, and practice those skills; the same goes for ACT skills to deal with obsessions.

And, practicing skills and living a fulfilling life also require replenishing your resources, taking moments to pause, and giving yourself a break.

To Keep in Mind

Everything we do, every action we take, every move we make uses many resources from our body and mind. Your reading of this workbook, learning ACT skills, and putting them into action is commendable and meaningful. And it also required time, effort, and energy on your part!

Values-based steps need to be nurtured. So when you withdraw from the bank account of your life, you also need to add a supply of resources for creating more fulfillment in the future. This is done by not overworking yourself.

Living with an overreactive brain – a content-generating and pattern-making machine that doesn't stop – is already challenging. Pushing yourself to your limits, even when creating a fulfilling life, could also lead to burnout.

So let's help you to renew your resources. You have a long-lasting run!

To Do

Here are my recommendations for you:

- Put this workbook down and take a two- to three-week break.
- Keep completing your Values-Dashboard, Shift Moves, and Life Tracker Logs weekly.
- Share with a friend or other trusted person what value you're working on that week, if you're comfortable doing so. I know it's hard to share what's happening, and yet it's enormously helpful to get support from people who care for you.
- Hold yourself kindly when things don't go perfectly. I mean it.
- Pause if you find yourself hooked on the thought, "I want to get rid of these obsessions" or variations of it. And as you might do with any uninvited guest at a party, just acknowledge he is there; no need to give him attention, talk to him, or kick him out, because that's energy you want to spend enjoying yourself and living your life.
- If you find yourself stuck, check in with yourself. HOW do you want to show up for yourself in that moment? What matters enough to put your skills into action? How do you want to show up to yourself in that moment of struggle?
- And please do me a favor: treat yourself. You have worked so hard. What could you do for yourself to appreciate all the work you have put into overcoming OCD episodes and living a purposeful life? Pick one or more nourishing things and do them.

Takeaways to share

Figure 32.1 Values forecast.

Living a meaningful life and doing what matters is ultra-different than living a reactive life organized by obsessions, fears, worries, and anxieties. Dozens of research papers show that people are healthier, have better relationships with others, perform better at work – whatever work they're doing – and are happier in general when living a life worth living.

This part was all about assisting you to design your life and start living it. To sum up, you learned that:

– Values are freely chosen qualities you want to embrace or HOW you want to show up for life and are ongoing actions, steps, and behaviors you choose to make. Values and HOWs are used interchangeably in this workbook.

– Your HOWs apply to different areas of your life – personal growth, relationships, work/career, spiritual, and health.

– Values are different than goals, feelings, wishes, and hopes about others' behaviors toward you.

  Goals are specific steps, of any size, you check off from your list toward your values, but your values are principles you are always striving for. *Feelings* are transitory experiences that shift hundreds of times, that we have zero control of, and are different than a value because values are qualities we want to be remembered for. *Expectations about how we would like to be treated* are that, hopes and wishes about how others should behave, but Amazon is still not selling a device to manage others.

– The only way to life your HOW is with your feet, hands and mouth.
  Values without actions are meaningless, and that doesn't mean that you have to make big moves all the time; living your values is about taking any size of an action – petite, medium, small, large, or extra-large – toward living a meaningful life.

– Keeping track of your values is not to torture you but to keep you engaged.
  You can use the values-dashboard or any other logging system that ideally is visible, tangible, and physical, so it keeps you driven.

– Living a purposeful life requires you to recharge, refill, and replenish your resources. Striving for overcoming OCD and doing what matters are an amazing choices you're making and are also hard work. If you only withdraw from your body and mind accounts, that's not sustainable, and it has a downside: burnout. So, taking breaks are required to have purposeful lives.

Life Tracker

Reflect on how you have been living your life and mark an "X" where it corresponds.

Having obsessions as thoughts your mind comes up with	Seeing obsessions as problems to be solved
Approaching life as it is	Avoiding life because of obsessions
Taking action toward what you care about	Organizing your life around obsessions
Holding your thoughts lightly	Going 100% along with what your mind tells you
Checking what really works in your life	Doing stuff in automatic pilot mode
Making room for uncomfortable internal experiences	Pushing them down as much as possible

PART VIII

Making W.I.S.E. M.O.V.E.S.

Welcome back!

I hope you had a chance to recharge, refill, and continue to put into action all the skills you learned to relate to your mind in a different way. Hope you had a chance to watch your obsessions as they came, use acceptance prompts, and surf the waves of overwhelming emotions and made bold moves toward living your HOWs.

As we begin a new section of this workbook, don't forget to complete your Values-Dashboard every week. Doing – and tracking – the stuff you love and that is fulfilling has accumulative effects in many areas of our life!

By now, you may have noticed the difference between choosing how to live your life versus arranging your actions around obsessions and taking reactive moves; they're quite the opposite, right? You have a very strong foundation to tame the content-generating and pattern-making machine of your brain!

Some obsessions have a force of their own that can be irresistible and hard to let go of, despite your best efforts. They may even feel as if you have inserted your fingers inside an outlet and there is this painful electrical reaction that shocks your body, and it's hard to ignore.

Part VIII will give you the ACT and ERP skills you need for handling resistant, intrusive thoughts by targeting specifically those situations, people, activities, and objects that start OCD episodes. No one can make the personal decision to feel the yucky stuff and commit to do it except you. You cannot kill, shut down, cure, or make your obsessions disappear; but by using ACT and ERP skills, you can learn new, flexible, and soft ways of responding to situations so they don't hold you back, bring you down, or block you from doing what matters to you.

Keep in mind that facing these resistant, persistent, and obstinate obsessions is not a marathon to win but a process to live by. I encourage you to find your own pace and rhythm as you go through this path of liberating yourself from OCD episodes.

The reality is that, at the end of the day, as much your brain throws tantrums, every time you take a step toward what you care about when facing those annoying obsessions, you're responding with the one thing that your brain cannot argue with, question, or dispute: your behavior!

Let's move into the combo of targeted ACT and ERP together!

Put Together Your Values-Guided Exposure Menu

I'm sure you have done your best to use all the ACT skills learned in this workbook and handle all those weird thoughts that your reactive brain came up with. How was that for you? What did you notice now that you're investing your time, efforts, and energy into things that matter to you?

Changing behavioral patterns, learning to get unhooked from thinking patterns, and making the best of every moment we're alive is hard work – not impossible, but hard work. And despite your best efforts, there may be some activities that are still hard to participate in and enjoy because of OCD triggers.

This chapter and the following ones will teach you targeted forms of facing ultra-resistant OCD-related situations, including doing values-guided exposures.

Values-based exposure work is not about torturing you, traumatizing you, or asking you to do anything against your values. Values-guided exposures are an extension of what you've been doing already: making room for obsessions; hanging in there with the fear, panic, anxiety, and distress that come with them; flexibly responding to all that internal noise; and doing your best to keep moving with your feet, hands, and mouth.

But quite likely, when reading the word "exposure," your mind may have some opinions about it. Am I right? So jot down here what your mind tells you exposure is about. Don't worry, this is not a test, you won't be graded, and I don't have a camera inserted in the book to verify if you do this exercise. But it truly does help to put on paper the ideas you have about important practices you will be invited to do moving forward.

_____

_____

_____

_____

Exercise 33.1 Inventory of challenging situations because of resistant-obsessions

What are the specific situations, people, places, activities, and bodily sensations that have been really hard to face because of intrusive thoughts?	How are these challenging situations affecting you when looking at different areas in your life: work, family relationships, parenting, friendships, and health?
Example: I have been avoiding going to brunch with my parents on Sundays, because I'm afraid I'm capable of lying to them and that I won't' tell them the truth of what happened, and they may have a wrong impression of me. I feel sick to my stomach at the thought I might lie to them. (Justin is afraid of being capable of lying and not saying the truth.)	Example: Well, they don't get to know what's going on in my personal life and I feel like an outsider. I guess my value is being seen fully by my parents, and right now I'm not being seen by them at all, we have almost no relationship.

My clients have all types of ideas about what exposure is, such as "pushing you to do things," "making you do weird things," "forcing what you're anxious of," and so on. Within ACT, exposure is not about throwing you into a pool of overwhelming fear, discomfort, and worry, but inviting you to choose what matters, what to feel, how to feel it, and when to feel it. You're always in charge!

To start, you need to make an inventory of all the situations that you're avoiding or approaching with compulsive behaviors because of resistant-obsessions. Using the form below, in the left column, write down all the situations that have been extremely challenging because of obsessions. In the right column, write down all the ways the challenging situations affect your day-to-day life. Try to come up with 10 situations and jot them down. (If you need an additional blank form, see the appendix.)

After completing this inventory, it's time to create your Values-Guided Exposure Menu! And yep, you read the word "menu" correctly, meaning that you get to choose what to face, when to face it, and how to do it! You're your own CEO, remember?

As an example, let's take a look at Deedee's Values-Guided Exposure Menu. Deedee has an obsession about accidentally setting her house on fire. When Deedee gets hooked into this obsession, she follows a nighttime routine of checking all the dials on the stove, touching the stove burners, checking whether the fans in the bathroom are off by flipping the on-off switch numerous times, and checking that all lights are off by flipping the on-off switch a bunch of times, too. Deedee's routine usually took her 30 minutes and sometimes longer, because she repeats the routine multiple times until it "feels right." At the end of the day, Deedee misses out on spending time with her partner and teenage kids and doesn't have much time to recharge for the next day.

Refer to your Inventory of Challenging Situations Because of Resistant-Obsessions. Choose 10 situations that you're willing to approach without compulsive behaviors as a personal commitment toward living your HOWs. Write down how you can approach each situation differently as a move toward your values.

Example from Deedee:
Going to bed every night without checking the stove, so I can chat with the kids before they go to sleep.

Letting John use the stove at night without checking after him to see whether he turned off the stove: not checking the dials of the oven or seeing if the dials of the burners are in the right position, so I can practice being flexible in my relationship with him.

Going to sleep every night without checking the fans in the bathrooms, so I can connect with John and do fun things with him.

Allowing my teenage boys to use the bathroom at night without asking them if they are sure they turned the fans and light switches off, so that I can be a caring mom and not a controlling one.

Asking John to cook dinner for the family one evening a week without checking the stove, so I can practice being flexible in my relationship with him.

Going to bed at night before John without compulsively asking him to do the nighttime routine instead, so I can teach my kids how to handle discomfort in life without being consumed by it.

Preparing a meal with teenage boys without checking what they're doing when close to the stove so that I can connect with them and teach them life skills like cooking.

Leaving the lights on in the bathroom at night for 30 minutes while having dinner and watching TV with my family so I can continue to teach my kids how to handle stressful moments in life.

Before we look at another example of a Values-Guided Exposure Menu, let's get some background on Dan, who has an obsession about contracting testicular cancer and his sperm being negatively affected because of battery radiation from computers.

Dan really wants to obtain a major in computer science. He knows that he'll need to sit a minimum of 15 hours in front of a computer for lab time, not counting other hours for homework and other projects using his laptop. Dan is quite nervous about this, and although he has been getting better at visualizing his obsessions as bubbles coming out of a bottle of champagne, riding the urges to do compulsions like checking the operating systems of the laptop, putting his cell phone far from him when working, and willingly choosing to go for coffee with friends in the service of his values of showing up for his friendships, he still struggles having a social media account himself or having dinners or long meals with people who may use their phone.

Dan's Values-Guided Exposure Menu looks like this:

Refer to your Inventory of Challenging Situations Because of Resistant-Obsessions. Choose 10 situations that you're willing to approach without compulsive behaviors as a personal commitment toward living your HOWs. Write down how you can approach each situation differently as a move toward your values.

Staying in a computer store for 15, 30, 45 minutes, and 1 hour to get better at being knowledgeable about different types of technology.

Going to, walking into, and working in a computer lab for 30, 60, 90, and 120 minutes to get better at being flexible with different situations that are out of my control.

Creating a personal website with five pages on my laptop while placing the laptop on top of my testicles, without pushing it away, to practice being flexible with uncomfortable situations that happen in day-to-day living.

Watching a TV show while having my laptop on my lap for 10, 20, and 30 minutes without pushing it away so I can get better at just relaxing, even though things are not ideal at times.

Now it's your turn to organize your Values-Guided Exposure Menu. Take another look at the Inventory of Challenging Situations Because of Resistant-Obsessions that you just compiled. Choose 10 situations that are really important to you and that you are willing to approach to get better at handling what comes with those resistant-obsessions. If you have more than 10 situations, you can use the following questions as prompts to help you to choose:

1. Which 10 situations matter enough to you that you're willing to face them and sit with the discomfort that comes along with obsessions?
2. Which values are you open to move toward that make it worthwhile for you to do the challenging work of facing the obsessions that come with those 10 moves?

Exercise 33.2 Values-Guided Exposure Menu

> Refer to your Inventory of Challenging Situations Because of Resistant-Obses-sions. Choose 10 situations that you're willing to approach without compulsive behaviors as a personal commitment toward living your HOWs. Write down how you can approach each situation differently as a move toward your values.
>
> Example: I want to start having dinners with my parents on Sundays because I care about being seen by them.

Your Values-Guided Exposure Menu is your road map to guide you to tackling resistant-obsessions in an organized and planned manner. You can always go back to it, change it, modify it, and adjust it as needed, especially as you continue to learn about different types of exposures and gain tips to maximize their impact. Your Values-Guided Exposure Menu is not a menu set in stone but a flexible one that will guide you in approaching your most triggering situations – so you can free yourself from being bossed around by sticky obsessions.

The next chapter will show you what to do when putting into action a values-guided exposure.

34

Make W.I.S.E. M.O.V.E.S. When Practicing Values-Guided Exposures

If you have been practicing all the exercises in this workbook wholeheartedly and have made a personal commitment to do so, you may have noticed that, little by little, you've been getting away from reactive moves driven by obsessions or ruling-thoughts.

I know it's quite painful to go from one reactive move into another one, over and over. But bit by bit, you have learned to date your mind and take it lightly. You've begun to watch all the thoughts it comes up with and to take your obsessions for what they are: symbols assembled together. You have learned to watch your emotions, and use acceptance prompts when needed. You've put in front of you what you care about, and you do what you care about. Quite exciting and different than making reactive moves, right?

And even if this shift isn't perfect, and you're still working on it, what matters is that by taking those steps you are creating a very solid foundation to get your life back! So let's get you moving in that direction!

In the previous chapter you put together your Values-Guided Exposure Menu to help you face the resistant-obsessions that are still taking you away from what you care about.

When reaching this crucial conversation with my clients about moving into targeted exposure work, it was clear to me that I needed to come up with a quick, short, and easy way to talk to them about the ACT skills they have been learning and could use in those pesky moments. Not an easy task, trust me. After many trials, rich discussions, torturing people close to me, and my commitment to make ACT and ERP skills more accessible, the uncomplicated acronym W.I.S.E. M.O.V.E.S. was born.

W.I.S.E. M.O.V.E.S is not just a catchy expression – it's a reminder for all my clients that they can approach and face every resistant-obsession they are getting fused with while building over and over a new behavioral pattern in those moments.

Let's break down this acronym in detail:

Watch your mind
Invite your obsessions
Stay with your experience
Either toward or away from your values

Make a choice
Observe what comes with the choice
Value your choice
Engage with what's next in your life
Soften up with self-compassion

Watch your mind

In Chapter 25, "Watching Your Mind," you discovered a bunch of ways for defusing from your obsessions by watching, saying, or physicalizing them or checking how it works when getting hooked on them.

No matter how distressing a situation is, no matter how loudly your content-generator machine shouts about what you can or shouldn't do, when facing any obsession (even the weirdest and more disturbing ones), watching your mind and defusing from it is the place to start.

It looks like this: You say to yourself the name of the obsession and visualize it as an object, physicalize it with a gesture, or say it in different ways.

Invite your obsessions

You have learned that the more effort and energy you put into fighting back, pushing down, neutralizing, or trying to control those pesky obsessions with avoidant or compulsive behaviors, paradoxically, you get the opposite result: the more OCD episodes you end up struggling with, the more that your brain keeps learning to get hooked in the fake-news of obsessions, the more that an ineffective behavioral response gets rehearsed – the less time you have to do the stuff you love.

Inviting the obsession means accepting it, making room for it, not necessarily liking it or approving it, but just acknowledging it's there without judging it, criticizing it, or trying to power through it.

To invite your obsessions, you can use your acceptance moves.

It looks like this:

Using acceptance prompts, tell yourself, "I don't need to fight this obsession in any way" or "fighting it makes it worse."

Stay with your experience

OCD episodes get strengthened when your brain comes up with the ruling-thought "you can't handle this" or variations of it, and then organizes thought patterns – more ruling-thoughts – and behavioral patterns – avoidance and compulsions – that, left to their own devices, make your life miserable.

You have been already making a shift toward practicing a new, helpful behavioral pattern: staying with your experience as it is, as it comes, and not as your mind tells you it is when dealing with resistant-obsessions.

Staying with your experience requires that you use the skill of riding the wave of the emotions that come with the obsessions by describing to yourself what you're feeling.

It looks like this: You take five deep and slow breaths, then describe to yourself what you're sensing in your body: "my heart is beating fast, my hands feel really sweaty." Then you follow that sensations in your body with curiosity.

Either toward or away from your values

You cannot change how you managed any OCD episode or how you behaved with yourself or others in the past, but you can change how you move forward and do your best to live your values in any step you take.

After watching your obsessions, inviting them in, and staying with your experience, you need to decide what to do next in these OCD-resistant moments – and that's where your values come into play as your constant compass, guiding your choice.

There are only two choices you can make at this point: moving toward or away from your values. You decide how you want to show up in that moment. And just to be clear, so you don't add any pressure on yourself and power through an exposure exercise, making a moving towards your values is much more powerful when choosing to experience with willingness what shows up when making that move.

It looks like this: you ask yourself any variation of the questions: what's important to me in this moment? What do I care about enough to face these obsessions?

What do I value enough that is worth this discomfort?

Make a choice

After asking yourself what matters when handling a pesky obsession, it's time for you to commit to a choice.

Committing to a choice is not about agreeing with a particular outcome; it's about committing to experience, sit with, and stay with what comes with that decision. You can commit to face something for as long as you are open to it and as close as you're willing to be to it. You're in charge, and nobody else!

It looks like this: you tell yourself "I fully commit to do _____" or "I choose to do _____ in this moment."

Observe what comes with the choice

With every choice you make, there is an experience that results from it.

If you decide to continue facing a particularly sticky situation, person, or place, continue practicing and repeating the skills of staying with the experience and making acceptance moves (e.g., describing to yourself what you're feeling or sensing when continuing approaching that situation).

If your urges to do a compulsion or run away from the sticky situation are over the roof, take a deep breath, acknowledge the push and pull you're having, and do your best to focus your attention on the activity that is in front of you.

Going back and forth describing what you're experiencing under your skin while continuing to approach and focus on what's in front of you may feel like a lot of work at the beginning, but it's how you strengthen a new way of handling your reactive brain, expand your life, and move toward your values.

Value your choice

Valuing your choice is really about appreciating your struggle, acknowledging your courage to face those triggering moments, and valuing your boldness to face your fears when doing an exposure.

It's human to make all types of choices in all types of directions in our life, including away moves at times.

It looks like this: giving yourself credit for making a choice in a triggering moment. For example, when you make a choice, you can give yourself a pat on the back right then or take note to celebrate later.

Engage with what's next in your life

As you recall from the chapters "Fall Out of Blind Love With Your Mind" and "Get Out of the Content of Your Mind," there is nothing wrong with staying in our heads at times. But how does it work if you do it all the time? How does it work when you're dealing with yucky obsessions and stay in your head calculating, planning, and fighting back?

After making a choice with your values-based exposure work, observing what comes with the choice, recycling the skills of staying with the experience, and riding the wave of uncomfortable feelings that come, then it's time for you to keep moving with your life.

It looks like this: asking yourself "What's the next thing I need to be doing right now?" and moving ahead with that activity.

Soften up with self-compassion

In the chapter "holding your mind lightly," you read about how our mind, as incredible as it is, at times can be a source of all kinds of criticisms, self-blame, and negative judgments. The reality is that it's already hard to have disturbing thoughts, but getting hooked on those criticizing thoughts makes it ultra harder.

After working so hard making a values-based exposure practice, it's possible that your mind may jump with thoughts like, "It's not enough. You could have done better. You should do more," and so on.

There are two ways to respond to these thoughts: putting into action all your skills to defuse from it and softening up in the moment with a caring response.

It looks like this:

- *Instead of buying into those thoughts or arguing against them, you can apply all the skills you have learned about watching your mind and do the same with this type of content. When the content-generator and pattern-making machine of your mind comes up with criticisms like "you're not good enough, you're stuck with OCD, you're not doing anything right," you can give a name to those negative self-judgments, e.g. MS. Critic; imagine what she looks like, say "here is Ms. Critic visiting me."*

– *Say to yourself, "gentle please, I just finished tough work facing my values" or "Ms. Critic, I know you care, thanks, but can't give you attention right now."*
– *Move along with what's next in your day.*

Here is a summary of the skills built in the acronym W.I.S.E. M.O.V.E.S.

Watch your obsessions
Invite your obsessions
Stay with your experience
Either toward or away from your values

Make a choice
Observe what comes with the choice
Value your choice
Engage with what's next
Soften up with self-compassion

If you need to revisit some of the skills, look to the Appendix section, where you'll find a list of chapters that are related to each skill.

What now? Grab a flashcard (or find your notes app), write down this acronym and what it means, carry it with you, and most important, start using it every time you decide to move forward with your Values-Guided Exposure Menu and encounter one of those resistant-obsessions.

Using your W.I.S.E. M.O.V.E.S. is not about having a rigid and strict sequences of steps but a quick reminder of all the skills you can use when doing values-based exposures related to OCD that show up in your day-to-day life.

Last clarifications before finishing this chapter:

– If you are working with a therapist, the process of completing exposure exercises will look different. While this workbook doesn't replace therapy, either way, you can still benefit from the skills in it, whether as a companion to your therapy or as a standalone.
– The exposure exercises from your Values-Guided Exposure Menu are usually more planned, organized, and longer (which is different than facing triggering moments on the go).
– You can make W.I.S.E. M.O.V.E.S. for every exposure practice you noted on your Values-Based Exposure Menu.
– You can make mini W.I.S.E. M.O.V.E.S. in the moment when encountering triggering situations, even if you haven't had a chance to do an organized exposure; you will read more about this in a later chapter.
– Your Values-Guided Exposure Menu is your road map to face OCD-resistant moments, and W.I.S.E. M.O.V.E.S. is what you do when facing those triggering moments.

Get Familiar With Different Types of Values-Guided Exposure Exercises

There are different types of exposure exercises to help you to face an OCD-related trigger: using situations, your imagination, and your body. Academically speaking, these different forms are known as situational, imaginal, and interoceptive exposure, respectively.

In this chapter you will learn about each one and how to connect them with your HOWs, so you can mix them up when working through your Values-Based Exposure Menu. Let's move on to them!

Practicing Values-Based Exposures in a Situation

This type of exposure, also called situational exposure, means *physically approaching an activity, situation, person, or object and getting in contact with all the discomfort that comes with it.*

In the chapter "Making W.I.S.E. M.O.V.E.S.," you learned that situational exposures are my favorite way to facilitate values-guided exposures, my go-to in my work, and where I stay a lot because in my heart, I'm just a passionate behavior therapist.

By now, you are aware that almost all exposures are situational, and you are already familiar with the nuts and bolts of how to make W.I.S.E. M.O.V.E.S. in a situation; so I'll continue with a different type of exposure practice.

Carrying Out Values-Based Exposures in Your Head

Another way to do exposure exercises is using your imagination – also known as imaginal exposures – based on a script you develop for that purposes.

You can practice values-guided imaginal exposure if one of the following situations is happening:

a. You are dealing with obsessions that you cannot approach in a values-based situational exposure (e.g., obsessions about stabbing your loved ones, contracting AIDS, exposing your private parts, molesting your child).

b. You have tried a values-guided situational exposure first, and even though you tried to adjust it, you're feeling terribly anxious, terrified, and fearful about that particular item.

c. You're still holding onto the obsession as the absolute truth, and you've stopped doing or are doing less of the stuff you care about (e.g., you still believe that you can acquire pancreatic cancer when having a stomach ache despite the doctors telling you that you're in good health).

In the chapter "Watching Your Mind," you already practiced different ways to visualize, say, and physicalize your obsessions, and some of those ways included writing words, poems, singing songs, and so on. Values-guided imaginal exposures are an extension of the skill of watching your mind.

Here are the key elements to writing a script for a values-based imaginal exposure:

1. Write the script in the present tense, as if it's happening right now.
2. Write the script in the first person, using "I" as a pronoun.
3. Write the script including as many details as possible that involve the five senses (e.g., describe what you see, hear, feel, sense, and smell).
4. Write the script describing your private experiences when having those obsessions (e.g., I feel . . ., my body will . . . I'm thinking . . .).
5. Write down the script including the worst-case scenario of getting hooked on your obsessions.
6. Do not include reassurance statements (e.g., everything was okay, I was fine; they were fine).
7. Don't worry about the length of the script; it doesn't matter. It's more important to have a script that has the elements described in points 1 through 6.

After writing your script, you can put into action a values-guided imaginal exposure in many ways. The traditional way is read it, record it, and listen to it.

You can set music to the script, sing it to the tune of your favorite song, or just read it plainly. You can pretend that you're a news reporter and say it as if you're delivering the news, a weather forecast, or an important alert. You can read it using a different tone of voice. And if you want more ideas, refer to the section "Saying Your Os." The ways to practice a values-guided imaginal exposure are endless, so don't be shy about getting creative. For instance, a client of mine wrote a script and said it aloud as if she were giving an inspirational speech at work for her staff.

In regard to reading or listening to a recording of your script, there is no research showing a difference whether you do it once or 30 times a day. Old models of imaginal exposure recommended doing it until your anxiety levels decreased; however, that's no longer consistent with current research on exposure work. So I encourage you to start with listening or reading your script at least once a day.

Here is a sample of a script for a values-guided imaginal exposure:

"After going to English class, I start coughing on and off. Hours later, after all my classes are over, I'm walking to the parking garage, and as I do so, I start coughing with blood. I'm scared, I don't know what's going on, I think I'm going to be sick indefinitely. I rush to my car, open the dusty door, and jump into my car. I throw my things in the back of the car, hold the wheel, drive with both hands, and feel how warm they are because my car has been exposed to the sun for a couple of hours. I start driving and continue coughing . . . I know I'm going to be sick for a long time, the doctors won't know what's happening with me, I'll discontinue my studies, and will be lying in bed, unable to move, looking pale, losing weight day by day . . . I'm anxious, petrified and I know it's coming . . . . I'll be sick for a long time."

Tiny steps matter, and if writing a whole narrative for an imaginal script is too much for you, start small. Every time you choose how to respond to those disturbing obsessions, you're getting closer to getting your life back on track and leaving behind old reactive behaviors.

Let's move onto another form of practicing values-guided exposures.

Implementing Values-Based Exposures With Your Body

Sometimes, the triggers or cues for an obsession are physical sensations – breathing, blinking, swallowing, not feeing full after eating, to name a few – that act as a barrier in a person's life, so an exposure focusing on these physical sensations is handy to expand your life. Exposures using your body are also called somatic or interoceptive ones.

In the past, most of the academic and clinical literature considered interoceptive or somatic exposures exclusive to panic disorder. But within ACT there is no reason for that limitation, since, as a therapy approach, ACT is more focused on processes or drivers of problematic behaviors than diagnostic categories. And also, it's a fact that clients struggling with OCD episodes get triggered with specific bodily sensations.

If you're dealing with obsessive thoughts because of a particular physical sensation, you have spent hours and hours monitoring your bodily reactions and doing all types of compulsions or reassurance-seeking behaviors, like calling doctors, searching for medical information online, comparing your bodily reactions from day to day, and dropping things in your life that you care about. If this describes you, then values-guided somatic exposures will help you to get unstuck from OCD episodes.

To practice values-guided exposure with your body, you need to identify the specific physical sensations that are related to your OCD episodes, and then do two things:

1. Think about regular physical activities that are part of your day-to-day life that may trigger some of those physical sensations (e.g., if your heart beating fast is a trigger for your fear of having a heart attack, one value-based exposure exercise could be going for a run for 30 minutes to trigger a faster heartbeat).

2. Practice interoceptive exercises that mimic or activate that particular physical sensation: holding your breath, swallowing fast, jumping up and down in the same place, breathing through a straw, staring into a mirror, drinking water really fast, running up and down the stairs, staring at a light, smelling strong odors, wearing a scarf around your neck a bit tight, shaking your head from side to another, stretching muscles for long periods of time so you experience a tingling sensation, or doing sit-ups with books on your stomach.

Now you're familiar with three different types of exposure exercises that you can mix up and add in your Values-Based Exposure Menu.

As I mentioned before, when working with my clients, I usually ask questions along the lines of, "When having this obsession, what do you do more or less of in your life? What would you like to start doing? Would you like to stop doing the things that get in the way of you being the person you want to be?" Because of my own biases, I focus more on values-guided exposures that physically get you in contact with a situation, person, object, or activity.

But you don't have to get hooked on my biases! Be curious about all types of planned exposures, see how they go for you, and do what moves you toward your values! Workability trumps biases!

Make the Best of Your Values-Guided Exposures

You need some tips before putting your Values-Guided Exposure Menu into action and starting to make your W.I.S.E. M.O.V.E.S.

Grab yourself a drink and a blanket and find a cozy place to read. Because this is the info you'll need to continue designing and living your life.

Let's begin.

Get Them Going: Choosing Where to Start Your Values-Guided Exposures

If you have read previous books on anxiety and OCD, most of the literature is based on habituation models (see chapter, "What About ACT and Exposure?" as a reference). In one way or another, most books usually teach readers to create an *exposure hierarchy*, ranking all items based on their fear level, start facing the item that has the lowest level of fear, and stay with that exposure exercise until the anxiety level reduces for that item, so a person is habituated to it. And the same procedure applies to all items on the exposure hierarchy.

But if we step back for a moment, there is something important to think about: our life doesn't come in hierarchies, fearful moments don't come in ladders, and our moments of struggles don't come in an organized manner. In fact, if you look at your daily life and how obsessions, distress, and worries show up, most likely you will find that they come in so many ways, in different situations, and with different intensities.

Also, research on exposure conducted by M. Craske et al. (2014) shows that you can do exposures in a random order and mix different ways of doing exposure practices; this approach is less time consuming at times, has fewer relapses, and has a strong impact on how you develop a new relationship with your mind and obsessions.

Here is my tip for you:

Start your values-guided exposure practice with a situation that truly matters to you, that you're committed to, and for which you're willing to face all the yucky discomfort that comes with it. If the exposure exercise gets too challenging and becomes unbearable, you can always adjust it by making some changes that you will learn in the next chapter. But before you start making adjustments, keep in mind that doing what matters and facing those resistant-obsessions is challenging and is going to be distressing – but that's not a reason to pull back all the way from your exposure practice. You might just need to do a little fine-tuning.

How difficult or easy or how much or little feared a particular situation is shouldn't be your criteria for choosing whether to approach it. Rather, *the deciding factor should be the importance of that particular situation, activity, or person in your life: That's your criteria.*

Once you start with one exposure practice, you can then move up or down on your Values-Guided Exposure Menu based on what's important to you, your willingness to face that situation, and whether you're open to getting out of your comfort zone in the service of your values.

Link Them Up: Practice a Values-Guided Exposure as a Move Toward Your Values

Doing an exposure exercise just because this workbook or your therapist or your loved ones say so is not good enough reason for you to face your fears. You do this work because it's in service of your values and the life you want to design for yourself and live.

Most of my clients have heard all types of "pushy messages" about doing exposures, and this workbook is not meant to add to those messages. Honestly, it's really up to you to make the decision to face resistant-obsessions.

In ACT, every values-guided exposure exercise you choose to do is about connecting it with the stuff that matters to you. As my good friend says, that's the beginning and that's the end. Exposure exercises in ACT are not about counting how many times you face your obsessions or power through them but to check how facing that particular situation, person, activity, or object gets you closer to being the person you want to be and showing up how you really want to show up in that moment.

Sometimes, when dealing with certain types of obsessions (e.g., aggressive, sexual, pedophile, harm), you may need to practice sitting with the discomfort that comes with those disturbing images as part of your values-guided exposure, but that doesn't mean you have to do something against your personal values. For example, if your obsession is about stabbing your children, it would be very inconsistent with HOW you want to show up as a mom to imagine stabbing them with a knife, right? Or if you're a religious person and your obsessive thought is about stabbing authority figures from your religious group, it wouldn't be consistent with your personal values to imagine stabbing those people, right? But using knives while cooking in the kitchen or chopping veggies while your children are running around would be a great values-guided exposure, right? Or carrying scissors in your bag when you're attending a religious service could be an exposure that is consistent with your values, right?

ACT doesn't approach exposure work by pushing you to the edge, and it doesn't deny, either, that exposure work comes with high affect; if you find value in practicing extreme forms of exposures in the service of your values, and if necessary, it makes total sense to practice them.

Mix Them Up: Combine Different Ways of Doing Values-Guided Exposures

In the next chapter you will learn in detail about three different ways of practicing values-guided exposures: using a situation, using your imagination, and using your body. In the meantime, you will read about how to combine them.

But before that, let me share my biased opinion as a passionate behaviorist: *Do your best to use situations to put into action your values-guided exposures!*

Here's why: When having an unwanted obsession – whether it's an annoying image, urge, or thought – an overreactive brain pushes to approach those triggering situations with either compulsive behaviors or avoidant behaviors. As you know, your brain relates everything with everything, creating a thinking pattern that connects not only the obsession with the upsetting situation but also with any other similar situation. Then your brain pushes you into a behavioral pattern to avoid and avoid again.

But every time you avoid a situation, person, or activity because of obsession, your life narrows and narrows.

Even if some obsessions (like fears of contracting AIDS, dying in a car accident, or becoming homeless) are imaginal by nature, you can still practice situational exposures. For example, reading about music figures dealing with AIDS, learning about symptoms of AIDS, shaking hands with someone who has AIDS, or visiting medical centers that do AIDS research are great situational exposures to lean toward the fears of contracting AIDS.

An effective and research-based way to get your life back and tackle all forms of behavioral avoidance is approaching all those situations that matter to you and making room for the distress that comes with them. That's why I'm biased about encouraging you do as many values-guided exposure practices using a situation as possible.

Vary Them Up: Practice Values-Guided Exposures in Different Contexts

When practicing values-guided exposures, you can vary them in many ways, like how long you stay in contact with the fearful situation (length), how physically close you are to that particular trigger (proximity), the times of day in which it happens, or locations in which you practice getting in contact with the obsession.

Let's think of Robyn for a moment. Robyn's mind comes up with intrusive thoughts about his relationships; he gets hooked on obsessions about his girlfriend cheating on him and becoming more attracted to other guys than to him. Robyn usually struggles when they have gatherings with other males that he finds handsome.

To handle his obsessions, Robyn Googles "signs of cheating," checks whether his girlfriend looks at other males, scrutinizes the way she talks to them, asks her how much she loves him, makes statements about how much he dislikes cheating in general, and at times asks hypothetically about how they would handle another person flirting with them.

When Robyn paused and looked at HOW he wants to show up in his romantic relationships, he recognized that he wants to show up as a "constant gardener," meaning that he wants to be fully present – instead of being consumed by his obsessions – and would like to create different memories with his girlfriend by taking trips, going to baseball games, cooking together, and other activities.

Applying the tip of *varying the context of values-guided exposures*, Robyn played with different variables, like inviting his girlfriend and a male friend to join him for a quick coffee for approximately 15 minutes before they went to work; inviting his girlfriend to dinner in a neighborhood he wasn't familiar with, where he wouldn't know if other males would be around; and asking his girlfriend to tell him about qualities of her crushes with male actors.

Robyn was mixing up the location, time, and people of his exposures. You can do the same.

Tune them up: Adjust Your Values-Exposure Activities as Needed

You have been encouraged to start your values-guided exposure practice by approaching a situation that is important to you. But if you have tried a particular exposure activity three to five times and are getting stuck, then it's time to tune it up.

Tuning up your exposure exercises is about making adjustments to better get in contact with the particular activities, situations, people, and objects.

Let's consider Pamela's challenges with obsessions about the possibility of harming her children by accident or because she isn't paying attention.

Pamela is so fused with this obsession that she compulsively washes her hands 15 times a day, changes her clothes if they touch common public objects or come in contact with a sick person, tracks what her kids are touching, scrutinizes a person to make sure they're not sick, and searches WebMD multiple times a day about potential signs of her kids getting sick.

When Pamela asked herself how she wanted to show up for her children, she identified "being present" as one of her values; in her Values-Guided Exposure Menu, she wrote as an exposure exercise the following activities: "spending 1 hour with my children in a park without asking them to wash their hands or changing their shoes."

Pamela was anxious and concerned and yet committed to go to the park with her kids. Once there, she quickly felt overwhelmed and had a hard time not scrutinizing how her kids were playing, who they were playing with, and all the stuff they were touching in the playground, and the idea of staying there for an hour was petrifying for her.

After trying this exposure practice three times and still not being able to pull it off, Pamela tuned it up. Instead of one hour, she decided to start with 15-minutes as a baseline and build her skills from there.

You can tune up your exposure exercises as Pamela did if that helps you to keep moving with facing your obsessions and expanding your life. Also, remember that you can move in any direction in your exposure menu; you don't have to practice them in any particular hierarchical order, necessarily.

Stay With Them: Watch Out for Subtle Compulsions and Avoidance When Practicing Values-Guided Exposures

When facing a triggering situation, activity, person, or object as part of your values-guided exposure, that's the moment to do your best to put into action your W.I.S.E. M.O.V.E.S.

For example, Jordana suffers with an obsessive thought of psychologically damaging her son Jacob when disciplining him. She genuinely attempts to discipline him when he screams back at her, calls her names, or throws things on the floor. But when buying into her obsession, Jordana avoids reprimanding him; asks her husband throughout the day to talk to Jacob or to get reassurance that she didn't hurt Jacob psychologically; calls her mom and friends to make sure it was appropriate of her to send Jacob for a time-out; asks for feedback from the different Facebook parents groups she's part of; or replays for hours and hours how she talked to Jacob.

One of Jordana's parenting values is teaching Jacob accountability for his behaviors, and as part of her moves toward that value, she's committed to asking Jacob to pick up his toys after playing without asking her husband for reassurance, without apologizing to Jacob if she hurt his feelings, and without rushing through this exercise or powering through it.

Jordana decided she would practice her exposure exercise on Wednesday after picking up Jacob from school, having lunch, and giving him his hour break to play. Jordana was a bit worried about this exposure because it was the first time that she was going to try to not engage on compulsions or avoid giving Jacob a direction. When the time came, Jordana asked him to pick up his toys so they could do homework. Jacob quickly said to Jordana that he didn't want to do so, he hated her, and he just wanted to be with Grandma in the afternoon.

Instead of getting hooked on "Jordana the terrible," Jordana pressed her foot on the floor, took a deep breath, and told Jason that he had 10 minutes to pick up the toys or he would be in time-out for 15 minutes. While Jason keep looking at her and screaming, Jordana didn't minimize her reactions and used her acceptance moves by saying to herself, "I don't like this feeling, but I will do nothing, it's going to pass on its own." Then she took another deep breath and described to herself her feelings: "I'm having a strong urge to text my husband, and my armpits are getting sweaty." Jordana continued going back and forth between describing her internal experience and watching Jacob. After 10 minutes of Jacob not picking up the toys, Jordan took another deep breath and told him that he needed to go to his room for 15 minutes for time-out because he didn't pick up the toys. Then she continued to practice acceptance moves and riding the wave of her reactions.

Jordana didn't use any safety behaviors or compulsions during her exposure practice. However, she could have easily started telling herself that she's a good mom, that good moms discipline children, that Jacob is not going to be psychologically damaged, and so on. While those comments seem benign, they take Jordana away from sitting with the internal discomfort she has when giving a direction to Jacob and him getting upset, perpetuating a cycle of obsessions and a chain of compulsions in the long-term.

When completing your exposure practices, watch out for anything you do with the purpose of making yourself "feel better," because that could be a compulsion and is taking away from getting in contact with the yucky stuff that comes when facing your obsessions.

And just to clarify, switching the focus of your attention between the activity, situation, person, or object that is part of your exposure practice and your internal experience when inviting your obsessions – riding the wave of feelings that comes along, defusing from your obsessions, or making acceptance moves – is not avoidance but a choice to flexibly pay attention to an aversive experience.

Be Curious About Them: Watch What Shows Up When Making W.I.S.E. M.O.V.E.S.

Being curious is not a technical principle but a matter of attitude and approach. It's the stance that will help you to overcome OCD episodes.

The attitude of curiosity I'm referring to is not the cold and disconnected one (like the immigration officer asking me for my passport when I come back to the States) but the one that doesn't get attached to any particular outcome. This curiosity is interested in what shows up, how it shows up, and how often it shows up.

Getting hooked on the thought of doing values-guided exposures to feel better or have less obsessions or practicing exposure exercises in a mechanical manner without pausing and learning from them is the antidote of curiosity.

So keep your eyes open when practicing your exposures and watch out for holding onto any particular result!

Following these tips to practice your values-guided exposures – and approaching fearful objects, situations, people, and objects – will help you to maximize the steps you're making, the effort you're putting into it, and the courage you're taking to build the full and meaningful life you deserve!

Next you will learn about different types of values-guided exposures using your imagination, a situation, and your body.

Settings for Making
W.I.S.E. M.O.V.E.S.

Avoiding situations, people, object, and activities	ON	(OFF)
Being curious with them	(ON)	OFF
Choosing one to start	(ON)	OFF
Doing compulsions	ON	(OFF)
Holding onto ruling-thoughts	ON	(OFF)
Linking them to your why	(ON)	OFF
Mixing them up	(ON)	OFF
Staying present with them	(ON)	OFF
Varying them up	(ON)	OFF
Tuning them up	(ON)	OFF

Figure 36.1 Settings.

37

Read About What You May Feel When Making W.I.S.E. M.O.V.E.S.

You have done a lot so far: You've put together your Values-Guided Exposure Menu to face those OCD-resistant episodes. You've learned about W.I.S.E. M.O.V.E.S. as a reminder of all the ACT skills you can do during an exposure exercise. You've also learned about different types of planned exposures: situational, imaginal, and interoceptive. And you've familiarized yourself with tips for facing those disturbing and resistant-obsessions.

Now moving along, you, like my clients, probably have some questions before you get started. Here are some of the questions I hear from my clients: how will I feel when doing values-guided exposures? Will it be too uncomfortable? How anxious am I going to be? Will my obsessions get better or worse?

I'm going to answer these and more right now. Take my responses for what they are, and keep in mind that there are no rules or predictions about what your internal experience will be.

Would My Anxious Feelings Change?

All the feelings of anxiety, fear, discomfort, and distress that come with obsessions may go up, down, left, or right and up and down, left or right again. This is very natural – you're not losing your mind. When making W.I.S.E. M.O.V.E.S., as it happens every time we do anything we care about – from cooking our favorite recipe to raising our kids, and from applying for our dream job to going on a date – our emotions move in all directions.

As uncomfortable, annoying, and overwhelming as all those feelings that come along in your W.I.S.E. M.O.V.E.S. are, you, I, and everyone around us don't have control of what we feel, think, or sense. Our minds, bodies, and emotions have a life of their own. We don't have a switch to turn our feelings on and off, but we do have the power to choose how to respond to them.

Tips: Using *acceptance prompts* and *riding the wave of feelings that show up to stay with your experience* are helpful skills in those moments.

Will I Have Fewer Obsessions When I Practice Values-Guided Exposures?

When making W.I.S.E. M.O.V.E.S., your brain, as the content-generating and pattern-making machine it is, may come up with more and more obsessions in the moment. As annoying as they are, those obsessions are not different than any other one you had before. The amount of obsessions may be different when you're intentionally practicing a planned, long, and organized values-based move than when walking in the street and one of those obsessions pops up, but obsessions don't require a customized treatment. An obsession is an obsession, whether it's an obsession about harming others, getting an illness, not being honest, or any other. We respond to any of them using visualizations, saying them, or physicalizing them so you can separate, detach, and disconnect from them.

Tip: Remember the skills of *watching your obsessions* and *inviting your obsessions* from the W.I.S.E. M.O.V.E.S acronym.

What if My Urge Is Too Strong?

When our brain perceives any form of threat – even when the seeming threat is just a thought – it mobilizes all our internal forces to either fight, flight, or freeze. When making W.I.S.E. M.O.V.E.S., our brain will naturally return to old behaviors and demand you fight back that obsession with avoidance and compulsive behaviors. It's not your fault; the brain is doing what it's supposed to be doing: protecting you the best it can, as it did in the past.

Making a shift from acting on those reactive moves, developing a new relationship with your brain, overcoming OCD episodes, and getting going with your life, requires that you willingly stay with your experience when practicing W.I.S.E. M.O.V.E.S.

Tip: Remember to acknowledge that internal struggle, take a deep breath, and focus on five things you see. Describe what you feel in your body. Next, describe four things you hear, and go back to describe what you're sensing in your body. Then count three things you smell, and notice bodily sensations. Then notice two things you can touch, and notice bodily sensations. Finally, describe one thing you can taste in your mouth, along with what you're feeling, sensing, and so on.

What if I Cause Harm to Others When Making W.I.S.E. M.O.V.E.S?

If you have been historically hooked on any of the ruling-thoughts from Chapter 11, "Do You Know Your Ruling-Thoughts?" – especially thoughts such as "Not doing anything about it is the same as causing it," "I need to know, for real," "My obsessions are so real that I know they're real" – then it's likely that they will show up in the middle of making W.I.S.E. M.O.V.E.S.

If you find yourself buying into these not-so-helpful thoughts, believing them as the absolute truth, remember this tip.

> Tip: Press your feet firmly against the floor, as if you have become a redwood tree. Take a deep breath, give a name to those ruling-thoughts (e.g., Mr. Knowing, Ms. Overprotective is here), and, as you have been doing with obsessions, defuse from them. For example, you can visualize them as leaves falling down from a tree or banners on taxi cabs. Say them in a voice that mimics your favorite actress, or make a gesture with your hand about having the thought (versus the thought having you).

What if I Feel Guilty, Regretful, or Remorseful When Doing an Exposure?

If you've been getting fused with aggressive obsessions, sexual obsessions, or harm obsessions, you may experience guilt and even shame when making W.I.S.E. M.O.V.E.S. If that's the case, it may be happening because you're still taking the obsessions literally rather than taking the content of your mind lightly. You may be still hooked on the ruling-thought "because I think so, it makes me so."

Most people confuse the feelings of guilt and shame, so here is a key distinction: *guilt* is an uncomfortable emotion about a particular behavior, such as spilling coffee in a book (as I just did). *Shame* is a distressing feeling you have about yourself as a person – not just in reference to a behavior – as if something is fundamentally wrong with you. When feeling shame, your mind may come up with any variation of the narratives: "I'm not good enough," "something is off with me," "I'm weird," "I'm very bad," and others.

For instance, Charlie used to buy into sexual obsessions about children. So as part of her values-guided exposure, she decided to spend time with her sister's daughter, since being connected with relatives was her value. When Charlie took her niece to the park, she felt a wave of fear and then a slight sense of guilt, as if by putting into action her values-guided exposure exercises, she was harming her niece.

It's tough to be in your shoes when these feelings do their best to crush, squeeze, and take you away from making W.I.S.E. M.O.V.E.S. But practicing over and over to hold those feelings, as with any other emotion, big or small, without running away from them is a core skill that will liberate you from being the prisoner of obsessions.

> Tip: If guilt or any other overwhelming feeling comes in the middle of making W.I.S.E. M.O.V.E.S., do your best to notice it, describe to yourself how it feels in your body, don't fight it, don't argue against it, just make room for it, take a deep breath, and still move forward with your exposures exercise.

When making courageous moves to live the life you want to live with your mouth, hands, and feet, all types of internal blocks may show up: more obsessions, overwhelming feelings, doubts, strong impulses to drop everything. But if you face all those internal experiences with willingness – like the sand on the beach allows the waves of the ocean to come and go without trying control them – *YOU* win!

Remove Your Compulsions From the Equation

In many parts of this workbook you learned how to step back, develop a new relationship with the content-generating and pattern-making machine of your mind, watch your obsessions, and disconnect from them as much as you can. These skills were foundational in learning how to make W.I.S.E. M.O.V.E.S. for taming resistant-obsessions. So far, so good, right? But as important as it is to make room for obsessions, it's also important to get a grip on all those compulsive behaviors that feed into OCD episodes, make your life miserable, and take you in the opposite direction of being the person you want to be.

To start, go back to the *inventory of compulsions* you completed in the chapter "What Are the Compulsions You're Doing?" and check if anything changed with those compulsive behaviors; if so, just update your inventory.

For some of my clients, compulsions are sometimes hard to spot, especially mental compulsions, because they look like any other regular behavior or thinking strategy. But it's what you do in response that makes a huge difference in building a life worth living.

Compulsions, public and private, are everything you do to neutralize those disturbing obsessions, no exemptions. For instance, searching online about a potential illness because you want to learn, you're curious, you're eager to understand more, is very different than feeling as if you cannot move forward with your day, you cannot let go of the possibility of contracting a particular illness, or you will be crushed by not knowing – unless you check online. *So again, the reason, purpose, and intention of your behaviors are key to differentiating a compulsion from helpful ways of thinking and of handling worries.*

Here is another scenario: if you have thoughts like "did I touch this? Would I get sick? And those thoughts come with a sense of urgency, sticky quality, and push you to do something about it, quite likely those are obsessions. If you spend hours thinking about it, tracing in your mind what you touched and how you touched those objects, as natural as those thinking strategies may seem, it's possible you're trying to figure things out/ruminating as a mental compulsion. So, here is the tip: the first doubtful thought – obsession – on the house, what you do after that, that's a compulsion.

Let's do an exercise. In Table 38.1, write down the 10 most upsetting compulsions you have that you're also willing to work on.

Now, read these basic principles to tackle those compulsions:

1. **Make a commitment to yourself to not do the compulsion.**

   This may sound a bit simplistic, but let's step back for a bit. Have you ever been in a triggering situation in which someone told you how to respond to it? Did people advise you to let your anxiety pass at times? Did they tell you not to worry or to stop being afraid? Did you listen to all those recommendations? Maybe at times you did, and other times you didn't.

   The fact is, being told what to do is very different than making a choice or decision on your own. I'm inviting you to make a commitment to choose how you want to handle all the different situations that come up.

   Not giving in to compulsions is not a decision that any person can make for you; it's really up to you to make that personal commitment with yourself to work on those compulsive behaviors and show up for yourself, others, and what you care about.

Exercise 38.1 Inventory of 10 compulsions you're willing to work on

Think back on this past week and jot down 10 compulsive behaviors that take you away from living your best life.	How does this compulsion affect your day-to-day life?	How willing and committed are you to work on this compulsion from 1 to 10 (1 = low & 10 = high)?

2. **When having the urge to do a compulsion, whether it's a tiny one or big one, public or private, turn up your skills.**

   As you've read over and over, the more you try to ignore, suppress, or answer your obsessions with any form of mental compulsion or behavioral reaction, the more time you spend in your head and the less time you spend living your life. It's not easy to handle those disturbing thoughts, and yet learning to watch them, distancing yourself from them, riding the emotions that come along with them – including urges – and practicing acceptance moves will give you the freedom you're looking for.

   It's the constant fighting, resistance, and pushing to control that adds more suffering when it's already hard to deal with obsessions. Think about this for a moment: what would you like your tombstone to say? Here lies Patricia, she was very busy fighting obsessions with hundreds of compulsions and avoidant behaviors? Or here lies Patricia, she was very busy loving, learning, and creating? Which tombstone would you choose?

   So, acknowledge you're having an urge to do a compulsion, describe what you're sensing in your body and check with yourself, what's the thing you can do that will take you closer to your values? As with any distressing urge or overwhelming emotion, you can connect with your body – press your fingers together, press your legs against the floor – and then use your senses to connect with what's happening around you – e.g., Use your eyes to describe what your see, use your lungs to inhale and exhale, use your neck your move your head around. Connecting and reconnecting with your body are handy skills to handle distressing feelings without making things worst.

   If you need a refresher of these skills, read Chapter 26, riding the wave of fear, anxiety, and overwhelming emotions.

3. **Use your Inventory of Compulsions as your guide to tackle compulsive behaviors**

   Check your Inventory of Compulsions, choose one compulsion to work on that affects your life, make a commitment with yourself to stop it, and do your best to use your skills when facing the urge to do the compulsion.

If you find yourself struggling with dropping any compulsions cold turkey, that's understandable. The primary focus of ACT is not to eliminate your compulsions to perfection but to get you back into your life. So, start small; if it's hard to resist those compulsions, start small. Start 1 minute, 2 minutes, 3 minutes, and so on. As long as you choose how to respond to that moment of stuckness, that's what matters.

Here are other options for you to continue working on those compulsions:

1. **Mess with it**

   Tammy had a fear of contamination and used to take a shower every night after dinner for 45 minutes to complete her routine. As a way to get her life back on track, she decided to mess with her compulsion by taking a shower sometimes in the morning and sometimes at the gym.

2. **Shorten it**

   Jacob was caught on an obsession about not following religious rituals and celebrations properly. As result, he compulsively prayed for more than six hours a day.

   To handle this compulsive behavior, he made the personal commitment to shorten it. So, instead of praying for six hours, he would pray five hours for one week, then for four hours the next week, and so on until he prayed for two hours a day, as he was doing before having OCD episodes.

3. **Delay it**

Nicole got fused with the obsession of losing her memory. She often went home and told her partner, Marina, everything that happened during the day as a way of reassuring herself that she was recalling all events correctly and to prove to herself that she wasn't losing her memory. This compulsion affected her relationship – it made it hard to be present with Marina and just enjoy her company.

Marina often got upset about listening to all the nitty-gritty details of Nicole's day and being asked about whether Nicole sounded okay and coherent, or if she noticed that Nicole skipped something or forgot a part of her narrative.

When Nicole asked herself HOW she wanted to be in her relationship with Marina, she realized that it was important for her to be fully present and engaging with her.

As part of her commitment to get her life back on track, Nicole decided that she would delay sharing her day with Marina for 30 minutes, because she knew that she wasn't just sharing her day but compulsively reassuring herself.

Nicole wanted to stop doing this compulsion completely and have regular conversations with Marina without getting hooked on the fear of not recalling everything or searching for signs of memory loss. But given that this was one of her most stubborn obsessions, she preferred to start tackling it little by little by delaying it.

4. **Make it hard to do it**

Let's think of Holly for a moment: she was anxious about mixing positive experiences with negative ones. For example, when unlucky numbers were generated on a digital clock, she would stop talking about trips, upcoming events, or family projects.

To make it harder to do this compulsion, Holly changed some of clocks in her house from digital to analog.

What could you do differently that would make it harder for you to go into compulsion land?

You can start taming those compulsive behaviors exactly where you are. If you're up for it, you can drop a compulsive behavior all at once or just parts of it by modifying it, delaying it, shortening it, or making it difficult to do it.

You can even schedule in your calendar the compulsion you decide to work on toward making your life more meaningful.

Radomsky et al. (2014), a researcher who has been studying OCD, and safety behaviors in particular, for more than 15 years, stated that

traditionally, psychologists thought that fading out or eliminating these behaviors entirely should be the primary focus of the therapy used to combat anxiety disorders. But we found that changing those behaviors and giving patients greater agency is much more effective.

Along those lines, within ACT, every action you take to tackle compulsions is about you being the owner of the decisions you make, especially about when and how to get back into your life.

Track Your Planned W.I.S.E. M.O.V.E.S.

Congratulations! You made it to the last chapter of this section.

This a short chapter with a super-important recommendation for you: keep track of your W.I.S.E. M.O.V.E.S. and the compulsions you're working on.

Make an extra effort to keep track of your progress, challenges, and victories as they happen – and make this log as visible as possible. If you can, save old versions of logs so that you can go back to it when needed and remind yourself of all the work you put into your life!

Teresa Amabile, a Harvard researcher, was very interested in what keeps people motivated at work, and her studies demonstrated that, contrary to popular beliefs, money, incentives, or material rewards don't maintain people's engagement; it was actually doing meaningful work and keeping track of that work that keep them going!

Given the amount of information we're exposed to on a daily basis – the number of emails we receive, texts we get, errands we need to run, movies we want to watch, work-related tasks we have to complete, and special moments we want to create with the people we love – it's easy to forget and even dismiss the importance of making values-based moves.

Use this calendar every week to plan three different values-guided exposures based on your Values-Guided Exposure Menu. Of course, you can plan more than that, up to you!

Exercise 39.1 W.I.S.E. M.O.V.E.S. weekly log

What are the values-guide exposure exercises am I willing to do this week that will make a difference in my life and will take me closer to HOW I want to be?	Mon	Tues	Wed	Thurs	Fri	Sat	Sun
What are the compulsions you are working on? 1. 2.							
How are you going to practice softening up with self-compassion this week? 1. 2.							

Takeaways to share

Figure 39.1 People chatting.

This is perhaps the longest part in this workbook, so you deserve a big pat on your back! Here are the takeaway points from this section:

- In ACT, all exposure exercises are practiced with the purpose of supporting you to create, design, and live a rich, meaningful, and fulfilling life every day! Every fearful situation you choose to face is in the service of your values!
- Your Values-Guided Exposure Menu is not a document carved in stone but a flexible roadmap that you can adjust, change, and modify as you face those resistant-obsessions and continuing living the life you want to live.
- The principles for practicing values-guided exposures are: (a) start with an activity that matters to you, (b) link every exposure exercise to your values, (c) mix the different types of exposures, (d) vary the situations in which you practice them, (e) make any adjustments you need to keep practicing them, (f) approach them with willingness, stay present with every exposure exercise, and (g) be curious with all the stuff that shows up when putting them into action.
- There are different types of planned values-guided exposures you can do: in a situation, using your imagination, and in your body; those exposures are academically called situational, imaginal, and interoceptive exposure, respectively.
- Remember to use the acronym W.I.S.E. M.O.V.E.S. when approaching any values-guided exposure exercise:

  • Watch your obsessions
  • Invite your obsessions
  • Stay with your experience
  • Either towards or away from your values
  • Make a choice

- Observe what comes with the choice
- Value your choice
- Engage with what's next
- Soften up with self-compassion

– You can start tackling compulsive behaviors by first making a personal commitment with yourself to do so; and second by *turning up your defusion skills, riding the wave of overwhelming emotions, and using acceptance moves as needed.*

– There is no right or wrong way to target compulsions; you can start by giving your best to stop doing them, cold turkey and all the way; if it's too challenging, you can shorten them, mess with the order of then, delay them, or even make it hard to do them. I encourage you to focus more on your willingness to choose how to handle the urges to engage in compulsion behaviors rather than stressing out about how perfect you're tackling them!

– When making W.I.S.E. M.O.V.E.S., it is natural that you may experience all types of shifts, because that's just what happens when doing the stuff that we care about. You may feel a shift in your emotions; your content- and pattern-making machine may come up with more obsessions; you may have more urges to do something about the obsession-problem; you may feel guilty, regretful, and even shameful; or you may have stronger urges to make sure that you're not causing harm to yourself or others. As annoying as all that sounds, always remember that our brains are shapeable, coachable, and adaptable. Change is possible!

– Keeping track of all the meaningful work you're doing when making W.I.S.E. M.O.V.E.S. and tackling compulsive behaviors, keeps you going!

Life Tracker

Reflect on how you have been living your life and mark an "X" where it corresponds.

Having obsessions as thoughts your mind comes up with	Seeing obsessions as problems to be solved
Approaching life as it is	Avoiding life because of obsessions
Taking action toward what you care about	Organizing your life around obsessions
Holding your thoughts lightly	Going 100% along with what your mind tells you
Checking what really works in your life	Doing stuff in automatic pilot mode
Making room for uncomfortable internal experiences	Pushing them down as much as possible

PART IX

Unpacking Blocks for Making W.I.S.E. M.O.V.E.S.

Since the moment I thought about writing this workbook and tackling this project, I was fully committed to doing my best to write a useful book that made ACT skills accessible and uncomplicated to readers so you can get the most of learning and applying them when dealing with obsessions and moving forward with your life.

So, I put together an eight-question survey and bothered every person I could within the OCD community to share it with their group. The survey included questions about the obstacles that people encounter before, during, and after practicing ERP. Based on the responses received, I did my best to organize the responses into themes and write chapters that addressed them. This part of the book is the result of that effort, and I hope you find it helpful!

To start, Chapter 40, "I Can't Do It: Reason-Giving Thoughts" addresses general blocks that make it hard for anyone to practice W.I.S.E. M.O.V.E.S. The chapters that follow it address more specific blocks that may show up in the form of values conflict, holding onto wishful goals (about what a values-guided exposure is about, obsessions going away, not feeling uncomfortable, or compulsively doing exposures), and lack of values clarity.

I strongly recommend that you read all chapters, even if you haven't encountered that particular block. And if you get stuck with your W.I.S.E. M.O.V.E.S, then you know what to do.

We live life by doing, not by talking about doing, so let's keep you moving!

40

I Can't Do It
Reason-Giving Thoughts

Has a friend ever invited you to go out to watch a movie, you enthusiastically said yes, and when the day of arrived, you changed your mind, just didn't want to go, and canceled on your friend?

When was the last time that you really wanted to go to a party, prepared for it months in advance, got your outfit, dreamed about how your hair would look like, but on the week of the party you got cold feet, started getting anxious about it, and decided to not go?

If similar situations happen from time to time, it's totally understandable that for one reason or another one we change our mind. But if these cancellations happen often, repetitively, or chronically, that's a different story. Those last-minute cancellations sooner or later affect who you want to be and how you want to show up for others. Do you agree with me on this?

Has it happened to you that, when getting ready to make W.I.S.E. M.O.V.E.S., your mind comes up with thoughts along the lines of, "It will be too much; I won't be able to handle it; It will be a disaster; how do I know it's going to work? Do I really have to do it?" And next thing you know, you're in a battle with those thoughts, sometimes trying to prove them wrong, other times giving up and going along.

It makes perfect sense that you may feel concerned and afraid of making W.I.S.E. M.O.V.E.S. because they do involve facing all those obsessions you are hooked on and take too seriously. It's not your fault; you're human. And seriously, this is what shows up when making bold moves toward your values.

Who wouldn't get hooked on those thoughts when having a reactive brain creating massive amounts of all types of content and screaming at almost everything that may look dangerous? It makes sense that, at times, approaching those stubborn obsessions is going to be ultra-hard. Naturally, your protective brain will give you reasons for not doing what you really want to do.

The problem is that every step you take in a valued direction comes with the potential of triggering obsessions and feelings of fear, anxiety, panic, and other unwanted emotions. It's like two sides of a coin: on one side you have the stuff you care about, and on the other you have the yucky stuff that comes with the obsession. But once you start walking down your values path and taking steps and of all sizes, you will notice the difference. And as I said before, once you experience how it feels to live your values and be the person you want to be, it's really hard to miss other ways of living life.

If you got stuck and couldn't keep going with your values-guided exposures, what got in your way? Jot down your responses in Table 40.1.

If you're not clear about what those blocks are, you can do two things:

1. Go back to your Values-Guided Exposure Menu and choose an activity, situation, people, or object to face. Then do your best to face it and see what comes up for you that makes it hard to go ahead with that particular exposure exercise. Those are your blocks!
2. You can complete the following worksheet for a week and see what comes up for you when thinking about your W.I.S.E. M.O.V.E.S.

After doing either option, you will be able to identify those internal barriers and see some patterns emerging; better to catch them now than later. For instance, when Alex spent one week noticing what was getting in the way of his doing values-based exposures, he realized that his reactive brain came up with thoughts like, "I'm exhausted; I'm burned out from dealing with OCD; I'm scared that I won't be able to handle to face my fears; what if things get worse when thinking about those awful images that I hate so much?"

Your turn.

Exercise 40.1 What gets in the way of your making W.I.S.E. M.O.V.E.S.?

What's a recent values-based activity you wanted to work on?	What gets in the way of your making W.I.S.E. M.O.V.E.S.? Is it a particular thought? What kind? Do you feel emotionally overwhelmed? Reflect on what's getting in your way of making W.I.S.E. M.O.V.E.S. and list them here.

What type of reasons did you come up with?

All those reasons that get in your way of making W.I.S.E. M.O.V.E.S. and living an intentional life are called *reason-giving thoughts* in ACT. And our minds are quite talented at coming up with hundreds of them – because that's what a content-generating machine does.

Now let's take a look at the impact and workability of those reason-giving thoughts in living your HOWs.

Exercise 40.2 Checking the workability of holding onto reason-giving thoughts

When thinking about W.I.S.E. M.O.V.E.S, my mind comes up with reason-giving thoughts like . . . (jot down those reason-giving thoughts)

When I take those reason-giving thoughts as the absolute truth, I take the following actions . . .

When I take that action, the short-term results are . . .

In the long-term, the outcome is . . .

Am I getting closer to or farther away from my HOWs?

If we pay close attention to our mind, we will notice that it's always trying to convince us to do something, to act, even if the action is taking a nap. And sometimes our mind tries its best to convince us to stop pursuing what we care about – not because it's against us, or our enemy, but because most of the time, is simply guarding us from anything that could go wrong. Think of your mind as a not-so-talented detective, a better-safe-than-sorry system that gets quickly activated, or as a prehistorical friend that didn't get the memo that the times have changed.

As you already know, our mind is just an unreliable source, because by nature it generates thousands of thoughts, letters, images, and words – it's impossible that all of them are true, accurate, or helpful.

Let's do two mini-exercises to see once again how our mind works dealing with accuracy:

1. For a moment, think to yourself, "I cannot lift my right arm," and as you hold onto that thought, extend your right arm above your body as if you're touching the sky, and hold it there for a couple of moments.
2. Tell yourself, "I can't swallow," and as you do so, swallow slowly and then fast.

How was it? What did you notice when having a thought and then taking a totally different action?

As simple and silly as this exercise looks like on the surface, it does show you that thoughts, even the most sophisticated reason-giving thoughts, don't have to control, lead, or monitor what you do, how you do it, and when you do it.

Reason-giving thoughts are no different from any other type of thinking the mind does, and it certainly doesn't have any magical powers. It's only our behavior, our public and private actions, that give them power and make them the governor of our life.

Given that our very protective content generator doesn't ever stop and goes on and on, and on and on again, we need to get better and better at deciding what to listen to and what to dismiss.

Getting out of OCD episodes and moving toward designing the life you want to live is not easy, and it's also not a straightforward path. And yet what's the alternative? Think for a moment of Dian Fossey, a primatologist and conservationist famous for her work with gorillas.

She was very clear that she wanted to show up as a person protecting animal life, and that's what she did. Fossey dedicated her career to protect gorillas in Rwanda from collectors of animal parts at a time when there was so much corruption between the government, the collectors, and the community. She never stopped doing so despite receiving more profitable job offers; she died living her values.

I share this story not to tell you that you have to live your life like Dian Fossey or that you should die for a cause; you don't need to be super-human, a superhero, or a super-guru, but doing what you care about comes with a large range of difficult circumstances, uncomfortable internal states, and challenging moments that are just unavoidable.

Now check for yourself: what's the price you pay by not making your W.I.S.E. M.O.V.E.S.? What does it cost you in your life?

Exercise 40.3 Confronting the costs of not making W.I.S.E. M.O.V.E.S.

What's the cost to my relationships in 1, 5, and 10 years if I don't make W.I.S.E. M.O.V.E.S?	What am I missing in my family life in 1, 5, and 10 years if I don't make W.I.S.E. M.O.V.E.S?	How would it look at work in 1, 5, and 10 years If I don't make W.I.S.E. M.O.V.E.S?
What's the cost to my health in 1, 5, and 10 years if I don't make W.I.S.E. M.O.V.E.S?	What's the cost to my recreational life in 1, 5, and 10 years if I don't make W.I.S.E. M.O.V.E.S?	What's the cost in my relationship with myself in 1, 5, and 10 years if I don't make W.I.S.E. M.O.V.E.S?

Take a couple of moments to reflect on your responses. And please know that I totally get it – it's not easy to be in your shoes, carrying a reactive brain hour after hour. But as hard as it sounds, every time you make moves toward what you care about, even a tiny step, you're getting closer and closer.

Moving forward, and to get your life back, think about two things: (1) what adjustments, changes, or fine tunings you need to make to your W.I.S.E. M.O.V.E.S., and (2) what skills you could use in those moments so you can approach that exposure exercise in which you encountered a block.

Let's go back to Alex. He decided to do his values-based exposures in the middle of the day, during lunchtime, because he noticed he wasn't very tired then. He also decided to call all those reason-giving thoughts, "Harry the Traitor." Alex realized that when buying into any variation of those thoughts, he was betraying himself, so when approaching making W.I.S.E. M.O.V.E.S., Alex imagined Harry the Traitor as an old king, touching his beard and speaking Old English, so that whatever he was saying didn't make sense when he was trying to boss Alex around.

Table 40.4 is a tool you can use to help guide you in troubleshooting these blocks:

Exercise 40.4 Troubleshooting blocks to start making W.I.S.E. M.O.V.E.S.

Which W.I.S.E. M.O.V.E.S. do I really want to do?
Jot down specifically what you want to be doing, including the day, time, length, etc.

These W.I.S.E. M.O.V.E.S. matter to me because . . . (answer the question, "What's the value that matters to me when facing W.I.S.E. M.O.V.E.S.?").

And, when making W.I.S.E. M.O.V.E.S., I'm willing to have these thoughts, sensations, emotions, and urges . . .

And when my mind butts in with reason-giving thoughts, I'm going to watch them as . . .
When making my W.I.S.E. M.O.V.E.S., I'm going to remember that . . .

This W.I.S.E. M.O.V.E. matters to me because . . . (try to answer the question, "What's the value that matters to you when facing that W.I.S.E. M.O.V.E.?").

Practicing W.I.S.E. M.O.V.E.S. is doable, possible, and feasible, but it sure isn't easy.

But if you ask me, when was making impactful and meaningful changes ever easy? If you look at your life or the lives of the people around you, do you ever experience any meaningful change happening easily and without effort? Getting a degree, caring for a friendship, living your faith, raising children, and any important changes in your life will always have some degree of difficulty.

W.I.S.E. M.O.V.E.S., like any new skill to regain your life, can be difficult to begin with, but with practice, commitment, and constancy, they do get manageable.

I Would Rather Be Safe

Values-Conflict or Fake-Value?

Felix is hooked on the obsession of feeling dirty; because of it, he avoids using credit cards, writing utensils from a public area, public restrooms, shared keyboards, and doorknobs. He usually wears long-sleeved sweaters so he can pull the sleeves down to hold any of those items when necessary. Felix doesn't like his OCD episodes because they've started affecting his relationship with his girlfriend: he now brushes his teeth immediately after kissing his girlfriend, asks her to take a shower before having sex, inspects the sheets on the bed, and changes his towel every day.

Felix loves his girlfriend and wants to commit to her and be a solid companion. So he put together his Values-Guided Exposure Menu. When he started to work on it, one of the items he chose to practice was "kissing his girlfriend for 2 minutes without brushing his teeth afterward." Felix did his best, but when the moment came after kissing his girlfriend, he felt a wave of fear come over his body and watched his thoughts about feeling dirty; he named those thoughts as "Here it comes, Felix, the cleaner." Felix even recalled the step of moving either away or toward his values, and he really wanted to choose a move toward his values in his relationship, but another thought popped up in his mind: "I won't be safe. I know it's an obsession, and yet, I'd rather be safe and not feeling dirty." Felix quickly went to the bathroom to brush his teeth.

The struggle that Felix experiences is the similar to the one faced by some of my clients: Felix was holding with white knuckles onto what appeared to be the value of "being safe and protected" versus the value of "being a solid companion" for his girlfriend.

Let's go over this matter in detail.

What's the conflict you have when making W.I.S.E. M.O.V.E.S. that could be related to your personal values?

_____

_____

_____

_____

_____

_____

Now let's consider Rebecca, who was committed to overcoming OCD and being an independent person. She practiced a bunch of defusion exercises and acceptance moves, put together her Values-Guided Exposure Menu, and little by little, she was making W.I.S.E. M.O.V.E.S to face her fears of contamination and being environmentally irresponsible at work and in public places.

Practicing values-guided exposures and messing up with her compulsions at home was much more challenging for Rebecca. Over the years, she demanded that her daughters and husband change their clothes as soon as they arrived home, leave their backpacks in the garage, take off their shoes, take short showers right away, wash their hands rigorously if they touched items in a public area (credit cards, doorknobs, stairs, handles, etc.), leave the laundry baskets in the garage, and never bring people inside the house.

Rebecca also refused to use any form of plastic or material that takes a long time to decompose, asked them to recycle almost all paper, including holiday cards, asked them to not flush the toilet if they only pee, refused to have a garden because of the water it required, and used only environmentally friendly cleaning products. Rebecca made her home a clean and environmentally friendly place, but her marriage and relationship with her daughters were a roller coaster despite how much she loved them.

Rebecca had a history of OCD-related symptoms with handwashing compulsions, but when she went to college to obtain a major in public health, her fears about contamination and hurting the environment increased, and a chain of compulsions and avoidant behaviors multiplied quickly. Later, when Rebecca obtained a master's in environmental law, things just got worse for her and her family.

Rebecca loved her children very much and felt frustrated with herself for her not allowing them to bring friends over or for having to always go to other people's homes for gatherings.

Rebecca's reactive brain latched onto the most precious things she cared about: protecting the environment, getting to know her kids, and being a compassionate and caring wife.

When facing a values-conflict related to obsessions, it's natural to get stuck. And because of all the intense emotions involved, it's natural that our problem-solving abilities falter at times. It's natural that your mind may say things like "it's better to be safe than sorry." Now can you imagine for a moment all the stress hormones that get released in our brain when we're struggling with a problem, when we're feeling scared, when we're feeling anxious? One of the consequences of being on edge is that we usually only see options as this or that, black or white, which makes it harder to get unhooked from the obsession.

So how do you know which are true values and which aren't? Let's explore potential values-conflicts with flexibility. Here are two considerations using Felix and Rebecca as examples:

a. First, let's check if what Felix referred to as his value of "being safe" is really a value. Values are qualities and life principles we want to stand for; they're answers to the questions HOW do I want to show up for life? Living our values is invigorating and energizing, and they give us a sense of purpose. Felix values being a companion to his girlfriend, but then he got stuck on the idea that "being safe" was another value. Even though it's written like a value, isn't it possible that Felix was holding onto a value of "safety" as a form of avoiding discomfort and distress?

Being safe, protective, or caring are certain qualities that we may want to embrace in different types of relationships and in different ways. But values are freely chosen qualities and come with all types of experiences, from troublesome to precious ones – and that's different than choosing a value to avoid feeling discomfort, to run away from the struggle, to minimize the distress that comes with certain actions, as Felix was doing.

b. Sometimes, there are two genuine values you want to embrace and live for, but you may be attached to them rigidly, as was the case for Lisa. For Lisa, making W.I.S.E. M.O.V.E.S. toward her relationship values was in conflict with her personal value of protecting the environment.

After reading about these two considerations, which one are you struggling with: Felix's situation of maybe holding onto a fake-value of being safe to avoid the discomfort, or Lisa's struggle between her personal and relationship values?

If you're dealing with a situation similar to Felix, go back to the chapter "Figuring Out What Matters," do the exercises one more time, and find the stuff that makes you tick.

If your struggle is like Lisa's, then move with the next prompts.

Exercise 41.1 Unpacking your values

What are the actions you could take for the value related to your W.I.S.E. M.O.V.E.S.?

1. _____

2. _____

3. _____

4. _____

5. _____

What are the actions you could take for the value that is competing with your W.I.S.E. M.O.V.E.S.?

1. _____

2. _____

3. _____

4. _____

5. _____

What's your reaction when looking at the lists of all those behaviors related to each one of your HOWs?

_____

_____

_____

_____

Doing what matters is an important step to living the life you truly want to live; and yet as humans, we're wired to hold and latch onto all types of things in ways that are both helpful and unhelpful at times.

Look at this continuum, think over the last month, and mark an X where each fit.

Lightly	Rigidly
Value related to your W.I.S.E. M.O.V.E.S.	

Lightly	Rigidly
Value in opposition to making your W.I.S.E. M.O.V.E.S.	

Now let's step back a bit and look at the impact of holding onto your values both lightly and rigidly.

How is it for you to hold lightly onto a value in the long-run?

_____

_____

_____

_____

What happens in the long-term if you hold onto any value on the rigid side of things?

_____

_____

_____

_____

_____

Given this values conflict, is there any way for you to act toward both values in a way that fosters flexibility, makes your life better, and moves you toward being the person you want to be? (For example, Lisa chose to stop asking her husband and daughters to take a shower after coming home, but she continued to request that they not flush the toilet if they're only peeing.)

_____

_____

_____

_____

_____

What ACT skills could you use to sit with the yucky discomfort that comes when making W.I.S.E. M.O.V.E.S and your mind shouts at you about not living accordingly to that personal value?

_____

_____

_____

_____

_____

Now that you have taken an in-depth look at another potential block that may get in your way of moving forward with your values-guided exposure, make sure to go back to your exposure plan and tune it up as needed.

If you take anything from this chapter, I hope that it's the awareness that there is a slippery road between living a value with flexibility versus holding onto it with rigidity or as an avoidance of the struggle that comes with facing obsessions.

Our brains are not perfect devices, and when going into protecting mode, they push us in all directions. By acknowledging that our brain is doing its job, to be best it can, and as it knows, we give ourselves the opportunity for new possibilities to come our way.

42

Why Am I Doing This?
Lack of Values Clarity

Here is another source of stuckness that many people encounter when practicing exposure exercises: you're clear about what matters to you and really want to move forward with your W.I.S.E. M.O.V.E.S., but when getting close to practicing a values-guided exercise, your mind comes up with the thought, "I don't care about it; it doesn't really matter; it's not related to who I want to be," and you end up not completing that particular values-based exposure.

If that's what has happened to you, let's start by jotting down all those items from your Values-Guided Exposure Menu that you didn't complete because they weren't related to your personal values.

For instance, Rena, a nurse working in an emergency facility, got hooked into obsessions about contamination and fears of making mistakes when writing things down.

At first, Rena thought that stress was the cause of her unwanted thoughts and fears, since she started having OCD episodes at the same time she was having sleeping problems, but after her sleeping got regular, she continued having OCD episodes – and they got worse.

Rena initially started wearing three pairs of synthetic gloves, avoided completing certain procedures, and washed her hands approximately 30 times a day. As time passed, she started getting triggered with stains and Band-Aids; if there was a blood stain or a Band-Aid, she monitored which colleagues stepped on them and had terrible urges to wash her shoes or wash her clothes, even though she didn't touch those stains directly.

Rena was eager to get back to having regular days at the hospital and at home; she imagined her obsessions as subtitles of a movie and carried in her pockets flashcards with obsessions words written on them. Rena put together her Values-Guided Exposure Menu and was ready to go. But when thinking about decreasing the amount of times she washed her hands or wearing two pairs of gloves instead of three, she told herself: "Why am I torturing myself in this way? Why do I have to do something so painful? What's the point of adding more stress to my life? I'm not sure this is what I want for me right now."

Battling with OCD episodes comes with moments like than in which your mind doesn't see the point of doing values-guided exposures.

Values are more than thinking who you aspire to be. They are also moments of choice, decision points, pivotal moments in which you are faced with two paths: one that unfolds into living the qualities you want to live and stand for and one organized around living in fear and anxiety and driven by all the discomfort that comes with obsessions.

If you're using this workbook, it is because you deeply want to make a shift; you care, and you want to get your life back. And yet making room for the discomfort that comes when doing what you care about is not always a straight or easy path; in fact, it has moments like Rena experienced at times.

The reality is that living our HOWs is never a straight path, and we do all types of things that take us to a cul-de-sac. Compulsions, avoidant behaviors, and holding onto ruling-thoughts are one form of detour; other times, we go into behavioral excesses like drinking, overeating, watching hundreds of hours of TV, eating as much sugar as possible, or using substances. And other times, we get hooked on thoughts that say, "What's the point?"

It's all part of being human.

If we step back for a moment, we can see how natural it is that your over-reactive brain, whose main and full-time job is to protect you, will come up with thoughts like that when you're getting close to doing something that can seem scary.

Here is my recommendation for moments like that: Instead of arguing back and fighting thoughts like "What's the point?" do your best to reflect on and answer the prompts in Table 42.1:

Exercise 42.1 Unpacking thoughts like "What's the point?"

> If you take thoughts along the lines of "What's the point?" as a matter of fact, what do you do in the moment and later on? What's the impact of behaving as the thought says in your day-to-day life and long-term?
>
> _____
>
> _____
>
> _____
>
> _____
>
> _____
>
> If you could make room for the group of thoughts like "What's the point?" without acting on them or taking them as the absolute truth, what would you be able to do that matters to you? Which actions would you take that are important to you?
>
> _____
>
> _____

_____

_____

_____

If all the thoughts similar to "What's the point?" represent a bridge between the life you want to have and the life you have right now, what would the life you want to live look like?

_____

_____

_____

_____

_____

Any reactions after reflecting on these questions?

The reality is that building and living the life we want comes with a dynamic dialectic of experiences, some of them more pleasant than others. And yet living our values has nothing to do with our feelings, thoughts, or sensations but with HOW we want to show up for the world, the commitment we make to do so, and the steps we take every moment.

I want to invite you to keep in mind that you have tried really hard to handle the obsession problem before; can you bring into your mind the outcomes of all those efforts? How did it work in the long-run? Did you behave as the person you want to be would behave? Were you able to have the relationships you want to have?

Quite likely none of the behaviors were effective, which is why you're practicing all the skills from this workbook. And now, and as you move forward, you're facing a new troublesome situation, a different color, but the same dilemma: living a life full of vitality, meaning, and purpose comes with the thought, "What's the point of doing that?"

So I invite you to not respond or dwell on any thoughts along the lines of "What's the point?" but to practice all the skills you have learned in this workbook, in particular watching your mind and defusion skills. You can choose a name and then visualize, say, or physicalize this thought.

For instance, Rena named these thoughts, "I don't care thoughts," and she imagined them as having the shape of gummy bears, about 2 to 3 inches in size, so she could hold them between her thumb and index finger and put them into her pockets.

Write down the name you choose and defusion skills you would like to practice when I-don't-care thoughts show up in the middle of your exposure work.

_____

_____

_____

_____

_____

Go back to your Values-Guided Exposure Menu and make any tune-ups you need to continue taking steps toward what you are about; it doesn't matter how big or small the step is; every step counts. Go for it!

I'm Doing Hundreds of Exposures

New Compulsion?

There comes a time when some of my clients will tell me, "I'm doing all types of exposures, hundreds of them, every day, and I'm still struggling!"

This is another block that could make you feel discouraged and hopeless about making W.I.S.E. M.O.V.E.S., because you're certainly doing what you supposed to be doing, right? But before you get bent out of shape, let's take a look at it.

To start, what are you hoping to experience or accomplish when doing values-guided exposures? Jot down your responses.

_____

_____

_____

_____

_____

What's your experience after you complete your values-based exposure exercises?

_____

_____

_____

_____

_Is there any part of you that is doing values-guided exposures with an agenda of:

a. Feeling better right away
b. Making your obsessions go away
c. Answering a question about an obsession
d. Preventing another OCD episode from coming in the future
e. Making the anxiety, fear, panic, and other related feelings go down

When practicing values-guided exposures, how would you describe your attitude toward it? Using the continuum below, mark an "X" where your attitude lies.

Hammering out   Pushing through   Flexibly choosing

If you're practicing your values-guided exposures hoping for one or a combination of the agenda items listed and pushing through or hammering out, chances are that you're doing exposures as a compulsion.

If that's the case, here is what you need to do:

- Stop doing any values-guided exposure exercises right away.
- Go back and read Chapters 26, "Riding the Wave of Fear, Anxiety, and Terrible Feelings," and 34, "Make W.I.S.E. M.O.V.E.S. When Practicing Values-Guided Exposures," and how to make the best of your values-guided exposures.
- After rereading, give your values-based exposures another trial run. But this time, if you catch yourself doing them as if you were a machine and completing them as a problem-solving technique, pause again.
- If necessary, go back to Part V, "Learning to Date Your Mind," before giving your values-based exposure exercises another shot.

Our brains are constantly trying to defend us from anything that could possibly go wrong. And by nature, some brains are just wired to be more reactive than others. When approaching an exercise toward being the person you want to be and the tiny possibility of an obsession showing up, it makes your overreactive brain shout danger alerts in a high-pitched, high-volume, and high-speed way so that you end up practicing values-guided exposures as a control strategy to neutralize obsessions.

It does make sense, right? Our brain is an old device doing its job. Yet none of this means that you cannot learn to respond flexibly to all those urges, to leave those obsessions untouched and unattended, and show up for your life as it matters to you.

Takeaways to share

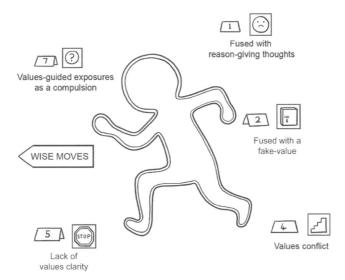

Figure 43.1 Crime scene.

As you make moves in your values-guided exposure menu, you might notice that obsessions move too; they can change in content, frequency, and form. Yet, keep in mind that every time you intentionally choose how to handle them, you're taking steps in the direction of the life you want to build for yourself.

Checking how you're approaching the process of facing obsessions, and keeping an eye out for potential obstacles will take you a step further down the path of showing up as the person you want to be. All OCD episodes can be overcomed, managed, and handled as they come your way.

The chart below summarizes that most common obstacles people encounter: how they look like, skills you can practice to tackle them, and chapters you can re-read as needed.

Table 43.1 Checking potential barriers for making W.I.S.E. M.O.V.E.S.

Potential obstacle that may show up	What does it look like?	Recommended chapters for you to go back and work on	Worksheets
Fused with reason-giving thoughts	I can't do it	24, "Always Check What Works"	– What gets in the way of your making W.I.S.E. M.O.V.E.S.? – Checking the workability of holding onto reason-giving thoughts – Confronting the costs of not making W.I.S.E. M.O.V.E.S. – Troubleshooting blocks to start making W.I.S.E. M.O.V.E.S.

(Continued)

Table 43.1 (Continued)

Potential obstacle that may show up	What does it look like?	Recommended chapters for you to go back and work on	Worksheets
Fusion with a fake-value Values-conflict	I'd rather being safe	29, "Figuring Out What Matters"	– Unpacking your values (Chapter 41, "I Would Rather Be Safe: Values-Conflict or Fake-Values?" has useful questions)
Lack of values clarity	Why am I doing this?	29, "Figuring Out What Matters"	(Chapter 42, "Why Am I Doing This: Lack of Values Clarity" has useful questions) – Unpacking thoughts like "what's the point?"
Doing values-guided exposures as a compulsion	I'm doing hundreds of exposures	26, "Riding the Wave of Fear, Anxiety, and Terrible Feelings" 34, "Make W.I.S.E. M.O.V.E.S. When Practicing Values-Guided Exposure Exercises" 36, "Make the Best of Your Values-Guided Exposures	(Chapter 43, "I'm Doing Hundreds of Exposures: New Compulsion?" has useful questions)

Life Tracker

Reflect on how you have been living your life and mark an "X" where it corresponds.

Having obsessions as thoughts your mind comes up with	Seeing obsessions as problems to be solved
Approaching life as it is	Avoiding life because of obsessions
Taking action toward what you care about	Organizing your life around obsessions
Holding your thoughts lightly	Going 100% along with what your mind tells you
Checking what really works in your life	Doing stuff in automatic pilot mode
Making room for uncomfortable internal experiences	Pushing them down as much as possible

PART X

Moving Forward

Congratulations! This is the last part of this workbook! Tons of appreciation for all the hard work you put into learning ACT and ERP skills and moving forward with your life!

In Part X you will read more suggestions, ideas, and exercises to keep moving forward with your life as it happens, and especially on how to handle those annoying situations that may show up when having a reactive brain.

Living life is not a Hollywood movie or fairy tale that ends with the classic line of "she lived happily ever after" – that's a telenovela's end. The truth is, you can have an amazing, rich, fulfilling, and meaningful life, but that doesn't mean that you're never ever going to feel down, get hooked on a ruling-thought, dwell on future thoughts, ruminate on past thoughts, or have an OCD episode.

I hope that you have learned that, when looking deeply in your heart and living your HOWs with valued actions day by day, those steps will give you direction and the capacity to experience the full range of experiences that get under your skin and happen outside of you as life happens.

Remember that there is learning by talking about values-based living and there is learning by doing values-based actions!

Intentionally disrupting OCD episodes with your actions will take you closer and closer towards a positive, impactful, and meaningful life!

Grab your favorite drink, get yourself comfortable, and make the best of this last part!

Make Mini W.I.S.E. M.O.V.E.S. On-the-Go

In Part VIII, "Making W.I.S.E. M.O.V.E.S.," you learned all the nitty-gritty steps and skills you need to know for practicing planned values-guided exposures. But life happens, life moves, and as you move throughout your day, triggering, upsetting, and obsession-provoking situations are going to emerge your way – that's unavoidable.

Think of Elena for a moment.

Elena has this hard-to-let-go thought about losing things. When she goes out, to avoid doing a long compulsion, she makes sure to carry her credit card in one of her pockets so she doesn't have to open her purse and potentially lose other personal items. Elena has been doing this type of organizing among many other avoidant and compulsive behaviors for quite a while: making a sound, saying the name of the item aloud, touching each item inside the bag, making another sound, and then zipping up the bag.

But on a Wednesday morning, when Elena went out with her friend for a stroll, she needed to get tissue paper from her purse to clean her runny nose. Elena didn't expect to need tissues, and she got panicky right away, felt triggered. But she didn't want to do all her compulsions, and she definitely didn't want her friends to see her doing them.

Elena couldn't have known this was going to happen; she couldn't have anticipated it. She certainly hadn't planned an exposure for this. Some people may argue that actually she could have anticipated it; and sure, Elena could have anticipated that her nose was going to run and be prepared for it. But imagine anticipating all the potential things that could go wrong and organizing your life around them? How would that be? A nightmare.

Life doesn't come fully organized, arranged, and assembled. And so even if you haven't planned a values-based exposure for a particular scenario, you can still make bold moves in those random moments. Behavioral therapists usually refer to such moves as exposures on the fly; I usually call them W.I.S.E. M.O.V.E.S. on-the-go. Of course, you can refer to them as you prefer.

Moments to practice W.I.S.E. M.O.V.E.S. on-the-go can include suddenly seeing someone sick opening a door; seeing a particular number on a clock; being asked by your teenaged daughter if she's making the right decision about college; hearing about a new disease; picking up your children from school and having an image about killing them in a car accident when driving; or having a dream about having a different sexual orientation, just to name some of the hundreds of other situations that could show up your way.

What about you? Think about last week and jot down those moments in which the unexpected happened and you were faced with a triggering situation, person, activity, or object.

_____

_____

_____

_____

I know you didn't plan those situations; they just happened. When facing them, you can use the same prompts you have been using for all values-guided exposures:

W – watch your obsessions
I – invite your obsessions
S – stay with your experience
E – either toward or away from your values

M – make a choice
O – observe what comes with the choice
V – value your choice
E – engage with what's next
S – soften up with self-compassion

When you're unexpectedly triggered, sometimes it can feel as if you're facing a crisis, and you may find yourself getting caught up in a hurricane of obsessions, urges, fear, despair, or frustration.

This is what making your mini W.I.S.E. M.O.V.E.S. on-the-go looks like:

– Start by always grounding yourself, bringing yourself back into the moment, noticing five things you can see, four things you can hear, three things you can touch. Move your body, wiggle your toes, balance your body. Reconnect with your body. Intentionally slow down your breathing. Acknowledge what's happening by saying to yourself, "I'm here, I'm getting triggered, and this is happening right now."
– After bringing yourself back into the present moment, use your defusion skills: name the obsession or imagine how it physically looks (e.g., obsessively – biciviulus; Mrs. Doubty-Doubty). Press your feet really hard into the floor, really look at what's in front of you in that precise moment, and make a choice. It's really up to you to choose either a move away or move toward your HOWs.

– Making a choice toward living your values is not about making a humongous step all the time; it is about really approaching things with flexibility, curiosity, and openness as they come and really checking in with yourself. What are you willing to do at that moment? You can opt for a tiny, medium-size, or long step, but it's really up to you to choose what actions you are willing to take, for how long, with whom, and so on. There are no absolutes about what you can do in that moment, and don't let your brain get tricky with the thought, "You have to always make a big step."

Let's say that you're talking to a person, and out of the blue, you get inundated by fears of contamination in your mind. At this point, you may ask yourself, how do I want to handle this moment? You may choose to stay three more minutes in front of them or keep the conversation going for five more minutes; and if you decide to do so, you can intentionally pay extra attention to the way this person is talking: Is she talking loud or soft? How is she moving her lips? What is she really saying? By focusing on what's important to you – the person you're talking – you're getting out of your head and minimizing the possibilities of being consumed by those obsessions. You're not fighting them but you're not giving them your attention.

Here is another scenario: If you're typing on the computer when suddenly an image of a person of the opposite gender to which you feel attracted shows up, and the obsession about being of a different sexual orientation comes along. In those moments, name the obsession, and then ask yourself, what's the action I can take right now that will make my life better? Next, use your body to ground yourself: press your feet into ground and see if you're up to continue typing for five more minutes, maybe 10, maybe even 30 minutes. And if so, focus on how it feels to be moving your fingers, how it feels to be touching the keyboard, notice the sound of the keyboard, the posture of your arms, and so on.

A third scenario: If you're at the grocery store and out of the blue a Latino person stands next to you and smiles at you and as you expected, your mind comes up with fears about blurting derogatory comments to this person. Then, acknowledge that you're getting triggered by saying to yourself, "It's happening, I'm getting triggered." Don't fight the feeling or try to resist it. Move your body a bit as if you're stretching your legs, notice how it feels moving your body, and then check what you're willing to do: if you decide to stay next to his person, you can ask this person a recommendation for a particular product, make a comment about a product, or gently smile back.

In some circumstances, despite your best efforts, you may engage in a mini-compulsions – e.g., telling yourself it's going to be okay; she knows I won't ever say anything rude; I didn't touch anything contaminated, and so on. If you ended up doing a micro-compulsion or an avoidant behavior, your brain may come up with problematic thoughts about who you are as a person. If you get hooked on the me-problem, then you may engage with a bunch of criticisms, harsh comments, and negative judgments that later on feed into a cycle of sadness, disconnection, and hopelessness.

So, it's very important that you value your choice (e.g., "I'm doing my best" or "I did the best I could"), observe your struggle with kindness, focus on what's next, and soften up with self-compassion. You have been working really hard, and it's very bold of you to be in your shoes with those obsessions jumping up and down, left and right, and trying to dictate your life.

The next chapter will show you how to make a shift from looking at yourself with harsh eyes and as a problem to be solved to looking at yourself with caring eyes.

For now, I invite you to pay attention to those unexpected and unplanned moments as they come and do your best to practice mini W.I.S.E. M.O.V.E.S. on-the-go.

45

Soften Up With Self-Compassion

How often does your mind say: "You didn't do enough; you haven't accomplished anything with those exposures, you're back to square one!" How often do you notice thoughts like, "I'm bad; I'm a freak; I'm a terrible person; I'm broken inside, what type of nutcracker am I?"

Do you relate to those thoughts? If so, you're not alone. Me, too.

From a place of honesty, I can tell you that my mind barks at me all types of things, including criticizing thoughts about my looks, writing, work, how I talk, my accent, and many other things, on and on. As annoying as it is hearing all those editorial comments, that's what the mind does. I could be very mad with my content-generating and pattern-making machine for coming up with those statements, but it's really not my mind's fault; as you know by now, it just happens that because of survival, our mind evolved having those functions – coming up with all types of content and connecting all that content all the time. The cave woman needed to have those rough thoughts – comparing, criticizing, judging – to survive, because those thoughts guided her in what to do next, how to fit in with the group, how to get as much food as she needed, and so on.

It's so hard to be human, because we're walking around with an ancient brain in the information era; we're not cave people any longer, but we carry a brain that was designed for those oooooooooold times.

In general, how do you respond to those harsh thoughts?

_____

_____

_____

_____

I usually see two types of responses when dealing with these harsh thoughts:

- *Fighting those thoughts, judgments, and stories by doing everything you can to prove them wrong.* Maybe you list your positive qualities, ask others to mention your attributes, look at yourself in the mirror and recite your positive attributes, or replace those thoughts with positive ones, and so on.

  Maybe you even feel successful for a little bit, until again, your mind comes up with another judging thought, and another one, and the cycle continues. The battle to prove your mind wrong is endless, and quite likely, you're never going to win.

- *Buying into those insulting, derogatory, and criticizing thoughts.* Perhaps you take them as absolute reality, a fact, as definitive signs of your character. As a result, you may end up acting and doing exactly as the thought says, which just makes things worse. Let's say that the judgy thought is "I'm weird because of my obsessions," and it pushes you to not apply for a job, go on a date, or take a fun trip. When that happens, the judgy thought can quickly send you into a downward spiral of hopelessness, despair, and loneliness.

Which one of those responses do you do?

Before we continue, let me clarify that I'm not saying that having those harsh thoughts doesn't hurt. They do hurt – but only if you buy into them right away or spend countless hours fighting against them. Think about those judgy thoughts again for a moment: what is a criticizing thought made of? What is an image made of? All those harsh, unkind, and comparing thoughts are another product of the content-generating and pattern-making machine of our minds; they're just letters, words, vowels, and images put together.

But if you have been fused with those self-stories forever, so that it seems almost impossible to remember a day that you didn't have those nasty thoughts about yourself, I want to invite you to try all the self-compassion skills you will learn in this chapter.

The good news is that our brains are adaptable, flexible, and coachable! To start, jot down anything and everything that comes into your mind when hearing the words "compassion," "self-compassion," and "compassion for others."

_____

_____

_____

_____

Perhaps you know a little bit about self-compassion, or maybe you already have a self-compassion practice. Either way, just to make sure we're on the same page, let me share key ideas about it – I promise I won't torture you with hundreds of academic definitions or theories about it.

First, compassion is about recognizing that we're all connected, all of us, even the people we don't know. While our struggles take different forms and may look different on the outside, we're all interconnected in one form or another because we do share common struggles, challenges, and difficulties that are part of being alive.

Second, compassion is about learning to make room for that the pain that comes with our struggles and to hold it without judging it or judging ourselves for having it.

Third, compassion is a real-time decision we make to lighten, alleviate, and soften our pain (not to get rid of it but to take it with care).

In this chapter, we'll focus on self-compassion exercises and I'll refer to it as the skill of acknowledging your own distress and responding to yourself with the same consideration and kindness that you would show to someone you care for who is in similar distress.

Now that we're on the same page, let's check what makes it hard to put self-compassion into action.

46

What Gets in Your Way of Being Kind to Yourself?

If we're wired to be compassionate, what gets in our way? Let's do a couple of exercises to answer that question.

Exercise: What Gets in Your Way of Being Kind to Yourself?

Read the sentence here and answer each question as it corresponds.

What would you do and how would you treat each person in the following situations?

Seeing a homeless person with two children in the street:

_____

_____

_____

Witnessing one person assaulting another person:

_____

_____

_____

Hearing about war veterans surviving in combat:

_____

_____

_____

Observing a pregnant woman falling down the stairs:

_____

_____

_____

Witnessing a teenager being bullied by his peers:

_____

_____

_____

Seeing your friend crying because her pet just passed away:

_____

_____

_____

How was it for you thinking about responding to those situations? Almost everyone I ask these questions responds with caring, concern, and worry, and they genuinely want to do something about it. Isn't that interesting, that the capacity to be gentle and considerate with others is there, but it may be different with ourselves?

Here is another question to ponder: What gets in your way of responding in the same or similar way when those harsh thoughts are about you? Jot down your responses as they come.

_____

_____

_____

_____

_____

_____

If there is a theme that showed up in your responses, what's that theme?

_____

_____

_____

_____

_____

A client told me once: "I don't deserve to be kind. It's scary because somehow it means that I'm giving myself a pass to have all types of thoughts, like these awful harm obsessions." My client's block was very real. He had obsessive thoughts of harming others, and he feared that if he were kind to himself he would be letting himself off the hook, as if he were condoning his unwanted scary thoughts – as if those thoughts defined him.

Here is a personal observation: I sometimes think that dealing with OCD makes my clients extra busy managing these obsessions because they're hooked on thoughts like, "I may miss something important if I don't pay attention to the obsessions," or "I may cause harm if I'm not monitoring my obsessions at all times." It is as if the idea of practicing self-compassion is letting your guard down and preventing you from not trying hard enough. Do you relate?

After recognizing those blocks to self-kindness, let me ask you a bit more the role of those blocks in your life: What happens in your day when you hold onto those thoughts with white knuckles and do what they tell you to do? What happens when you take those blocks literally and refuse to be kind with yourself? Do you show up for life as you want to step up? Or do you stay where you are?

Quite likely, the more you hold onto those thoughts, it hurts more and feels like living in hell at times. It's not your fault; things are a bit harder when having a reactive brain, and it's actually courageous to walk in your shoes.

Let me briefly share key ideas about compassionate responses. Paul Gilbert (2014), a clinician and researcher from the United Kingdom and founder of Compassion-Focused Therapy, has proposed that the interaction between the incentive, affiliation, and threat systems of our brain allow us to go back and forth between our internal and external worlds. The incentive system is in charge of behaviors connected with wanting and pursuing; the affiliation system gives us a sense of safety and connection; and the threat system regulates our need for safety. All these systems get activated and interact constantly through different daily life experiences with stuff that happens around us and inside us.

You may wonder why learning about those systems is important when dealing with OCD. Here is why: when dealing with OCD or any form of anxiety, the stream of loud obsessions your mind comes up with activates the threat system in your brain, blocking automatically the path to connect with the affiliation system that is in charge of any soothing or caring behavior for yourself. Basically, when you're in threat mode and get so busy managing the fake-threat of the obsessions, you don't give yourself a chance – at a brain level – to access a soothing response or acknowledge that you're hurting, and paradoxically, you end up prolonging the struggle with obsessions.

If on top of that you get hooked on thoughts about not deserving to be caring with yourself or why you shouldn't be kind with yourself, then you deprive yourself from fully learning to let go of internal blocks and be your best version.

It's hard to be compassionate with yourself, because to be caring with yourself requires that you get in contact with your own pain, acknowledge that you're hurting, recognize that you're human, and face your own vulnerabilities when having those disturbing thoughts. But if you learn to practice gentleness, caring, and self-compassionate responses with yourself, chances are that you can teach your brain another way to step back from feeding into the OCD cycle, minimize the exhaustion that comes from fighting obsessions, and have more energy to do the stuff that really matters to you.

Time to make a shift, right?

Self-Compassion Reflective Exercises

So glad you made it to his chapter! The next pages will show you different ways to soften up and practice the same caring responses you have with others with yourself.

Keep in mind that the goal of these exercises is not to get rid of those criticizing, judgy, or blaming thoughts that your mind comes up with but to practice making room for the struggle that comes with them because of obsessions. Imagine if, instead of running away from all those hurtful thoughts or acting quickly on them, you learn to have them as they come – and you put your energy, efforts, and time into doing the stuff you care about? It could be quite amazing, right?

Now, less blah blah blah and more hands-on caring behaviors for you!

Let's start with self-compassion exercises that are more of reflective time and will require that you find a private place for you to practice them.

Exercise: You Are Not Alone and You're Not Broken

Some clients I work with struggle with a sense of isolation, feeling as if they're broken or a problem to be solved; they find it shameful to share with others about their obsessions and what they're dealing with. This gets much more accentuated when the obsessions are related to sexual, harm, and aggressive content – fears of being a pedophile, attacking others, or causing harm to loved ones or suicidal obsessions, to name a few.

Whatever story the content-generating machine of your mind came up with about yourself because of the struggle with obsessions that you're holding onto, I can tell you right away that caring behaviors are much needed for you to keep moving forward, designing, and living the life you want to live!

To start, read the directions here, record them in your cell phone or in any other device, and then listen to them. This exercise may take approximately 15 minutes.

Sit in a relaxed position, or if it's better for you, lean your body against a wall, but do your best to find a comfortable position. For the next couple of moments, see if you can start focusing on your breathing as it happens. Every time you inhale and exhale, notice the passing sensations of the air while you breathe in and breathe out. Notice the rhythm and pace of your breathing, the sensation of air as it enters your nostrils and moves through your body. You can even notice the temperature of the air as it moves and leaves your body a few moments later.

If your mind brings distracting thoughts at this moment, it's natural. You're invited to notice these distracting thoughts as they come, and without reacting to them, name them for what they are, *distracting thoughts*, or choose any other name that resonates with you. Let these distracting thoughts drift by like clouds in the sky, and gently go back to focusing on the flow of your breath.

Imagine for the next couple of moments one of those situations in which you struggle with an OCD episode. See if you can bring that image into your mind as clearly as possible and hold onto it for a couple of moments. Silently describe the feeling or feelings that show up for you; don't worry about finding the perfect name for your feelings, but just choose one of them that closely represents what you're feeling. See if you can locate any sensations in your body and notice whether that sensation stays in the same location or moves through your body. See if you can notice this sensation without pushing it away or trying to get rid of it, just letting it be. Notice the stream of thoughts, if any. See if you can notice how difficult that moment was, how difficult it was to be in your shoes in that situation. You were doing the best you could in that moment, and you are aware that you are not perfect as a person, as no person is. See if you can notice your reactions in this moment while acknowledging that every human being and every person in this planet has made mistakes while doing their best in the moment.

See if you can make room in this moment to accept that everyone naturally fights obsessions when they pop up, that everyone may judge themselves because of obsessions; that everyone shares being imperfect, being stuck at times, and being harsh with themselves. You are not alone. See if you can tell yourself with a soft and caring tone of voice that your pain when dealing with disturbing thoughts is the same pain that others suffer when dealing with OCD episodes. You are in the same boat with others, sharing the pain and imperfections of being alive. See if you can make room to accept this experience – your experience and the experience of others – accepting it for what it is.

Notice how it feels in your body to accept your struggles and others' struggles. Notice any reaction in your body in this moment of acceptance without blaming yourself or getting hooked in a criticizing story. Notice if there is even a tiny sensation taking form in your body, and see if you can name the feeling that comes with that sensation. See again if you can tell yourself, in a kind and soothing voice, that it's not easy to be in your shoes. It's not easy to be dealing with OCD episodes. It's not easy to feel alone, and yet you're not alone.

Slowly go back to paying attention to the flow of your breath as it happens, while breathing in and breathing out. Allow yourself to take a couple of slow and deep breaths before finishing this exercise.

Exercise: From Receiving a Compassionate Response to Being Self-Compassionate

Budget 15 to 20 minutes for this exercise. As with the previous exercise, read the guidelines, record them in a slow and paced tone of voice, and then listen to it.

- Ground yourself in the moment by focusing on your breathing, noticing the qualities of it every time you're inhaling and exhaling.
- Bring into your mind all those self-criticizing thoughts or stories about who you are that show up in your mind because of OCD.
- Say them slowly and aloud to yourself for a moment.
- Notice any reaction you're having in this moment: Check any sensation showing up in your body. When you notice them, say to yourself, "I'm sensing _____" or "This is a _____ sensation." You can scan your body starting at your head, moving into your shoulders and neck, your chest, your stomach, your hips, your legs, your calves, and your feet.
- Name the emotion or emotions showing up by saying "I'm feeling _____" or "Here is the feeling of _____."
- If this emotion and sensation were waves in the ocean, imagine their size. Are they small waves, medium ones, or big waves? Are you on the ascending side, the peak of it, or on the descending side?
- Imagine for a moment that a person who cares about you – perhaps your partner, a relative, or your best friend – is next to you, has listened to those criticizing and self-derogatory stories, and is responding to you. What would they say? Imagine for a moment their voice; imagine what they're saying and how they're responding to you.
- Notice your reactions to receiving a response from a person you care about. How did it feel? What thoughts came to you? What sensations showed up?
- Take a couple of moments to notice those sensations, one by one. Scan your body again from top to bottom, and allow yourself to notice what's showing up in this moment.
- Continuing with this exercise, take a deep breath or a couple of them, and bring into your mind the self-criticizing thoughts you worked on at the beginning of this exercise.
- Notice your reactions to this self-criticizing voice again by paying gentle attention to those feelings, thoughts, sensations, and even urges that may have shown up.
- As you did in the first part of this exercise, notice and describe to yourself those sensations, feelings, thoughts, and urges by saying, "I'm having this _____ feeling, thought, or urge."
- Now imagine that a very caring, kind, and soft voice within you has listened to the derogatory narratives and is responding to you. This compassionate voice notices your struggle when hearing those words and sees your suffering. This compassionate voice knows how it feels to be in your shoes when having those self-blaming thoughts and sees your pain.
- See if you can make room for this compassionate voice and imagine what it will tell you right now; see if you can make room for this compassionate voice by

softening your tone of voice, relaxing your facial muscles, and really talking to yourself from a place of caring.

- Slowly imagine the compassionate responses and, if you find yourself fighting against them or resisting them, acknowledge the fight and take a deep breath, make sure your back is straight but not tight, and relax your body intentionally starting from the head and moving down.
- As you scan your body, practice again noticing what's showing up. Notice and describe those sensations, emotions, or urges showing up to you.
- Gently go back to paying attention to your breathing and slowly noticing how it feels bringing air into your body and breathing out. Notice the temperature of the air moving through your body and leaving it.
- And to finish this exercise, take five deep and slow breaths.

After practicing these exercises, take a couple of moments to reflect on this question: What type of relationship do you really want to have with yourself when those criticizing, harsh, and self-judgmental stories show up?

_____

_____

_____

_____

There are many reflective exercises you can practice to continue developing compassionate behaviors toward yourself:

- Imagine a safe, nurturing, and soothing place for yourself.

  This place can be somewhere in nature, a room in the house you grew up, a sweet spot you have at home, etc.

- Write a caring, kind, and compassionate letter to yourself.
- Carry with you an object that reminds you that you can respond with kindness when having negative judgments toward yourself.
- Ask for caring behaviors to others when needed.
  Sometimes, all that you need is to hear from someone else that they care about you or that they get that you're struggling. It's okay to ask for those small gestures from the people you trust.

Try these exercises and see which ones you relate to the most, and hope you can make them a weekly practice. The next chapter will show you how you can practice self-compassion exercises on-the-run as another alternative to bring gentleness into your day-to-day life as it happens.

48

Self-Compassion Exercises On-the-Run

Let's be real: it's not a surprise that many of us find it challenging to squeeze even five minutes into our day to practice self-compassionate exercises, given all the errands, responsibilities, and fun stuff we need and want to do.

Most of the clients I work with usually say, "I don't have the time, I would like to, but it's so hard to find the time." So in this chapter you will read some tips to practice gentleness, caring, and self-compassionate behaviors as your day unfolds.

For a moment, let's take a look at any regular activity you do, like visiting a friend, taking a shower, going to a restaurant, preparing to apply for a job, or even driving on the freeway. It's possible that you may get triggered when engaging in any of those activities. I know it's not ideal or easy, and your mind may come up with thoughts like:

- "Oh my God, I felt his energy. There is something off about him. Now I'm a mess."
- "What happens if I really stab that person? I'm a monster!"
- "I can't get out of this situation, and I'm just going to make it worse, as I always do."
- "I may offend someone – I'm a terrible person."
- "Did I make a mistake when making that turn? I'm just a walking disaster."
- "My son touched the stain, is he going to get sick now? I'm a bad parent, no one would stop protecting her kid, but I just did. I'm an awful parent."

In moments like that, when your mind keeps going on with different scary thoughts, judgy stories about yourself, and you don't have a chance to practice a long meditative exercise, you can still practice a brief self-compassion exercise on-the-go:

Adjust your posture, lift up your shoulders, intentionally relax your facial expression, and take a deep breath. You can even place your hand where you notice your struggle, give a name to those negative stories, and acknowledge them, (e.g., "Here is Mr. Criticizing" or "Here is Miss Sassy"). Then, imagine a caring voice within you, and acknowledge to yourself that you're scared, that you've felt like this before, that this is not your fault but a reaction of your brain, that you're feeling vulnerable and that's a normal feeling to have.

The key is to acknowledge that you're hurting in those moments and respond to yourself with kindness and appreciation for that moment of struggle.

Incorporating self-compassion exercises into your daily living may feel awkward at the beginning, as it does with any new practice. Maybe your mind tells you that "self-compassion is just a soft move and that it won't make a difference." But in reality, self-compassion is faaaaaaaaar from being a soft move or letting your guard down – it's actually the opposite. Compassionate behaviors are courageous moves that ask you to face your pain, your hurt, and your struggles with OCD episodes, and they gives you the foundation to continue shifting from reactive moves into W.I.S.E. M.O.V.E.S. and from surviving into thriving!

49

Life Is Imperfect!

In the midst of writing this book, in the United States more than 2,000 children were separated from their parents and placed in what the government called "chain-link partitions," the father of one of my students got diagnosed with cancer, my sister lost her job, and my 60-year-old aunt fell and injured her arm.

"*La vida es absolutamente imperfecta, y punto*," as my aunt says many times. *Life is absolutely imperfect, period.* That's a fact.

Imagine for a moment that almost everyone and everything around you functions in an absolutely perfect way: the neighbor parking her car next to you, your kid doing his homework, your mom asking you the right questions, your car functioning beautifully all the time, and so on. How would it be? Maybe it would be amazing, exciting, and super-nice. And yet that's just a fictional world that we can easily get trapped in.

If we look at our lives and our friends' lives, we'll recognize a collection of unfortunate situations that happen, from the random ones when we cannot find the pen we like to write with, to waiting for more than an hour in traffic, to feeling rejected by the person we love, to losing our darling pet, and on and on. Life has many messy moments, and we don't know when those messy moments are coming, how often they will come, or how intense they're going to be. They happen.

A natural response from our brain in those moments is to come up with hundreds of thoughts, theories, and hypotheses of what's happening or why it's happening, and a turmoil of emotions come and go. And when dealing with OCD, some of these messy moments may turn on the obsession switch and toss you up and down, left and right, and push you to do a compulsive behavior.

Here are some of the things my mind does when dealing with messy moments.

After taking an airplane: I wish I didn't get sick every time I travel.

After coming back from Bolivia: I would love for the weather in the Bay Area to be humid.

When teaching: I wish my students would do all the required readings.

When writing: I wish I could be more creative.

After dealing with anxiety: It's a bummer to feel this way; I wish I didn't feel so anxious at times.

After being robbed: It's not fair; I shouldn't be going through this. Why does this happen?

When feeling lonely: I don't understand why I feel this awful way, I don't wish this empty feeling on anyone.

Despite our efforts and intention, life gets messy, and there is no switch to change what's happening around us, either. In moments like that, our mind does what it is supposed to be doing: coming up with tons of thinking content at the speed of the light, in all directions, and with all types of connotations. Our content-generating machine will always be doing its own thing, like an old over-protective device, one that doesn't respond to the commands "stop being bossy" or "stop being afraid."

It's only when we distinguish what we have control over and what we don't, turn up the acceptance dial, and drop all those control strategies that we learn to handle those unexpected, untidy, and chaotic moments!

Let's take a look into this last paragraph a bit further in the next chapter.

50

The Illusion of Control

Here is an important piece of reality: There are things that you can change, have control over, and have the decisional power to make happen; and simultaneously, there are hundreds of other things that you have zero control over.

For example, if you decide to take a vacation, you can choose the location, the time of the day to fly, the airline, the number of stops, and so on. If it's too cold in your office, you can turn off the heater; if you're thirsty, you can get a drink; and so on.

There are other types of situations that just are what they are; we don't like them, we don't love them, we may even hate them, and yet that's just how they are. When I teach a class, I don't have control over my students' reactions to my lecture; when listening to one of my favorite songs, I don't have control of how I feel; when flying, I don't have control of the thoughts that my mind comes up with. As much as I dislike the cold weather, I don't have control of temperature in the area. As much as I hope, we just cannot change the messiness and unfair situations that happen every day in the world.

Although this reality may sound a bit fatalistic to some, here is why it's important: hundreds of times, out of the blue, disturbing obsessions, anxious thoughts, fearful images, or annoying worries will show up as often as situations in which people disappoint you, say the wrong things, and so on.

But if you get attached to the illusion that you can control every single thing, when in reality you can only control *your* behaviors, that's recipe for disaster. For instance, look at all the costs that come with trying to control the obsessions problem with compulsions, avoidance, and holding onto ruling-thoughts?

I'm not saying that you shouldn't advocate to change unfair or biased situations; I'm just saying that when different upsetting situations happen around you or bothersome triggers show up under your skin, you need to distinguish between what you can change and what you cannot change.

Dropping the illusion of control – and learning to accept what needs to be accepted – are amazing skills, and trust me, they will save you hundreds if not thousands of headaches!

51

How to Handle Those Unexpected Moments

Living life is not a Hollywood movie but a journey that gets written every minute based on how you respond to, handle, and deal with all those imperfect, unplanned, and unrehearsed moments. Close to the end of the book, here are my last tips for you.

What to Do When an Obsession Shows Up

By now you know that you don't have control over when or how often an obsession shows up or how intense it is. But you have all the power to decide how to respond, handle, and deal with it! Whether it's an obsession about harming another person, becoming a zombie, making mistakes, not doing things right, causing harm to others by accident, or wondering about your sexual orientation, you can choose not to engage with it, leave it unattended, practice W.I.S.E. M.O.V.E.S. on-the-go, and focus on what's in front of you.

What to Do When an Upsetting Situation Happens

When encountering a difficult situation, whether because someone disappointed you, you didn't get the job you wanted, the Amazon order arrived late, you can't find your favorite pen to write with, or any other upsetting situation, you can practice values-based problem-solving as a skill to handle those troublesome moments and ask yourself: how do I want to show up for this? It sounds simple, but it's a powerful question to answer ourselves when things get rocky for us.

In Table 51.1 you will find different prompts to figure out how to show up for upsetting situations that come your way while continue to be the person you want to be. Give it a try!

Exercise 51.1 Values-based problem solving

Directions: Not everything goes as we would like it to go, and more often than not, we have to face problems of all types. Within ACT, you're asked to learn to solve a problem not only as a technique but as another step toward your values. Choose a situation you're struggling with, and do your best to answer these questions. It's better if you choose a situation that you may be ambivalent about or one in which you have high stakes.

Can you describe the situation in as much detail as possible?

_____

_____

_____

_____

_____

What's the stuff you have control of?

_____

_____

_____

_____

What's the stuff you don't have control of at all?

_____

_____

_____

If you step back for a moment, what really matters to you in this situation? (Watch out for any "feeling hooks" when checking your values.)

_____

_____

What is your emotion machinery coming up with about it? (What are your feelings, sensations, urges, memories, images, thoughts?)

_____

_____

_____

_____

What are the potential actions you could take? Determine whether each action takes you closer to or farther away from your personal values.

Potential actions	Closer to values (1–10)	Farther away from values (1–10)

Based on your responses, what did you decide?

_____

_____

_____

Let's be real: whatever decision you choose is not struggle-free – and your emotional machinery, with a loud inner voice and tons of bodily noise, will be there. What emotions, thoughts, sensations, or urges do you need to make space for when choosing the behavior that takes you closer to your values?

_____

_____

_____

After you take action about this problem, answer the following:

What was the action you decided to take?

_____

_____

_____

What are the payoffs of this behavior in the short-term and long-term?

_____

_____

_____

What to Do When Feeling Overwhelmed

Sometimes we feel very overwhelmed, and it's as if an emotional switch is turned on and off, we feel like we're living in hell, and those exhausting emotions drag us around like a puppet. Do you know what I'm talking about? Quite likely, yes, we all have been there!

Here is what to do:

a. Anchor yourself: You can ground yourself by taking a deep breath and pressing your feet really hard against the floor, so you feel your body.
b. Notice, describe, and name those sensations to yourself: "Here is _____."
c. Recognize the strong urge to act right away.
d. Remember that you can ride the wave of any emotion.
e. Ask yourself, "How do I want to show up in this moment?"
f. Choose a values-guided behavior.

Remember when my visa didn't arrive on time for my trip to the UK? Here's how I used these skills: I noticed how quickly my emotions of frustration, disappointment, hurt, and sadness got activated throughout the day. I named them as "the disappointment feelings," acknowledged them in my body, and recognized the strong urge to act on them. I took a deep breath, over and over, to be able to step back and check what was really important in that moment, such as paying attention to cooking dinner, listening to the person in front me, searching for the perfect color of the wall I was going to paint, or describing the sensations while hiking. I went through that cycle hundreds of times; it wasn't easy to practice these skills, and yet they were very handy.

I was careful not to engage in hours of dwelling about the poor service I received because it was so easy to slip into the waterfall of angry thoughts and get stuck. I shared with friends and family what I could, when I could, and carefully noticed when my body was getting too agitated. Then I breathed and paused. It wasn't easy to get unstuck; I explained what happened to my friends, squirming with frustration and disappointment.

It was on the fourth or fifth day of being in emotional misery that my body slowly went back to its natural baseline. I wasn't organizing my actions around frustration, and I wasn't the puppet of my emotions any longer. I was still upset, sad, and disappointed, but instead of fighting against these feelings, minimizing them, or pretending they weren't there, I knew that the best thing I could do was to let them be. I made space for them, even though I didn't like them at all.

Life gets complicated, and yet you can get unstuck from tricky situations by going back to your values, your HOWs, over and over. I can honestly tell you that amazing things happen when we rely on our values to guide our actions, especially when things get messy and we feel like losing our mind. Choosing to be the person we want to be is revitalizing and energizing, and once you experience that, you will see how hard is to go back to the old ways of being.

Takeaways to share

Figure 51.1 Falling into a whole

You just learned new skills to take along in the ride of living your life when different tricky moments present! Let's recap the key points:

- Practicing mini W.I.S.E. M.O.V.E.S. on-the-go is a great way to handle those moments when unexpected triggers caught you by surprise (same principles but different than planned values-guided exposures).
- Self-compassion is not an esoteric practice, but a very courageous behavior because it requires that you get in touch with any painful feeling you're having as it is and as it comes, without hiding from it or pushing it down.
- You can practice self-compassion exercises – reflective ones or on-the-go when your mind jumps at you with criticizing, judgy, and harsh thoughts.
- Self-compassion exercises won't make "ouch thoughts about yourself" go away, but they are an additional skill to keep shifting from reactive moves into wise ones and from surviving into thriving.
- When dealing with upsetting situations, whatever size they are, you can always use a values-based problem-solving approach to it (worksheet in Chapter 51)
- When dealing with overwhelming emotions, here is a summary of the steps you can follow: anchor yourself with your body, take a deep breath, notice and describe what's happening under your skin, acknowledge your strong urges to act, make room for the chain of the emotions, ask yourself, "How do I want to show up in this moment?" and lastly, choose a behavior.
- Keep in mind that living your values is an ongoing process of choosing how you want to be as your day unfolds – and not a one-time thing or a perfect thing.

Life Tracker

Reflect on how you have been living your life and mark an "X" where it corresponds.

Having obsessions as thoughts your mind comes up with	Seeing obsessions as problems to be solved
Approaching life as it is	Avoiding life because of obsessions
Taking action toward what you care about	Organizing your life around obsessions
Holding your thoughts lightly	Going 100% along with what your mind tells you
Checking what really works in your life	Doing stuff in automatic pilot mode
Making room for uncomfortable internal experiences	Pushing them down as much as possible

Departing Words

Congratulations, you made it all the way to the end of this workbook!

I truly, truly, truly hope that all the skills, exercises, activities, reflective questions, tips, and information you read in this manuscript have put you in the direction of living your life and making the best of it!

I want to leave you with a few more recommendations as you continue to move forward. Of course, more recommendations, that's just me, right?

Make Your *Watching Your Mind Skills* Your Go-To Skills!

Every time the content-generating and pattern-making machine of your mind shouts at you ridiculous, weird, and not-so-weird content, watch your mind, go back to your favorite defusion skills, or create new ones.

It's fundamental that you keep practicing falling out of blind love with your mind and continue dating it with caring, curiosity, lightness, and in the moment. (It gets too busy to live in our heads.)

Make W.I.S.E. M.O.V.E.S. Every Moment You Can!

One of the best ways of living life is by connecting with what matters to you!

It doesn't matter how big of a step you take toward your values – what's most important is that you take a step.

In designing and living the life you want to live, quite likely there are going to be annoying and disturbing obsessions showing up, but you don't have to be bossed around by them. You have to remember that you can make your W.I.S.E. M.O.V.E.S. – planned or on-the-go – to handle those sticky moments.

Make W.I.S.E. M.O.V.E.S. as often as you can!

Go Back to Your HOWs Over and Over!

When situations get rocky, either because things are happening under your skin or in your surroundings, make room for the hurt, frustration, or disappointment that comes with those moments and ask yourself: "How do I want to show up in this moment? How do I want to be remembered by the people I love?"

I promise you, living your values is one of the most energizing, revitalizing, and amazing paths you can take in life!

Practice Kindness Toward Yourself Even When You Don't Feel Like It!

If your brain jumps at you with harsh criticisms, negative evaluations, or any other form of "ouch story," and you're getting hooked on those thoughts, take a deep breath and put your self-compassion skills into action.

A kind, caring, and gentle response when you're hurting will take you farther than harsh ones.

Make Your Life Tracker a Tool to Gauge How You're Living!

Using the life tracker form from this workbook, make the time to check in with yourself. How are you organizing and spending your time?

Having already-established checking points with yourself will keep you on the path you want to be on.

Make the Best of Your Life!

I know that sometimes things are far from ideal and we feel like losing our mind, all the way. But being the best version of yourself is not about being the perfect version but about having the humbleness to recommit over and over toward being the person you aspire to be. And here is a secret: once you move into the direction of your values, there is no return!

I can honestly tell you that I felt so alive when writing this workbook because I know how much more resources are needed when dealing with OCD. I see the struggle in my clients' lives day after day, from the 7-year-old kid who is afraid about becoming a zombie, the teenager dealing with obsessive thoughts about contracting an illness and making mistakes, the 20-year-old feeling petrified about having sexual images involving her parents, or the 40-year-old man fearful of the obsession of causing accidents to others because of the lack of attention.

As challenging as OCD is, I have seen how powerful blending ACT and ERP skills is, not just by paying close attention to the research happening over the years but also by witnessing firsthand my clients' shifts from being tortured by obsessions to making bold moves toward living the life they want to live and being the person they want to be.

It's really because of their encouragement and feedback that I wrote this workbook.

Last, I really want to make the point that you're not broken and you're not alone. It just happens that you have a reactive brain, and you're just wired to think a lot.

With tons of appreciation,
Dr. Z.
Don't forget to check the website www.actbeyondocd.com for extra resources.

Appendices

Appendix I: Online Resources

From the Community

ACT for OCD for children, teens, and adults
www.actbeyondocd.com

OCD stories
www.ocdstories.com

Intrusive thoughts
www.Intrusivethoughts.org

Professional Organizations

International OCD Foundation (IOCDF)
www.iocdf.org

American Association of Anxiety and Depression (ADAA)
www.adaa.org

Association of Contextual Behavioral Science
www.contextualscience.org

Association of Behavior and Cognitive therapy
www.abct.org

Appendix II: Shift Moves Log

SHIFT MOVES LOG

Looking back at this past week, how would you say you did using your ACT skills?

	Mo	Tu	Wed	Th	Fr	Sat	Sun

Watching moves

Acceptance moves

Riding the waves

Appendix III: Values-Dashboard

VALUES-DASHBOARD

Circle the area(s) you want to focus on this week

HEALTH • WORK • RELATIONSHIPS • SPIRITUALITY • PERSONAL GROWTH.

What matters to you? How do you want to show up? What's the value you choose to focus on this week? Jot it down here.

What actions are you willing and committed to take this week toward living your HOWs? Be as specific as possible.	Mark an X when you complete that specific action						
	Mon	Tue	Wed	Thu	Fri	Sat	Sun
1.							
2.							
3.							

At the end of the week, jot down any observations:

Appendix IV: Chapters Reference for Making W.I.S.E. M.O.V.E.S.

Skills	Chapters
Watch your obsessions	1 Obsessions Are the Norm!
	18 Get Out of the Content of Your Mind!
	20 Keep in Mind the F of Thinking, Not What It Looks Like!
	25 Watching Your Mind
Invite your obsessions	16 Let Your Mind Do Its Own Minding
	21 Make Room for Disturbing Content in Your Mind!
Stay with your experience	19 Stay "In the Moment," Not in Your Head!
	26 Riding the Wave of Fear, Anxiety, and Terrible Feelings
	22 Watch Out for Fake-Acceptance!
Either toward or away from your values	29 Figuring Out What Matters
Make a choice	30 Living Your HOWs
Observe what comes with the choice	26 Riding the Wave of Fear, Anxiety, and Terrible Feelings
	27 Acceptance Moves
Engage with what's next	19 Stay "In the Moment," Not in Your Head!
Value your choice	31 Counting Your HOWs Moves
Soften up with self-compassion	23 Hold Your Mind Lightly!
	48 Self-Compassion Exercises On-the-Run

Appendix V: W.I.S.E. M.O.V.E.S Log

What's the values-based exposure exercise you're willing to do that will make a difference in your life?	Mon	Tues	Wed	Thurs	Fri	Sat	Sun

About the Author

Online Classes With Dr. Z.

Dr. Z has developed a skills-based curriculum for an online class that teaches Acceptance and Commitment Therapy (ACT) and Exposure Response Prevention (ERP) skills for anyone struggling with OCD.

More information: www.actbeyondocd.com

Dr. Z's Newsletter

Dr. Z. runs a weekly newsletter, Playing-it-safe, and shares cutting-edge tips, resources, and skills to get unstuck from worries, fears, anxieties and obsessions.

More information: www.thisisdoctorz.com/playing-it-safe-newsletter/

Books Written by Dr. Z.

McKay, M., Fanning, P., & Zurita Ona, P. (2011, July). *Mind and emotions*. New Harbinger.

Zurita Ona, P. (2017, July). *Parenting a trouble teen: Deal with intense emotions and stop conflict using acceptance and commitment therapy*. New Harbinger.

Zurita Ona, P. (2018, August). *Escaping the emotional roller coaster: Acceptance and commitment therapy for the emotionally sensitive*. Exisle.

Zurita Ona, P. (2019, December). *ACT workbook for teens with OCD: Unhook yourself and live life to the full*. JKP.

Working With Dr. Z.

Dr. Z is the founder of the East Bay Behavior Therapy Center (EBBTC), a boutique center specialized exclusively in empirically-based treatments, including Acceptance and Commitment Therapy, for children, teens, and adults struggling with OCD, trauma, anxiety disorders and related conditions, perfectionism, procrastination, and mild to moderate emotional regulation problems. Dr. Z developed an Intensive Outpatient Program (IOP) for OCD and other anxiety conditions that offers intensive exposure treatments -15-hours a week- for children, teens, and adults.

More information at www.eastbaybehaviortherapycenter.com

About the Author

Professional Consultation and Trainings With Dr. Z.

Dr. Z offers ongoing consultation to professionals interested in learning the applications of ACT for specific struggles such as OCD, anxiety, trauma, and emotion regulation.

More information: www.thisisdoctorz.com

Dynamic Presentations

Dr. Z loves to give dynamic presentations that are jargon-free, full of hands-on skills to put into action right away, and with many insights from current behavioral science and social psychology. The overall frame of her presentations can be summarized in this sentence, "less talking, more practicing, and more living."

More information: www.thisisdoctorz.com

Bibliography

Abedi, M., Esfahani, M., & Kjbaf, M. B. (2015). Evaluation and comparison of the effects of time perspective therapy, acceptance and commitment therapy and narrative therapy on severity of symptoms of obsessive-compulsive disorder. *Journal of the Indian Academy of Applied Psychology, 41*(3), 148–155.

Abramowitz, J., Taylor, S., McKay, D. (2009). Obsessive Compulsive Disorder. *The Lancet, 374*, 491–99.

Abramowitz, J. S., Deacon, B. J., Woods, C. M., & Tolin, D. F. (2004). Association between protestant religiosity and obsessive-compulsive symptoms and cognitions. *Depression and Anxiety, 20*, 70–76.

Abramowitz, J. S., Moore, K., Carmin, C., Wiegartz, P. S., & Purdon, C. (2001). Acute onset of obsessive-compulsive disorder in males following childbirth. *Psychosomatics, 42*(5), 429–431.

Akuchekian, S. H., Almasi, A., Meracy, M. R., & Jamshidian, Z. (2011). Effect of religious cognitive-behavior therapy on religious content obsessive compulsive disorder. *Procedia-Social and Behavioral Sciences, 30*, 1647–1651.

Arch, J. J., Eifert, G. H., Davies, C., Plumb Vilardaga, J. C., Rose, R. D., & Craske, M. G. (2012). Randomized clinical trial of cognitive behavioral therapy (CBT) versus acceptance and commitment therapy (ACT) for mixed anxiety disorders. *Journal of Consulting and Clinical Psychology, 80*(5), 750–765.

Armstrong, A. B., Morrison, K. L., & Twohig, M. P. (2013). A preliminary investigation of acceptance and commitment therapy for adolescent obsessive-compulsive disorder. *Journal of Cognitive Psychotherapy, 27*(2), 175–190.

Baghooli, H., Dolatshahi, B., Mohammadkhani, P., Moshtagh, N., & Naziri, G. (2014). Effectiveness of acceptance and commitment therapy in reduction of severity symptoms of patients with obsessive – compulsive disorder. *Advances in Environmental Biology*, 2519–2525.

Barney, J. Y., Field, C. E., Morrison, K. L., & Twohig, M. P. (2017). Treatment of pediatric obsessive compulsive disorder utilizing parent-facilitated acceptance and commitment therapy. *Psychology in the Schools, 54*(1), 88–100.

Becker, C. (2002). Integrated behavioral treatment of comorbid OCD, PTSD, and borderline personality disorder: A case report. *Cognitive and Behavioral Practice, 9*, 100–110.

Bibliography

Bluett, E. J., Homan, K. J., Morrison, K. L., Levin, M. E., & Twohig, M. P. (2014). Acceptance and commitment therapy for anxiety and OCD spectrum disorders: An empirical review. *Journal of Anxiety Disorders, 28*(6), 612–624.

Craske, M. G. (2012). Preface. In: P. Neudeck & H-U. Wittchen (Eds.), *Exposure therapy: Rethinking the model and refining the method* (pp. vii–xii). Springer.

Craske, M. G., Kircanski, K., Zelikowsky, M., Mystkowski, J., Chowdhury, N., Baker, A., et al. (2008). Optimizing inhibitory learning during exposure therapy. *Behavior Research Therapy, 46*, 5–27.

Craske, M. G., Liao, B., Brown, L., & Vervliet, B. (2012). Role of inhibition in exposure therapy. *Journal of Experimental Psychopathology, 3*(3), 322–345.

Craske M. G., Treanor, M., Conway, C. C., Zbozinek, T., & Vervliet, B. (2014). Maximizing exposure therapy: An inhibitory learning approach. *Behavior Research Therapy, 58*, 10–23.

Doron, G., Derby, D., & Szepsenwol, O. (2014). Relationship obsessive compulsive disorder (ROCD): A conceptual framework. *Journal of Obsessive-Compulsive and Related Disorders, 3*, 169–180.

Forman, E. M., Herbert, J. D., Moitra, E., Yeomans, P. D., & Geller, P. A. (2007). A randomized controlled effectiveness trial of acceptance and commitment therapy and cognitive therapy for anxiety and depression. *Behavior Modification, 31*, 772–799.

Fostick, L., Nachasch, N., & Zohar, J. (2011). Acute obsessive compulsive disorder (OCD) in veterans with posttraumatic stress disorder (PTSD). *The World Journal of Biological Psychiatry, 13*, 312–315.

Gershuny, B. S., Baer, L., Radomsky, A. S., Wilson, K. A., & Jenike, M. A. (2003). Connections among symptoms of obsessive-compulsive disorder and posttraumatic stress disorder: A case series. *Behavior Research and Therapy, 41*, 1029–1041.

Gilbert, P. (2014). *Mindful compassion*. New Harbinger.

Gordon, W. (2002). Sexual obsessions and OCD. *Sexual and Relationship Therapy, 17*(4), 343–354.

Harris, R. (2019). *ACT made simple* (2nd ed.). New Harbinger Publications.

Huppert, J., & Siev, J. (2010). Treating scrupulosity in religious individual using cognitive behavior therapy. *Cognitive and Behavior Practice, 17*(4), 382–392.

Lee, E. B., Barney, J. L., & Twohig, M. P. (2017). Obsessive compulsive disorder and thought action fusion: Relationships with eating disorder outcomes. *Eating Behaviors, 37.*

Lee, E. B., Homan, K. J., Morrison, K. L., Ong, C. W., Levin, M. E., & Twohig, M. P. (2018). Acceptance and commitment therapy for trichotillomania: A randomized controlled trial of adults and adolescents. *Behavior Modification.* https://doi.org/10.14544551879436

Lee, E. B., Ong, C. W., An, W., & Twohig, M. P. (2018). Acceptance and commitment therapy for a case of scrupulosity-related obsessive-compulsive disorder. *Bulletin of the Menninger Clinic, 82*(4), 407–423.

Levy, H., & Radomsky, A. S. (2014). Safety behaviour enhances the acceptability of exposure. *Cognitive Behaviour Therapy, 43*(1), 83–92. https://doi.org/10.1080/16506073.2013.819376

Manjula, M., & Sudhir, P. M. (2019). New-wave behavioral therapies in obsessive-compulsive disorder: Moving toward integrated behavioral therapies. *Indian Journal of Psychiatry, 61*(Suppl 1), S104.

Nijdam, M. J., Van Der Pol, M. M., Dekends, R. E., Olff, M., & Denys, D. (2013). Treatment of sexual trauma resolves contamination dear: Case report. *European Journal of Psychotraumatology, 4.*

Olatunji, B. O., Tart, C. D., Shewmaker, S., Wall, D., & Smits, J. A. (2010). Mediation of symptom changes during inpatient treatment for eating disorders: The role of obsessive – compulsive features. *Journal of Psychiatric Research*, 44(14), 910–916.

Ong, C. W., Clyde, J. W., Bluett, E. J., Levin, M. E., & Twohig, M. P. (2016). Dropout rates in exposure with response prevention for obsessive-compulsive disorder: What do the data really say? *Journal of Anxiety Disorders*, 40, 8–17.

Ong, C. W., Lee, E. B., & Twohig, M. P. (2018). A meta-analysis of dropout rates in acceptance and commitment therapy. *Behaviour Research and Therapy*, 104, 14–33.

Pepperdine, E., Lomax, C., & Freeston, M. H. (2018). Disentangling intolerance of uncertainty and threat appraisal in everyday situations. *Journal of Anxiety Disorders*. https://doi.org/10.1016/j.janxdis.2018.04.002

Porges, S. W. (2001). The polyvagal theory: Phylogenetic substrates of a social nervous system. *International Journal of Psychophysiology*, 42(2), 123–146. https://doi.org/10.1016/S0167-8760(01)00162-3

Rachman, S., & de Silva, P. (1978). Abnormal and normal obsessions. *Behaviour Research and Therapy*, 16(4), 233–248. https://doi.org/10.1016/0005-7967(78)90022-0

Radomsky, A. S., Rachman, S., Shafran, R., Coughtrey, A. E., & Barber, K. C. (2014). The nature and assessment of mental contamination: A psychometric analysis. *Journal of Obsessive Compulsive and Related Disorders*, 3(2), 181–187. https://doi.org/10.1016/j.jocrd.2013.08.003

Rohani, F., Rasouli-Azad, M., Twohig, M. P., Ghoreishi, F. S., Lee, E. B., & Akbari, H. (2018). Preliminary test of group acceptance and commitment therapy on obsessive-compulsive disorder for patients on optimal dose of selective serotonin reuptake inhibitors. *Journal of Obsessive-Compulsive and Related Disorders*, 16, 8–13.

Salkovskis, P. M., & Harrison, J. (1984). Abnormal and normal obsessions: A replication. *Behaviour Research and Therapy*, 22(5), 549–552. https://doi.org/10.1016/0005-7967(84)90057-3

Samantaray, N., Chaudhury, S., & Singh, P. (2018). Efficacy of inhibitory learning theory-based exposure and response prevention and selective serotonin reuptake inhibitor in obsessive-compulsive disorder management: A treatment comparison. *Industrial Psychiatry Journal*, 27(1), 53–60.

Sasson, Y., Dekel, S., Nacasch, N., Chopra, M., Zinger, Y., Amital, D., & Zohar, J. (2005). Posttraumatic obsessive compulsive disorder: A case series. *Psychiatry Research*, 135, 145–152.

Shabani, M. J., Mohsenabadi, H., Omidi, A., Lee, E. B., Twohig, M. P., Ahmdvand, A., & Zanjani, Z. (2019). An Iranian study of group acceptance and commitment therapy versus group cognitive behavioral therapy for adolescents with obsessive-compulsive disorder on an optimal dose of selective serotonin reuptake inhibitors. *Journal of Obsessive- Compulsive and Related Disorders*, 22.

Twohig, M. P., Abramowitz, J. S., Smith, B. M., Fabricant, L. E., Jacoby, R. J., Morrison, K. L., & Ledermann, T. (2018). Adding acceptance and commitment therapy to exposure and response prevention for obsessive-compulsive disorder: A randomized controlled trial. *Behaviour Research and Therapy*, 108, 1–9.

Twohig, M. P., Hayes, S. C., Plumb, J. C., Pruitt, L. D., Collins, A. B., Hazlett-Stevens, H., & Woidneck, M. R. (2010). A randomized clinical trial of acceptance and commitment therapy versus progressive relaxation training for obsessive-compulsive disorder. *Journal of Consulting and Clinical Psychology*, 78(5), 705–716.

Bibliography

Twohig, M. P., Whittal, M. L., Cox, J. M., & Gunter, R. (2010). An initial investigation into the processes of change in ACT, CT, and ERP for OCD. *International Journal of Behavioral Consultation and Therapy*, 6(1), 67–83.

Vakili, Y., & Gharraee, B. (2014). The effectiveness of acceptance and commitment therapy in treating a case of obsessive compulsive disorder. *Iranian Journal of Psychiatry*, 9(2), 115.

Van Der Miesen, A. I. R., Hurley, H., & De Vries, A. L. C. (2016). Gender dysphoria and autism spectrum disorder: A narrative review. *International Review of Psychiatry*, 28(1), 70–80. https://doi.org/10.3109/09540261.2015.1111199

Van Kirk, N., Fletcher, T. I, Wanner, J. L., Hundt, N., & Teng, E. J. (2018). Implications of comorbid OCD on PTSD treatment: A case study. *Bulletin of Menninger Clinic*, 82(4), 334–359.

Williams, M. T., & Wetterneck, C. T. (2019). *Sexual obsessions in obsessive-compulsive disorder: A step-by-step, definitive guide to understanding, diagnosis, and treatment*. Oxford University Press.

Index

Note: Page numbers in *italic* indicate a figure, and page numbers in **bold** indicate a table on the corresponding page.

Index

saying prayers **73–74**; *see also* mental compulsions

saying words, numbers, or phrases **72**; *see also* mental compulsions

scanning thoughts, sensations, feelings, reactions, or emotions **74**, **77**; *see also* mental compulsions

scenarios **75–77**

scripts 210–211

scrupulosity OCD **44–45**

self-compassion: barriers to 263–266; explained 206–207, 259–261, 281; as go-to skill 284; on-the-run exercises 271–272; reflective exercises 267–270

self-criticism 139–140, 206, 260

sexual orientation OCD **45–46**

"Shake It Off" 145

shame 221–222

shifting your moves 145–146; acceptance moves 163–166; log 288; practicing 168–169; riding the wave of terrible feelings 157–161, 169; shift moves log 168; skills list 169–170; tracking 170; watching your mind (*see* watching your mind); in W.I.S.E. M.O.V.E.S. 230

Silva, P. 5

situational exposure 209

soft responding 140; *see also* self-compassion

somatic exposure 211–212

somatic OCD **30**

somatosensory OCD **30**

staying in the moment 129–130

staying with your experience 204–205

Streep, Meryl 185–186

suicidal and self-harm OCD **47–48**

Swift, Taylor 145

taking a break 191–194

thinking patterns 12, 53–54

thinking strategies 118; *see also* mental compulsions

tracking progress 170, 227–230

traps 148, 155, 160–161

types of OCD **30–31**, **31**; aggressive **26–27**; contamination **27–28**; existential **28–29**; gay OCD **45–46**; harm **26–27**; homosexual **45–46**; just-right **31–33**; mental **39–40**; meta **33–34**; metaphysical **28**, **34–36**; moral **44–45**; pedophile **36–37**; perfectionistic **36**; postpartum **37–38**; pure **39–40**; relationship **40–42**; religious **44–45**; responsibility **42–43**; scrupulosity **44–45**; sexual orientation **45–46**; somatic **30**; somatosensory **30**; suicidal and self-harm **47–48**

underestimating your ability to cope 84

unexpected moments 277–282

upsetting situations 277–279, 281

values 175, 177, 178, 179, 180; dashboard 183, 186–187, 189–190, 289; explained 175, 193, 240, 246; fake 241; forecast 193; lack of clarity 245–248; as verbs 175; and W.I.S.E.

M.O.V.E.S. 240–244, 241–242; *see also* HOWs; life principles

values-based problem solving **278–279**

values-guided exposure exercises: imaginal 209–211; interoceptive 211–212; situational 209; types of 209–212

values-guided exposure menu 197–202; and challenging situations inventory 198, 199, 200, 201; creating 200–201, 201; and reason-giving thoughts 234

values-guided exposure practice 203–207, 213–218; adjusting 216–217; attitude toward 250; being curious 218; combining 215; either toward or away from your values 205; engage with what's next 206; invite your obsessions 204; linking 214–215; make a choice 205; as new compulsion 250; observe what comes with the choice 205–206; principles for 229–230; settings 218; soften up with self-compassion 206–207; starting 213–214; staying with them 217–218; stay with your experience 204–205; value your choice 206; varying 215–216; watching your mind 204

visualizing obsessions 148–151

watching your emotions 157–158; *see also* emotions; riding the wave of terrible feelings

watching your mind: explained 147, 169; as go-to skill 283; and imaginal exposures 210; physicalizing obsessions 152–153, 153; practicing 155; saying obsessions 151–152, 151; traps 155; and values-guided exposure 204; visualizing obsessions 150–151, 150; workability 153–154, 154; *see also* defusion

weirdness of thoughts 4

what-if scenarios **75–77**

"What's the point?" **246–247**

willingness 134

W.I.S.E. M.O.V.E.S./exposures 193; acronym meaning 204, 207, 229–230, 256; blocks to 231–252, 234, 238; chapters reference 290; cost of not making 237; either toward or away from your values 205; engage with what's next 206; feelings during 219–222; as go-to skill 283; invite your obsessions 204; log 291; make a choice 205; observe what comes with the choice 205–206; on-the-go 255–258, 281; remove compulsions from the equation 223–226; settings 218; soften up with self-compassion 206–207; stay with your experience 204–205; tracking 227–230; types of values-guided exposure exercises 209–212; and values 240, 241–242; values-guided exposure menu 197–202; values-guided exposure practice 203–207; value your choice 206; watch your mind 204; weekly log 228

words, counting **72**; *see also* mental compulsions

words, saying **72**; *see also* mental compulsions

workability 80, 141–144, 153–154, 154, 186, 235